The East Asian Currency Crisis

For Amareshda
and Dipakbabu

THE EAST ASIAN CURRENCY CRISIS

Mihir Rakshit

OXFORD
UNIVERSITY PRESS

OXFORD
UNIVERSITY PRESS

YMCA Library Building, Jai Singh Road, New Delhi 110001

Oxford University Press is a department of the University of Oxford. It
furthers the University's objective of excellence in research, scholarship, and
education by publishing worldwide in

Oxford   New York

Athens   Auckland   Bangkok   Bogota   Buenos Aires   Cape Town
Chennai   Dar es Salaam   Delhi   Florence   Hong Kong   Istanbul Karachi
Kolkata   Kuala Lumpur   Madrid   Melbourne   Mexico City   Mumbai Nairobi
Paris   Sao Paolo   Shanghai   Singapore   Taipei   Tokyo   Toronto   Warsaw
with associated companies in Berlin Ibadan

Oxford is a registered trade mark of Oxford University Press
in the UK and in certain other countries

Published in India
By Oxford University Press, New Delhi

© Oxford University Press 2002

ISBN 019 565723 3

Typeset at Inosoft Systems, Delhi 110 020
Printed at Roopak Printer, NOIDA
Published by Manzar Khan, Oxford University Press
YMCA Library Building, Jai Singh Road, New Delhi 110 001

Preface

This book grew out of a series of papers I wrote on the East Asian currency crisis for *Money & Finance* over the period 1997–9. Apart from providing a running commentary on the different phases of the crisis as they unfolded, the papers try to unearth the major domestic and international forces at work before and during the currency turmoil. These articles have been reproduced without revision in the second section of the book entitled 'Unfolding of the Asian Crisis', so that the reader can see the evolution of my understanding and views over the course of the crisis. A revision of the papers, it also seems, would have necessitated some changes in emphasis, but not in any retraction of my views in respect to the genesis of the financial turmoil, reasons for its rapid contagion, inappropriateness of the IMF sponsored policies, or factors behind the relatively early resolution of the crisis.

In order to enable the reader to have a deeper understanding of the issues examined in connection with the Asian experience, the first section, 'Currency Crises: Manifestations and Theories', discusses the evolution of the international financial system and currency regimes since the Second World War; the nature of the Latin American as well as the European currency crises in the two decades following the breakdown of the Bretton Woods arrangement; and the theories advanced in the context of these crises. The final part of the book, 'Stock Taking: Analytical and Prescriptive', recapitulates how the East Asian experience differed from the earlier episodes of currency turmoil, examines some of its analytical implications and evalutes in this connection the efficacy of alternative domestic and international policies for guarding against upheavals in the foreign exchange market and limiting their damaging impact.

The book contains an unusually large number of footnotes and appendices. This is intended to keep the text uncluttered with theoretical details and equations and to enable general readers to follow the narrative without losing the main thread of the discussion. However, readers interested in further studies and aspiring for a thorough grasp of the subject are advised to go over the appendices and footnotes most of which elaborate the textual arguments or provide their rigorous, theoretical backup. The format of presentation chosen here has been found extremely well suited not only for students, academics and policy-makers, but also people engaged or interested in business and finance. The book, it is hoped, will be of interest to both the specialist and the laity.

It would have been impossible to write the book without the excellent infrastructural facilities provided at ICRA's Monetary Research Unit. In the course of preparing the manuscript, I enjoyed the benefit of unstinted support and cooperation from all members of the unit. Special thanks are, however, due to Sumon K. Bhaumik for helpful suggestions and to Suchismita Bose, Sakuntala Sarkar and Paramita Mukherjee for their untiring assistance during the gestation period of the work.

Mihir Rakshit

Contents

Tables

Figures and Boxes

BOXES

Abbreviations

ASEAN   Association of South East Asian Nations
EU   European Union
ERM   (European) Exchange Rate Mechanism
IMF   International Monetary Fund
NPA   Non-performing Assets
GDP   Gross Domestic Product
GNP   Gross National Product
ICOR   Incremental Capital Output Ratio
FDI   Foreign Direct Investment
FII   Foreign Institutional Investment
OECD   Organization for Economic Cooperation and Development

1

Introduction

Very few economic events other than the Great Depression have
attracted so much attention or stimulated such a spate of writings
as the currency turmoil raging in the East Asian economies during
1997–9. This is despite the fact that such crises were by no means
rare; nor was the Asian experience the most serious in terms of its
intensity and duration. Not only do currency crises have a long
history, but since the early 1970s they have also become a fairly
regular phenomenon, especially in Latin American countries.
Compared with the East Asian currency upheaval, the Latin
American crises during the 1970s and early 1980s were, in fact,
deeper and caused much greater damage to the afflicted economies.
What then accounts for such world-wide interest among both
economists and the general public in the fortunes of the Asian
economies during the closing years of the last millennium?

Part of the answer to the question lies in the sheer unexpectedness
of the event and the difficulty of reconciling it with the generally
accepted theories of currency crises developed over the past two
decades. Before the Asian debacle, currency crises had come to be
associated with countries in Latin America, notorious for their
fiscal profligacy, hyperinflation and lack of export competitiveness.
Occasional balance of payments problems were also not unknown
to advanced countries like Great Britain, France, and Italy. However,
the problems faced by these countries were relatively minor and
it was fairly obvious that their troubles originated in deteriorating
trade balances along with depressionary pressure in the domestic
economy—a lethal combination for a fixed exchange rate system.
The East Asian economies, on the other hand, had throughout
been models of fiscal rectitude; had enjoyed unprecedented GDP

and export growth for more than two decades; and were widely expected to become the most prosperous part of the world in a generation or two. The fall of East Asia had, thus, all the hallmarks of a Greek tragedy[1] and could not but attract attention from all onlookers.

The Asian experience has also forced economists to think anew on open economy macroeconomics and has generated heated debates on important policy issues. Perhaps the most controversial issue in this connection has been that of the IMF assistance programmes for the beleaguered nations: economists are split down the middle, one side maintaining that these programmes helped in resolving the crisis while the other side holds that they aggravated the problem, subjecting the countries to needless suffering. No less diverse in this context have been economists' views on the role of capital mobility and the need for its control. More importantly, from a longer term perspective—thanks to the gyrations in Asian financial markets—economists are now better aware of the limitations of their discipline; have come to recognize some important, but hitherto neglected, interlinkages between the domestic and the international economy; and have renewed their search for policy packages (including reorganization of global financial institutions) that can hopefully make nations less vulnerable to currency crises, or at least, contain their deleterious impact.

There are thus reasons aplenty for a close scrutiny of the Asian crisis. However, before coming to consider the background and course of the crisis, it appears appropriate to start with the basic question: what is a currency crisis?

CURRENCY CRISES: FEATURES AND MANIFESTATIONS

As in the case of the proverbial elephant, we know a currency crisis when we see one, but find it difficult to provide a precise definition. The easiest way out of the problem is to identify the major, distinguishing features of the phenomenon, though the list may fail to demarcate some borderline cases.

The single most important characteristic of currency crises consists of a large devaluation or steep depreciation of the exchange rate

---

1 In a Greek tragedy, let us recall, the fall of the hero was ordained by the gods, and not due to any intrinsic weakness in his character.

within a short period, exhibiting a break from the previous trend. Since instability of exchange rates is considered detrimental to international trade and commerce[2], a precipitous fall in the value of a country's currency signals the failure of attempts on the part of the government to avoid such crises. However, government intervention for averting large devaluations imply that movement of the exchange rate alone may not always be the best indicator of a currency crisis. To appreciate why, note that currency crises are a manifestation of pressure or excess demand in the foreign currency market. Government measures to rein in market forces may temporarily prevent a meltdown in the exchange rate; but this does not necessarily mean the absence of pressure in the currency market or that all is well in the country's economy.

In the olden days the government generally took recourse to quantitative restrictions on imports and controls on capital movement in order to prevent a fall in the exchange rate. These measures basically amounted to a rationing of the available quantum of foreign currency for uses approved by the authorities. Crises in such instances were manifested, not in a sharp exchange rate devaluation, but in other, no less unpleasant forms: countries could not import essential goods in order to sustain production, consumption or capital accumulation; there emerged flourishing black markets in foreign currency; and clandestine capital flight through over-invoicing of imports, under-invoicing of exports and other ingenious ways, became the order of the day. All these were reflections of disequilibrium in the balance of payments[3], which, in a number of instances, ultimately forced the authorities to devalue the currency. Even when the government stuck to the exchange rate, the underlying forces were similar to those operating in a currency crisis.

2 Owing to the high risk traders and investors then have to face. Such a risk occurs, it is of some importance to note, when there are large, frequent ups and downs in the exchange rate. However, by common consent, currency crises refer to steep devaluations and not sharp appreciations of a country's exchange rate. This is partly because politicians and people at large take pride in the 'strength' of their currency, but mostly since it is much easier for the central bank to avoid large, unwelcome appreciation of the exchange rate by supplying domestic against foreign currency.

3 i.e., excess demand for foreign currency for financing *net* imports plus *net* outflow of capital, with no official restrictions on current and capital account transactions in the balance of payments.

Over the last three decades progress of financial liberalization has gone hand in hand with major changes in the mode of public intervention. In order to attain their goals, central banks in most countries now operate through the market, rather than subverting it through quantitative controls and rationing. The commonly adopted policy for avoiding a sharp fall in the exchange rate is sale of foreign currency by the monetary authorities. The pressure due to demand supply gap in the currency market is then manifested in a corresponding reduction in foreign exchange reserves of the central bank. When the pressure is large and persistent, in the absence of other supporting measures, the forex reserves soon get exhausted and the central bank becomes incapable of defending the currency. Before matters come to such a pass, the central bank generally goes in for restrictive monetary policies—by way of open market sale of securities along with increases in the Bank Rate (BR) and the cash reserve ratio (CRR) of commercial banks. These policies are designed to raise interest rates, and hence, tend to make the holding of domestic financial assets relatively more attractive than their foreign counterparts and reduce excess demand in the foreign currency market.

Indeed, a sufficiently high interest rate may eliminate the excess demand altogether and put a stop to the central bank's loss of foreign exchange reserves. The reason lies in the relation between the exchange rate and interest rates. In order that there is no incentive for capital outflow nor inflow, the domestic interest rate must equal the interest rate prevailing abroad plus the expected rate of depreciation of the domestic currency plus the risk premium on account of exchange rate volatility.[4] Development of pressure in the foreign exchange market implies that economic agents expect a devaluation of the currency and given the interest rates prevailing in the domestic and international markets, want to raise their holding of bonds denominated in foreign currency. However, if the domestic interest rate is raised sufficiently to compensate for loss on account of the expected devaluation or additional risk, there need not be any rush to exit from the country's currency, and the

---

4 The equality implies that the risk adjusted returns on holding of domestic and foreign bonds are the same so that there is no incentive for switching from the former to the latter or vice versa. See Annexe 2.1 for further details.

exchange rate may stay put without any drain from the central bank's forex reserves. In this case the (original) pressure in the foreign currency market shows up in the widening of the gap between domestic and foreign interest rates.

The implication of the foregoing analysis is that while a meltdown of the exchange rate is generally the most glaring attribute of currency crises, the temporal behaviour of the exchange rate may, on its own, fail to reveal the emergence, duration, and intensity of a crisis. Along with exchange rate variations it is also important to examine changes in foreign exchange reserves and interest rates. Even when the currency is not undergoing a free fall, persistently large declines in the central bank's foreign exchange reserves and steep hikes in interest rates strongly suggest the existence of a crisis situation in the country's external balance. In fact, it is not inconceivable that a sharp devaluation marks the end rather than the beginning of a currency crisis.[5] Thus, when the central bank willynilly lets the currency fall in line with market expectations, the exchange rate and interest rate may stabilize thereafter with no further erosion of the central bank's holding of foreign assets.

As the perceptive reader must have recognized, a criterion comprising more than one indicator may often pose problems in identifying some episodes of currency crises. When the financial sector of an economy is characterized by a falling exchange rate, decumulation of foreign currency reserves, and rising interest rates, the situation indubitably represents a currency crisis. What if all the indicators do not move in the same direction? Or even if they do, how do we compare relative intensities of different currency crises? The usual procedure adopted by economists for answering these questions is to take a weighted average of the three indicators and use it as an index of pressure in the currency market.[6] As in the case of other indices, there is no fully satisfactory way of deciding upon the weights or the critical value of the index separating the crisis from non-crisis situations. However, instances where movements in the three indicators give contradictory signals are extremely rare and there is little disagreement among economists in their

5 See the discussion of the currency crisis in Brazil in the late 1990s (Rakshit, 1999a).

6 See, for example, Girton and Roper (1977) and Eichengreen, Rose and Wyplosz (1995).

identification of most episodes. There can be some borderline cases where the labelling may have to be somewhat arbitrary. But this is no great deficiency of the three-way test, given the complexity of the phenomenon and multiplicity of factors simultaneously working in the economic system. Indeed, search for too precise a criterion for identifying currency crises goes against the Aristotelian dictum in his tract, *The Nicomachean Ethics:*

It is a mark of a trained mind never to accept more precision in the treatment of any subject than the nature of that subject permits; for demanding logical demonstrations from a teacher of rhetoric is about as reasonable as accepting mere plausibility from mathematics.

PLAN OF THE WORK

Though the focus of our current endeavour is on the East Asian currency crisis, an adequate appreciation of the phenomenon requires some acquaintance with international financial arrangements and theories of currency crises. Part I of the book, tries to make the reader familiar with these topics, without going into too many details. In Chapter 2 we examine the evolution of the international financial system since the Second World War, with special reference to exchange rate regimes and integration of global capital markets, and draw attention to the increasing frequency of currency crises since the late 1960s. We also summarize in this chapter the theories advanced in order to explain the Latin American (and other episodes of) currency turmoil, occurring between the early 1970s and mid 1990s. Part II, comprising Chapters 3 to 6, discusses the origins, manifestations, and resolution of the Asian crisis over the period 1997 9. Chapter 3 records our response following the outbreak of the crisis and is devoted entirely to Thailand, which was the first to experience severe pressure in the foreign exchange market and had to let its currency float in mid 1997. Since the fall of Thailand was so unexpected and could not be easily explained in terms of conventional wisdom, we take a close look at the country's macroeconomic indicators preceding the crisis, advance some hypotheses regarding chinks in the Thai armour and draw a few tentative policy conclusions.

The next chapter discusses the rapid spread of the Thai crisis to the rest of East Asia within a few months despite the defensive measures adopted by the countries concerned and the series of rescue operations on the part of the International Monetary Fund. Our analysis of economic forces behind the contagion helps to identify some crucial weaknesses of policies pursued by the crisis countries and suggests how and why, instead of arresting the contagion and effecting a rapid resolution of the crisis, the IMF bailout programmes tended to make matters worse. East Asia's fall from grace within so short a time span made economists search for the roots of the Asian troubles and offer various explanations, even while the crisis was at an early stage. Chapter 5 provides a critical assessment of some of these hypotheses and suggests an alternative explanation in the light of empirical evidence and theoretical considerations. The last chapter of Part II provides an overview of different phases of the currency turmoil and seeks to analyze the interplay of economic forces, including policy responses that seemed to govern the course of the crisis, its turning points and its resolution.

The concluding chapter of the book draws the main theoretical and policy lessons of our study of the East Asian experience. In the light of the analysis in earlier chapters, we draw attention to some important analytical issues brought to the fore by the Asian crisis, and suggest measures at the domestic and international level that may make countries less vulnerable to currency crises and help limit their damaging impact.

2

Post-War International Finance and Currency Crises
Some Perspectives and Theories

BRETTON WOODS SYSTEM AND ITS COLLAPSE

Though currency crises or acute balance of payments problems are by no means new phenomena, there is little doubt that they have become increasingly frequent and severe since the breakdown of the Bretton Woods system in 1973. In order to provide a backdrop to our discussion of the Asian currency crisis in the subsequent chapters, it is useful to have an idea regarding the evolution of global financial arrangements during the second half of the twentieth century, the nature of the problems countries have been facing in the foreign exchange market, and explanations of currency crises offered by economists between the late 1970s and mid-1990s.

The international financial system prevailing for nearly three decades after the Second World War was based on Articles of Agreement of the International Monetary Fund, signed (initially) by 44 countries at Bretton Woods, New Hampshire in July 1944. Under this agreement countries fixed their exchange rates in terms of the US dollar and the United States, in its turn, was required to maintain a fixed dollar price of gold, at the rate of US$ 35 an ounce.[1] It is worth noting some salient features of the IMF system that differentiated it from the gold standard regime (see Box 2.1) of the olden days.

1 The Bretton Woods system may thus be regarded as a gold exchange standard, with the dollar playing the role of the main reserve currency.

The Bretton Woods system was also a fixed exchange rate system; but in the light of the domestic economic difficulties that countries had experienced under the gold standard and the priority that governments came to attach to maintaining full employment, the IMF articles included quite a few provisions to enable countries to maintain both internal and external balance. First, in order to enable a country to mitigate the adverse impact on the domestic economy of random or cyclical shocks by following an expansionary fiscal or monetary programme[2], the IMF permitted a country to temporarily access the gold it had contributed to the IMF's reserves pool and also stood ready to advance short term loans upto a limit.[3] If the shocks are indeed random or cyclical, and there is nothing wrong with the long term balance of payments situation of the country, the country should have no problem in repaying its debt without suffering unemployment or unrealized growth potential.

Second, when the country faces a long term, adverse change in its export or import markets, temporary loans from the IMF will be of little avail in tackling the balance of payments problems. Maintenance of external balance with full employment then requires real devaluation of the country's currency.[4] Since adjustments in prices and wages are generally slow, in the absence of a (nominal) devaluation the country will have to suffer prolonged unemployment and depression or face persistent balance of payments deficits. It is to obviate such problems that the IMF's Articles of Agreement contained an escape clause under which countries were allowed to devalue their currencies if there was a fundamental disequilibrium in their balance of payments.

2 Without taking recourse to beggar-thy-neighbour policies like high tariffs and devaluations these measures would generally lead to a shrinkage of world trade and amount to exporting unemployment.

3 Expansionary policies for purposes of neutralizing the adverse impact of an external shock on domestic output and employment tend to enlarge the balance of payments deficit which the country may find difficult to meet from its own foreign exchange reserves. In the absence of IMF support the country will then have to suffer from unemployment or abandon the fixed exchange rate system.

4 A real devaluation is nothing but a fall in the amount of importables the country can get in exchange of one unit of its exportables. Thus, a real devaluation can be effected by a nominal devaluation with no change in domestic prices, or by a fall in domestic prices with the nominal exchange rate remaining unaltered.

Box 2.1
CURRENCY CRISES UNDER THE GOLD STANDARD

Under the gold standard in its pristine form, countries tied their currencies to gold which served as the means of settling international transactions and constituted the central bank's asset against which the local currency or reserve money was issued. The implication was that any balance of payments deficit or surplus would be immediately reflected in a corresponding increase or decrease of reserve money. The fixed exchange rate system and the one-to-one correspondence between reserve money and the central bank's gold holding made the countries extremely vulnerable to shocks, especially from external sources, and posed serious obstacles to maintenance of full employment in the system. Large gold losses due to trade deficit or capital outflows reduced domestic money supply by a multiple of the loss[1] and set deflationary forces in motion[2]. Pursuit of an expansionary fiscal policy was constrained by the fact that such measures tended to raise trade deficits and enlarge the central bank's loss of gold reserves.

In most instances currency crises under the gold standard were manifested, not so much in the abandonment of the standard by the crisis countries, but more in a substantial fall in gold reserves along with severe unemployment, large scale underutilization of resources, and falling prices. The genesis of such crises lay in the operation of cyclical factors in the domestic sphere, loss of external markets, or outflow of 'hot money' due to speculative reasons; but irrespective of the source of these crises, countries adhering to the gold standard had to pay a heavy price in terms of unemployment, output loss, and stunted growth. Perhaps the most important reason why governments stuck to the gold standard except in an emergency like war, was its single minded devotion to the maintenance of external balance alone.[3] However,

1 Thus, if the outflow of gold amounts to (say) 100 units and the money multiplier (which is nothing but the increase in aggregate supply of money resulting from a unit increase in reserve money) is 3, the fall in domestic money supply will total 300 units.

2 If the outflow of gold is due to trade deficit, resulting from a fall in export demand, the country becomes subject to two types of depressionary pressure. The first consists in the decline in domestic output and employment due to a fall in external demand, reinforced by operation of the foreign trade multiplier. The second is the pressure on the domestic money market created by a contraction in money supply.

3 The absence of a macroeconomic theory of effective demand and the notion that departures from full employment were only transitory under the free play of market forces also played a role in preventing governments from taking any active measure for raising the level of output and employment.

Contd.

Box 2.1 Contd.

during the inter-war period, and especially after the Second World War, democratically elected governments could ill afford to sacrifice internal balance of the economy at the altar of the gold standard or any other irrevocably fixed exchange rate system.

The First World War led to the abandonment of the gold standard as the countries had to rely on monetized deficits to mobilize their resources for the war effort. But after the cessation of hostilities, first the United States (in 1919) and then other countries returned to the gold standard. However, the Great Depression forced practically all countries off the standard once again and the international economic scenario in the 1930s was characterized by beggar-thy-neighbour policies by way of competitive devaluations, high and retaliatory tariffs, multiple exchange rates, and preferential trade agreements among groups of nations. The result was a severe shrinkage of international trade and loss of allocative efficiency without any significant expansionary impact on output and employment at the global level.

The framers of the Bretton Woods agreement were heavily influenced by the inter-war experience. In order to promote international trade and undo damages from beggar-thy-neighbour measures, a fixed exchange rate system was adopted and countries were called upon to gradually dismantle trade barriers and go in for convertibility of their currencies on current account. However, in order to insulate their domestic economy from the ravages of international capital movements, countries were left free to institute capital controls. What is no less important is that cyclical shocks in the international market for goods and services were sought to be cushioned through the IMF's short term lending facilities, permitting the countries to borrow from the institution when there was a downturn in the world demand for their exportables and make repayments as the demand revived. Finally, maintenance of internal and external balance without triggering off competitive devaluations was facilitated by allowing a country to devalue its currency, provided there was an adverse, permanent shift in the country's international trade environment leading to a fundamental disequilibrium in the balance of payments. In the absence of such an escape clause, the country would, it was felt, have to suffer from prolonged depression and unemployment until domestic prices and wages had fallen enough to restore balance on both fronts.

Third, both in the pre-World War I era and during the inter-war period speculative capital movements, or what was called 'hot money', seriously impaired countries' abilities to maintain internal and external balance under the gold standard. Hence, under the Bretton Woods system, countries were not barred from imposing capital controls. When such controls are in force, balance of payments deficits will be limited primarily to trade deficits and countries could be expected to tide over temporary shocks, even substantial ones, without being forced to abandon the IMF exchange rate system or being subjected to a sharp contraction in their gross domestic product.

Though the IMF charter did not enjoin capital account convertibility, one of the basic objectives of the system was full convertibility of currencies on the current account, since otherwise there would be serious impediments to international trade in goods and services.[5] Since both the war ravaged and developing economies needed time for reconstruction and development of their production system, currencies other than the US (and Canadian) dollar were, in fact, not fully current account convertible in the aftermath of the Second World War[6]; but under the IMF agreement countries were required to gradually abolish all restrictions on the use of their currencies for effecting current transactions entering the balance of payments.

By the late 1950s and early 1960s[7] not only did currencies of practically all developed countries become fully convertible on current account, but there was also some relaxation of capital controls. The result was a growing integration of major financial centres of the World and opening up of avenues of private gains

5 Convertibility on current account implies that the currency can be freely used for settling all current transactions, e.g. exports and imports. These transactions do not directly affect future receipts from or payments to the rest of the world. Transactions on capital account on the other hand involve acquisition of foreign assets or getting indebted to the rest of the world, and hence, change the country's asset–liability position vis-à-vis other countries. A currency is said to be fully convertible when it can be used for all current or capital account transactions.

6 The period 1945–60 was characterized by a dollar shortage: given the paucity of dollar reserves of central banks and near total absence of private capital flows, the current account deficits of most countries were limited by the amount of official aid or loans from the USA and the World Bank, the IMF's sister organization responsible for providing long term loans for development.

7 By then West European countries and Japan had registered a remarkable recovery, thanks to their massive investment and fast development, supported by inflow of resouces from the USA through the Marshall aid and other programmes.

through speculative attacks on a currency, if the country ran persistent currency account deficits and was expected to devalue the currency under the IMF's escape clause relating to fundamental disequilibrium. Indeed, throughout the 1960s and early 1970s there were frequent bouts of balance of payments crises in Europe and countries found it increasingly difficult to maintain full employment and external balance under the Bretton Woods system. The collapse of the system came when the US external balance itself appeared to be in 'fundamental disequilibrium'.[8] There was a massive speculative attack on the dollar in early February 1973, and the world's major currencies were allowed to float on 19 March the same year.[9]

POST-BRETTON WOODS FINANCIAL SYSTEM

The international financial system has undergone radical transformation since 1973 and it is important to keep its major features in mind in order to appreciate the alternative theories advanced for explaining the currency crises in the post-Bretton Woods era.

8 Note that under the IMF articles the USA could not devalue its currency without upsetting the whole system.

9 There were three major reasons behind 'the fundamental disequilibrium' in the United States' external balance. First, as Triffin (1960) had already anticipated, growth of world trade led to a corresponding increase in dollar reserves of the world's central banks, thereby making the gold holdings of the US Federal Reserve Banks inadequate to exchange gold for dollar at the fixed rate, should the central banks of other countries want to substitute gold for dollar holdings. Indeed, speculation of traders as early as 1968 forced central banks to institute a two-tier gold market, one for inter-central bank and the other for private transactions. Even this proved infructuous and gold losses forced the Federal Reserves to stop selling gold to other central banks at the stipulated rate. Second, productivity growth in Japan and Germany and other European countries in the post War period along with persistent US inflation and current account deficits emitted clear signals regarding overvaluation of the dollar and made the currency a prime target for sustained speculative attack. Third, with all other currencies tied to the US dollar under the Bretton Woods system, a general devaluation of the dollar would require agreement on the part of all countries, many of whom were unwilling to put their external balance in jeopardy by revaluing their exchange rates.

EXCHANGE RATE ARRANGEMENTS

The currency float adopted by the major countries was initially intended to be temporary. However, following the quadrupling of petroleum prices over 1973–4, industrial economies faced serious inflationary depression.[10] This, along with the fact that there were considerable inter-country differences in the impact of supply shocks and inflation rates, made the major nations stick to the flexible exchange rate system[11] so that they would be better able to maintain their external and internal balance. The formal recognition of the Bretton Woods' breakdown came in 1976 when, at the insistence of the major members, the IMF agreement was amended, conferring upon each country the right to adopt any exchange rate system it liked, though members were called upon not to follow beggar-thy-neighbour policies through manipulation of exchange rates.[12]

However, the collapse of the Bretton Woods system did not imply that all currencies of the world were thenceforth driven entirely by market forces. Countries did not, in fact, follow a uniform policy and the global financial market came, over time, to be characterized by the co-existence of several exchange rate regimes, of which the following were the most important.

First, practically all developing economies and quite a few developed countries pegged their exchange rates to the US dollar or the German mark[13], though the market rate was permitted to move within some narrow band around the central parity. The currency peg, however, was not irrevocable and in a number of

10 In canonical Keynesian models price increases are associated with a rise in levels of output and employment, the reason being that it is the aggregate demand that drives production and prices in these models. When, however, there is an autonomous increase in the domestic cost of production due to (say) hike in prices of imported oil or other commodities, domestic inflation will be accompanied by a fall in output.

11 The reason is that a fixed exchange rate system prevents a country from making effective use of monetary instruments, as we shall see in the next section. Note also that a fixed exchange rate system cannot be sustained if inflation rates differ across countries and frequent supply or demand shocks call for more or less continuous realignment of nominal exchange rates for preserving external-cum-internal balance.

12 The IMF was, however, powerless to prevent such practices since its clout was confined only to countries receiving its financial assistance.

13 In some cases the peg was to a (trade) weighted basket of currencies.

instances, countries went in for substantial devaluations or gave up the peg altogether[14] either in order to avoid depression or under persistent speculative onslaughts.

Second, in the context of their own or others' experience relating to inflation and balance of payments problems, a few emerging market economies like Argentina, Hong Kong, Bulgaria, and Estonia ultimately opted for a currency board system under which not only was the exchange rate permanently fixed against the dollar (or the mark), but the supply of domestic currency was also fully backed by foreign exchange reserves in terms of the main currency.

Third, members of the European Union strove to maintain some alignment among their own currencies and the arrangement was formalized with the establishment of the European Monetary System[15] (EMS) in 1979. Strictly speaking, the EMS was not a fixed rate regime in as much as the currencies could move above or below their central parities by some pre-stipulated margin. Again, both in the 1980s and the 1990s, not only were there a number of realignments in the central parities, but the margins themselves were often changed. Indeed, until the establishment of the euro, the mark was by far the most important currency in Europe and both the intra-European exchange rates and in the relation between the EMS currencies and the dollar or the yen were significantly influenced by the German economy.

Finally, the exchange rate system among the major currencies like the dollar, the yen, and the mark cannot be easily pigeonholed. The USA, Germany, and Japan generally let their exchange rates float, but intervened in the currency market (backed up by monetary easing or tightening) when the emerging (market driven) exchange rate trends were deemed to be detrimental to their economies. The

14 The central bank very often intervened in the foreign currency market even when the exchange rate was officially a floating one.

15 And led ultimately to the institution of a common currency, the euro, from 1999. It should, however, be noted that all members of the European Union did not belong to the EMS or the euro zone. The EMS started with 8 countries and included some other members in the late 1980s and 1990s and ended up with 11 (out of 15) members of the European Union under the full fledged monetary integration effected in 1999. Meanwhile, Great Britain joined the EMS in 1990, was forced to quit the system under the speculative attack of George Soros *et al.* in 1992, and chose to stay out of the Euro zone 'for the time being'.

problem, however, was that the exchange rates between the dominant currencies would necessarily be governed jointly by the forces operating in, and the policies followed by, all the major countries. Under this scenario, there occasionally emerged conflicts of interest and some major players indulged in beggar-thy-neighbour policies, trying to export their inflation or unemployment to their trading partners. Policy co-ordination among large industrialized nations[16] was often attempted and an informal agreement made for joint intervention in the currency market in order to keep their exchange rates within some implicit[17] target zones. But these attempts generally came to naught when some country was subjected to major shocks and found it necessary to effect substantial changes in the exchange rate, even if the process entailed considerable economic loss for other nations.

International Capital Flows: The period 1973–96[18] witnessed the growing integration of global financial markets and an enormous increase in inter-country capital flows. The enabling factor behind these developments was the relaxation of controls on capital movements. We have already noted how currencies of nearly all industrialized economies became current account convertible by the late 1950s and how the second half of that decade also marked the move towards capital account convertibility by these countries. Free use of currencies for current transactions, even without *de jure* capital account convertibility, stimulates capital flows among financial centres, as traders try to gain through delaying or hastening the payments or settlements when exchange rates are expected to change in the near future.[19] The process of globalization of the

16 Consisting mainly of the USA, Japan, Germany, Great Britain, France, and Canada.

17 Not officially announced.

18 Spanning the post-Bretton Woods years until the outbreak of the Asian Crisis.

19 Thus, if the domestic currency is expected to depreciate or interest rates are higher in foreign financial centres, exporters will try to postpone converting their foreign exchange receipts into domestic currency, while importers rush to effect early or advance payments (enjoying a discount on prices). Note that such moves amount to short term capital outflows and tend to put pressure on the domestic currency. The problem is magnified when exporters and importers can effect capital transfers through under- or over-invoicing their transactions.

capital market was interrupted for a short while when the financial turbulence leading up to, and in the aftermath of, the Bretton Woods breakdown forced quite a few countries to reinstitute capital controls. However, the two major players, the USA and Germany, started relaxing their controls from 1974; Japan began opening up its financial markets from the late 1970s; Great Britain lifted restrictions on domestic agents trading in international assets in 1979; and in the 1980s the European Union initiated a programme under which not only were member countries' financial markets to be fully unified, but the EU market was also to be gradually integrated with others in the rest of the world.

Much more significant (at least for our subsequent discussion) was the relaxation of capital controls by emerging market economies. The steep rise in petroleum prices in the 1970s played havoc with the external balances of non-oil exporting developing countries and created an urgent need for capital inflows (in the absence of which they would have been forced to suffer substantial contraction in output and employment). Moves were afoot in the next decade for liberalization of the domestic financial sector in a number of emerging economies and by the early 1990s many of them had introduced a substantial degree of convertibility in the capital account of their balance of payments.

The sharp increase in inter-country capital flows during the post-Bretton Woods system was facilitated by other important developments during this period. First, the huge current account surpluses accumulated by the OPEC countries were deposited with financial institutions of advanced nations[20], which in their turn, lent them to non-oil exporting developing countries, attracted by the relatively high interest rates prevailing therein.[21] Second, financial deregulation in both domestic and external sectors magnified the flow of foreign direct investment (FDI), as multinationals sought to

20 In fact, mostly in the USA.

21 Over the period 1973–8 (i.e., between the first and the second oil shock) the external debt of non-oil developing countries increased by 250 per cent, from US$ 130 billion to US$ 336 billion. Under the impact of the second oil shock the figure balooned to as much as US$ 600 billion by end 1982. This increase in (non-oil) developing country debt closely corresponded to the accumulation of foreign assets by oil-exporting nations during this period and largely reflected the recycling of funds by developed country financial institutions.

locate their production activities where costs were lower and from where market access would be easier. Third, the last two decades of the twentieth century saw enormous growth in financial resources mobilized by pension funds, mutual funds, and other types of financial intermediaries. These institutions, in their bid to raise returns and reduce risk, diversified their portfolios among liquid assets supplied by a wide variety of countries, both emerging and emerged, played a leading role in the development of a globalized capital market, and were constantly engaged in shuffling their portfolios in response to changing prospects of various economies across the world. Fourth, movements of funds from one financial centre to another was made easy by the revolution in information technology and the emergence of facilities for trading in financial assets practically anytime, anywhere.

Since integration of the world's financial markets is closely related with currency crises and contagion, it is useful to take stock of the evolving nature of international financial flows since the demise of the Bretton Woods system. In the aftermath of the Second World War, inter-country capital movements consisted almost entirely of official aid or assistance to the war ravaged economies of Europe, Japan, and developing countries in Asia, Africa, and Latin America. The recovery of industrialized nations saw sustained growth of private capital flows from the early 1960s; but until the oil shock, these flows were mostly from one advanced country to another. An interesting feature of inter-advanced country capital movements was that gross flows were many times the net flows, as countries bought each other's financial assets—a tendency that became increasingly pronounced with the growth of financial intermediaries and integration of global capital markets.

The post-Bretton Woods period also saw a qualitative change in capital account transactions of developing countries. There was a quantum jump in capital inflows into these countries during 1973–82[22] and again since the late 1980s. It is worth emphasizing

22 As we have already indicated in fn. 21, the sharp rise in non-oil developing country debts during this period reflected re-cycling of petro-dollars. The decline in capital flows to these countries over 1983–9 was due to the fact that current account balances of oil-exporting countries turned negative from 1982 onwards and there was a rise in interest rates in the USA and other industrialized nations (so that investment in emerging economies became less attractive).

some aspects of developing country capital inflows since 1989 until the outbreak of the Asian currency crisis at this stage. The surge in foreign investment in developing countries during this period was much larger than that over 1973–82: capital inflows in these countries over 1990–6 averaged a whopping US$ 147.7 billion per annum as compared to a relatively modest annual average of US$ 36.4 billion during 1973–82. The flows reached their peak at US$ 214.8 billion in 1996 before declining to US$ 129 billion in 1997 (IMF, May 1996, and December 1998). Second, the period 1973–82 saw a sharp rise in private capital flows; but capital receipts from official sources not only remained dominant but also exhibited a significantly rising trend until the late 1980s.[23] Only since 1989 was there a sea change in the composition of capital movements, with private flows going up by leaps and bounds and official flows registering rapid declines and becoming quite an insignificant source of external finance for developing countries.[24] Third, globalization of financial markets went hand in hand with the increasing importance of short term loans and portfolio investment, as banks and other financial intermediaries became key players in these markets. We have already noted how balance sheets of advanced economies came to be characterized by large cross holdings of each other's liquid financial assets. So far as the developing economies were concerned, during 1973–82, multinational banks, as we have seen, were instrumental in recycling large quantities of petro-dollars to these countries. This source of capital inflow dried up between 1984 and 1989, but emerging economies experienced a surge in foreign portfolio investments and bank loans from the late 1980s and in a short

23 Despite the quantum jump in private capital flows to developing countries during 1973–82, the annual average of official flows (at US$ 18.4 billion) was still marginally higher than its private counterpart (at US$ 18.1 billion). In fact, over 1983–8 the average of annual official flows increased to US$ 29.5 billion, while that of private flows plummeted to US$ 11.6 billion.

24 During 1984–9, net private capital flows and net official flows to developing countries respectively averaged US$ 12.5 and US$ 26.5 billion per annum. The corresponding figures for 1990–6 were US$ 141.7 and US$ 17.4 billion respectively. Indeed, in 1996 net official flows amounted to only US$ 2.4 billion compared with the US$ 214.8 billion inflow from private sources.

while these components became a significant part of total capital inflows.[25]

POST-BRETTON WOODS CURRENCY CRISES: THEORIES AND CONJECTURES

The collapse of the Bretton Wood system, as we have seen, was preceded by a series of balance of payments crises during the 1960s and early 1970s. However, under the new exchange rate regimes that came to be adopted since the breakdown of the IMF system, currency crises became much more frequent and pronounced, and posed a serious challenge to economists in unravelling their origins and manifestations. Theories developed for explaining the post-Bretton Woods currency crises over 1973–96 are generally grouped under two heads, the first generation and second generation. The former were advanced in the context of the Latin American currency turmoil in the 1970s and early 1980s, and the latter sought to provide insights into the speculative attacks on some currencies under the European Monetary System (during the 1980s, and especially in 1992–3) and into the Mexican debacle of 1984–5.

FIRST GENERATION MODELS

Currency crises in Latin American economies like Mexico (1973–82) and Argentina (1978–81) were characterized by the failure of central banks to defend the currency peg in the face of speculative attacks and by sharp depreciation of currencies following the abandonment of the peg. The speculative attacks culminating in the crises came in the wake of expansionary fiscal and monetary policies and building up of inflationary pressure. It is this connection between domestic economic policies and sustainability of the pegged exchange rate that lies at the heart of the first generation models.

The earliest version of the first generation theories was presented by Krugman (1979), drawing on the work of Salant and Henderson (1978) relating to the unsustainability of the government's attempt

25 Over 1984–9, out of an annual average of US$ 12.5 billion (net) private capital inflows, the two components totalled –US$ 0.5 billion. During 1990–6, they were worth US$ 77.0 billion out of an annual average amounting to US$ 141.7 billion.

to fix the price of gold (or some other commodity), given the fact that its price would tend to rise over time under the free play of market forces.[26] The focus of the Krugman model is on the fundamental inconsistency between economic policies pursued at home and maintenance of a pegged exchange rate—an inconsistency that cannot but end in a currency crisis and abandonment of the peg.

To appreciate the basic logic of the Krugman framework, consider the case where the government runs large and persistent budget deficits financed by borrowing from the central bank. This leads to a sustained increase in the supply of money, with the rise in the central bank's holding of government securities. However, under a fixed exchange rate system and perfect capital mobility, the domestic interest rate equals the rate prevailing in the international market[27], and money supply becomes completely demand determined.

The implication is that increases in the central bank's holding of government securities will be offset by the fall in its foreign currency reserves, as the incipient decline in domestic interest rates resulting from monetized deficits induces investors to hold larger quantities of foreign bonds at the expense of domestic bonds.[28] Quite clearly, such a process is unsustainable, since persistence with deficit financing by the government will sooner or later leave the central bank with no foreign exchange reserves to maintain the exchange

26 Unsustainability of the government's scheme to stabilize the price, irrespective of the volume of gold held in government coffers, is easily demonstrated. So long as the 'natural' price of gold, (i.e. the price prevailing under market forces, with zero gold holding on the part of the government) is less than the official price, traders will not try to buy gold from the government. However, as the natural price rises over time, at some point the natural price equals the official price and then exceeds it. The situation is then ripe for a speculative attack and the government will be unable to maintain the official price, remembering that when speculators have bought the entire government holding, the price prevailing in the market equals or exceeds the official price. See Annexe 2.1 for a parallel with the currency market.

27 Otherwise, capital flows from the low- to the high-interest market and eliminates the inter-market interest differential in the process. The implicit assumption here is that domestic and foreign bonds are perfect substitutes.

28 See Annexe 2.1 for a more detailed exposition. Were the exchange rate perfectly flexible, the quantity of domestic money would have been supply driven and the economy would have experienced rising prices over time.

rate peg. Indeed, as Krugman (1979) shows, even before the central bank has lost all foreign exchange reserves (under the normal process), it will pay private economic agents to mount a speculative attack at some stage, rob the central bank of its remaining reserves, and force it to let the currency float.[29] If domestic policies remain unchanged after the abandonment of the peg, the economy experiences rising prices, and the exchange rate depreciates over time.

The Krugman model has subsequently been refined and extended in a number of ways[30]; but its basic message and conclusions have proved quite robust and require recapitulating at this stage. First, contrary to the widespread view among politicians and policy makers, speculative attacks on a currency and its collapse need not always be the outcome of chaotic, unfounded expectations or be traced to market manipulation of powerful, malevolent agents, exploiting their monopolistic position in the global currency market.[31] In the canonical currency crisis models advanced by Krugman *et al.*, foreign exchange markets are highly competitive, and traders' actions are based on rational expectations, formed in the context of the continuing expansionary policies followed by the fiscal and monetary authorities. The speculative onslaught on a currency, even while the central bank may have a considerable kitty of foreign exchange reserves—a common feature of many a balance-of-payments crisis—is grounded on solid economic logic according to these theories and need not, thus, reflect loss of nerves or pure panic in the currency market.

Second, given the inconsistency between domestic economic policies and the fixed exchange rate system, no amount of foreign

29 The economic rationale of the speculative attack lies in the fact that even when the central bank has considerable amount of foreign exchange reserves left, the exchange rate after the abandonment of the peg will be higher than the rate at which speculators buy foreign currency from the central bank. See Annexe 2.1.

30 See Flood and Garber (1984) and Agenor, Bhandari, and Flood (1992).

31 The periodic balance of payments crises faced by Great Britain since the late 1950s was for long considered the handiwork of the 'gnomes of Zurich', until George Soros became the villain of the piece from the 1980s, especially since the UK was forced to quit the European Monetary System in 1992. Indeed, the Malaysian prime minister also held Soros directly responsible for the outbreak of the East Asian currency turmoil in 1997, though the charge appears to be ill founded.

exchange reserves held by the central bank can prevent, or even postpone, the currency crisis. That the fundamental inconsistency will eventually exhaust the forex reserves, irrespective of their initial size, is not very difficult to appreciate. What is no less significant is that, rational economic agents will mount a speculative attack whenever the free market exchange rate (after the collapse of the pegged regime) is expected to be higher than the pegged rate. Since the free market exchange rate (in these models) does not depend on the central bank's existing foreign currency reserves, their size will be immaterial for the timing of the attack. Note also that the speculative attack, *a la* the first generation theories, cannot but be successful since (a) all economic agents are aware of the current and future states of the economy; and (b) size of the domestic money supply exceeds the central bank's foreign exchange reserves.[32]

Third, though currency crises in the Krugman formulation originate in expansionary monetary policies, the focus of the theory is basically on economic fundamentals governing the long run equilibrium exchange rate. These fundamentals consist not only of monetary and fiscal policies, but also of other factors affecting the time profile of production, prices, and interest rates in both domestic markets and the rest of the world. The canonical models suggest that if the equilibrium exchange rate, driven by the fundamentals, consistently deviates from the pegged rate, speculative attacks and currency crises become inevitable.

Second Generation Models

The first generation models were built, as we have seen, on the basis of the Latin American currency crises in the 1970s and early 1980s. However, the models seemed unable to explain some subsequent episodes of currency turmoils, especially the 1992–3 European currency crisis. The period 1992–3 was characterized by speculative attacks on quite a few currencies under the European Monetary system (EMS), for example, the British pound, French franc and

32 Since the reserve money supplied by the central bank is issued against its forex reserves and holding of government (or other domestic) securities. The implication is that when all economic agents compete among themselves to exchange domestic money for foreign currencies, the central bank's reserves are exhausted and the exchange rate is henceforth driven entirely by market forces. See Annexe 2.1 for more details.

Danish crone. The attacks forced Great Britain out of EMS, enabling it to effect a substantial devaluation of the pound, and led, in August 1993, to a widening of the permitted fluctuation bands for currencies belonging to the (European) Exchange Rate Mechanism (ERM) from ±2.25 per cent to ±15 per cent around the par.

There were several respects in which the ERM experience did not fit in with the canonical crisis theories. First and most important, the crisis could not be attributed to long term fundamentals. Indeed, after an initial dip following the widening of the band, the currencies of France, Belgium, and Denmark recovered by the end of 1993 to their pre-August 1993 values and did not show any marked upward or downward trend over the next two years. Nor was there any significant change in the unemployment rates or other important economic indicators of the three countries during this period. Hence the difficulty of rationalizing this episode of speculative attack in terms of the Krugman framework. Again, unlike the Latin American central banks, countries in Europe never faced the problem of exhaustion of their foreign exchange reserves in the face of speculative attacks on their currencies. By the second half of the 1980s, global financial markets had become well developed and there would have been little difficulty for Britain, France or other countries under the EMS to secure large foreign currency loans to ward off speculative attacks. Third, both the EMS experience and some other episodes of currency turmoils suggest that, contrary to the canonical conclusions, private agents are generally uncertain regarding the timing of the speculative attack or its success. Finally, the widespread evidence regarding speculative attacks on a country's currency in the wake of crises in some other economies implies that (a) currency crises need not be due to weak long run fundamentals; or (b) the perceived 'fundamentals' may be quite different from the ones focused in Krugman type analyses.

BEHAVIOUR OF THE GOVERNMENT AND PRIVATE AGENTS

In the context of the newer varieties of currency crises, the second generation models try to explain why a pegged exchange rate regime may endure indefinitely in the absence of a speculative attack, but can collapse if the currency is subjected to a massive onslaught. The explanations in these models centre round the behaviour of the government and currency traders, both trying to choose among alternative courses of action on the basis of their payoffs.

Perhaps the most unsatisfactory feature of the canonical framework relates to the mechanical way in which the central bank is supposed to behave, defending the currency peg till the last iota of its foreign exchange reserves and letting the currency float only when the reserves are exhausted. The implication of such behaviour is that (a) either the central bank, unlike private agents, is devoid of any foresight whatsoever, or (b) maintenance of the fixed exchange rate dominates all other objectives of the government, despite the knowledge that the peg can be sustained only for a short while. Since both the hypotheses fly in the face of all evidence in recent decades[33], the second generation models (for example Obstfeld, 1994, 1996) take explicit account of the government's objectives and trade-offs between promoting one goal at the expense of others.

Thus, while a fixed exchange rate may be deemed desirable, the government cannot be indifferent to employment, growth or the other objectives. In view of the multiplicity of goals that governments try to further, defending the exchange rate in the face of a speculative attack may turn out to be too costly. To be more concrete, when the defence involves a severe monetary squeeze and a sharp rise in interest rates, the cost in terms of enhanced unemployment, a lowering of the growth rate, a weakening of the domestic banking system[34], and the increased burden of servicing public debt may be considered unacceptably high compared with the benefits of sticking to the currency peg.

33 Recruitment of highly professional economists by central banks and ministries of finance militates against the first hypothesis, while the second is ruled out by the proactive role governments are expected to play in promoting social well-being. This is not to deny that there can still be some policy makers like Montagu Norman, the longest serving governor of the Bank of England during the inter-war years, who relied solely on his 'instincts' and was reputed to have told one of his subordinates, 'We have appointed you as our economic advisor; let me tell you that you are not here to tell us what to do, but to explain to us why we have done it'.

34 Since bank deposits have a much shorter maturity period than loans extended by banks, a rise in interest rates reduces the gap between the banks' lending and borrowing rates of interest. This, along with the capital loss on securities in their portfolio and depressed business conditions (consequent upon the monetary squeeze), may severely erode the viability of banks, especially when their initial balance sheets were not too strong.

Note that in this case (a) were there no speculative attack on the currency, the pegged exchange rate would have endured; and (b) it is the *attack itself which raises the cost of maintaining the peg* and makes its abandonment the optimal policy option for the government. To put the matter in a slightly different manner, in the second generation models the fundamentals themselves are not independent of the speculative onslaught on the currency, so that private agents' expectations may often become self-fulfilling.

As in the Krugman type models, in the second generation theories too currency traders are motivated solely by considerations of private gains and losses. However, in the newer formulations uncertainty and informational frictions play a big role in determining whether a currency is attacked or if the attack will be successful. There could be several sources of uncertainty, the most important of which are the following. First, though the traders know that the fundamentals are attack dependent, they may not have full knowledge of the government's trade-offs between different goals, the policies the authorities will adopt in the event of a speculative attack, and other relevant pieces of information. Again, the types of information available can differ widely across agents. This tends to make most individual agents uncertain regarding whether a concerted attack on the currency will indeed be crowned with success.

Second, even if everybody knows that the exchange rate under the attack contingent equilibrium is higher than the pegged one[35], the success of the attack depends on whether it is mounted by the large majority of traders or by a relatively small minority. This knowledge makes the outcome uncertain since the behaviour of a trader depends not only on his perception of the fundamentals, in the broader sense, but also on his expectations of others' behaviour.

In the context of the nature of uncertainty considered above, factors that lead to a convergence of traders' beliefs regarding the fundamentals and co-ordinate their decisions tend to play a crucial role in triggering off a currency crisis. Economists have suggested alternative modes in which traders' expectations and behaviour may converge and an attack equilibrium can come about in the presence of imperfect information. When market participants have

---

35 i.e., there will be depreciation or devaluation of the exchange rate following the speculative attack.

only partial knowledge of the true state of affairs, they may be influenced, often unduly, by others' behaviour, believing that such behaviour is based on more accurate information. Thus, if a group of traders have some negative information and sell the currency, some others may follow suit, discounting their own private information.[36] This, in its turn, tends to promote information cascades as more and more traders come to expect an attack equilibrium. The result is herd behaviour, manifested in a cumulative exit from the currency.[37]

Again, informational uncertainty and herd behaviour in currency markets may also be traced to globalization of capital markets and rapid growth of pension and other funds. When fund managers can deploy their resources in a large number of markets across the world, their incentive to collect detailed, country-specific information is considerably weakened. Lacking any firm basis for forming expectations, investors then tend to attach undue weights to gossip and rumours. No less important is the fact that fund managers are generally judged on the basis of their performance in relation to that of others. Even though a manager may not believe that there are strong grounds for a speculative attack, he will be loath to be a contrarion, lest the attack being mounted by his fellow managers turns out to be successful.[38] Under these conditions minor events can push the market to an attack equilibrium, setting off a currency crisis, even though the pegged exchange rate could have prevailed indefinitely in the absence of a co-ordinated attack.

Finally, globalization of capital markets and advancement of technology now enable financial intermediaries to reallocate their portfolios or tap credit lines almost instantaneously, with very little cost. This has made pegged exchange rates highly vulnerable. In the absence of any significant transactions costs and problems of arranging for credit, it pays a trader to take a position against the currency if there is some probability of a crisis: in case the crisis

36 Knowing it to be partial and imperfect.

37 Theories of herd behaviour were originally developed for share markets. See Shiller (1989) for evidence of herd behaviour during the 1987 share market meltdown in the USA and Banerjee (1992) for a theory of the phenomenon.

38 The Keynesian perception is worth remembering in this context: 'Worldly wisdom teaches us that it is better for reputation to fail conventionally than to succeed unconventionally' (Keynes, 1936).

materializes, the trader gains; but he does not suffer even if the peg endures. When these costs are high, investors attack the currency only if they feel that there is a reasonable chance of the currency's collapse and the expected gains are large enough to outweigh the cost. It is thus not very difficult to see that large reductions in transaction costs or market frictions tend to make international capital flows highly dependent on rumours and relatively unimportant developments (Krugman, 1997), rather than longer term fundamentals.[39]

FUNDAMENTALS AND SELF-FULFILLING EXPECTATIONS

While self-fulfilling expectations play a pivotal role in second generation models, we must emphasize that they do not suggest that a currency can face speculative attack under all circumstances, irrespective of the state of economic fundamentals. Indeed, these theories generally distinguish between three sets of circumstances. Under the first set, the fundamentals are so strong that a currency crisis is ruled out and speculators fail to post any gain under the attack contingent equilibrium. Under the second set of situations the fundamentals are so weak that even without any speculative attack a devaluation or depreciation of the currency is inevitable sooner or later. This, in fact, is the situation highlighted in the first generation theories. Here a speculative attack, based on rational expectations, hastens the currency's collapse, but does not constitute an independent source of the crisis. The second generation theories suggest that between these two polar areas lies, a large intermediate zone, where a successful speculative attack is possible, but not inevitable. It is in this intermediate zone that the outcome is uncertain and self-fulfilling expectations assume enormous significance. When the economy is situated in this zone, a fixed exchange rate, as already noted, can persist indefinitely, provided there is no major attack on the currency. However, when a sufficiently large number of traders expect an attack, the expectation becomes self-fulfilling, since the defence of the currency then becomes too costly.

The important point to note in this connection is that the underlying fundamentals in the second generation theories must

---

[39] This is also the main reason behind Tobin's proposal for a tax on currency transaction (Tobin, 1978).

comprise a much wider set of factors than those highlighted in the canonical models. To be more specific, the set includes anything that affects the cost of defending the currency or the government's decision in the event of a speculative attack. Hence, apart from the authorities' degree of commitment and ability to defend the exchange rate[40], the currently prevailing state of the economy (and not simply its long term prospects) can have a crucial bearing on currency crises: the larger the size of the public debt, the weaker the domestic banking system and the stronger the recessionary forces operating in the economy, the higher will be the probability of an attack-contingent devaluation or depreciation of the country's currency.

The second generation theories are certainly an advancement on the canonical ones in understanding the nature of currency crises and giving a reasonably satisfactory explanation of the ERM and some other episodes of currency turmoil during the late 1980s and early 1990s. However, the new models do not constitute a general theory and have mostly been built to indicate how currency crises may materialize in some specific situations. Indeed, while the mechanics behind some past, individual instances of currency crises are better understood in terms of these models, they have not been of much use for purposes of prediction. Nor do economic agents appear to always abide by the tenets of these theories: in practically all cases, most market participants did not appear to have any inkling of the impending turmoil until the eleventh hour, even though economists, with the benefit of hindsight, could subsequently detect some fairly clear negative developments for quite some time before the crises.

Given the fact that first generation models were too rarified to explain most currency crises and that the second generation ones were tailored to specific instances, it is not very difficult to appreciate why the Asian debacle came as a complete surprise to almost everybody and did not quite fit in with earlier experiences and theories. Indeed, economists and analysts, well versed in the then prevailing theories, failed, not only to anticipate the problem, but also to foresee the widening and deepening of the crisis, even after the fall of the Thai baht in mid-1997.

---

40 The degree of commitment depends on the relative weights attached to different goals and the ability on the size of the foreign exchange reserves as well as sources of external credit that can be easily tapped if and when required.

SUMMARY

Under the Bretton Woods system, instituted in July 1944, all countries fixed their exchange rates in terms of the US dollar and the United States herself was committed to buy and sell gold at the rate of US$ 35 an ounce. In order to tide over their balance of payments difficulties of a transient nature, countries could use the gold they had contributed to the IMF reserves and avail of short term borrowing facilities from the institution, provided they agreed to its stipulated conditionalities. There was also an escape clause in the IMF Articles of Agreement under which the member countries could devalue their currencies if their balance of payments was deemed to suffer from long term, fundamental disequilibrium. However, under the IMF system the US dollar could not be devalued unilaterally.

Gradual integration of advanced-country financial markets opened up prospects of currency speculation and during the 1960s the UK and some other European economies found it extremely difficult to maintain internal balance under the fixed exchange rate regime. The proximate cause of the system's collapse was the mounting budget deficit and deterioration of the balance of payments position of the USA. These developments, coupled with the rise in the open market price of gold, made currency traders believe that the USA would not be in a position to sustain the gold–dollar parity stipulated under the IMF agreement. The result was a massive speculative attack on the dollar, culminating in the fall of the Bretton Woods system in March 1973.

The post-Bretton Woods era saw the evolution of various exchange rate arrangements. The large majority of countries pegged their exchange rates to some major currencies[41] like the dollar or the mark, but the market rates were generally permitted to move within some narrow bands. The major currencies—the dollar, the mark and the yen—were driven primarily by market forces, though the three central banks often intervened in the currency markets and tried, not always successfully, to co-ordinate their policies in order to avoid violent swings in the exchange rates.

Between 1973 and 1997, movements of private capital, consisting of foreign direct investment, bank loans as also portfolio investment by pension and mutual funds, went up by leaps and bounds. The

41 Or some basket of currencies.

period was also marked by increasing frequency of currency crises, first in Latin America and then in other parts of the world.

The first generation models of currency crises, developed in the context of the Latin American currency turmoils in the 1970s, focused on the inconsistency between expansionary fiscal and monetary policies on the one hand and the pegged exchange rate system on the other—an inconsistency that makes the collapse of the system inevitable. The models also underline why a speculative attack, launched before the central bank's foreign exchange reserves are exhausted under the normal process, is perfectly rational and how the attack advances the timing of the crisis.

Contrary to the teachings of the first generation models, the currency turmoils buffetting the European Exchange Rate Mechanism in the early 1990s suggested that there could be successful speculative attacks on a currency, even though there was no deterioration in the country's longer term fundamentals. The second generation models, developed to explain such crises, suggest that when the government has multiple objectives and continuously evaluates the relative gains and losses of sticking to or abandoning the exchange rate peg, there may be a large number of situations where the peg can endure indefinitely in the absence of a speculative attack, but in case of a large scale attack, defence of the currency becomes too costly.

The second generation models identify a much wider set of factors causing currency crises than the first generation ones. However, not only does the outcome in the new models remain largely uncertain, but they also fail, as the Asian experience has shown, to identify some of the crucial elements triggering off and deepening a currency crisis.

ANNEXE 2.1   THEORIES OF CURRENCY CRISES

First Generation Models

In order to highlight the basics of the first generation models we present a simplified version of the Krugman (1979) formulation without losing its essential elements. Let us assume that:

(a)   The central bank fixes the exchange rate[1] at $\bar{E}$ and is committed to defending the peg until its foreign exchange reserves are exhausted.

1 Amount of domestic currency per unit of foreign currency.

(b)   Government expenditure exceeds revenue and the deficit is entirely financed by borrowing from the central bank.

(c)   There is perfect capital mobility and the country is too small to affect the interest rate or other variables in the rest of the world.

(d)   Domestic prices are perfectly flexible and ensure full employment throughout.

(e)   Output, the price level, and the interest rate in the rest of the world are given.

(f)   Private economic agents know the policy stance and are rational.

Assumptions (a) and (c) imply that the domestic interest rate r equals r^*, the interest rate prevailing abroad[2]:

$$r = r^* \qquad (A2.1.1)$$

Without any loss of generality we assume that all money is reserve money and is issued against foreign exchange reserves (F) and government securities, B, held by the central bank:

$$M^s = \bar{E}.F + B \qquad (A2.1.2)$$

Money demand, M^d, depends on income and the interest rate:

$$M^d = P.L(Y, r^*) \qquad (A2.1.3)$$

where P = domestic price level and Y = domestic output, assumed to be at the full employment level.

The money market equilibrium condition implies that

$$\bar{E}.F + B = P.L(Y, r^*) \qquad (A2.1.4)$$

or

$$\bar{E}.F = P.L(Y, r^*) - B \qquad (A2.1.4a)$$

The reason for writing the money market equilibrium condition in the second form is that under the assumptions relating to the exchange rate and all that, the central bank does not have any control over M^s. If M^d exceeds M^s, the incipient tendency for a rise in the domestic interest rate will induce capital inflows, and hence, a corresponding increase in F, until money supply rises to equal M^d. An initial excess of M^s over M^d will similarly be eliminated through a fall in the central bank's foreign exchange reserves.

The commodity market equilibrium with full employment and flexible prices is given by the condition:

$$D\,[Y, r(= r^*),\ G, R, Y^*, E.P^*/P] = Y \qquad (A2.1.5)$$

2 Under the interest parity condition (with no risk premium),
$$r = r^* + (E^e - E)/E$$
where E^e is the expected exchange rate. Under the pegged regime, $E^e = \bar{E}$. Hence the equality of r and r^*.

where Y = Full employment output, G = government expenditure, R = government revenue, Y^* = foreign output and P^* = foreign price level. Note that $E.P^*/P$ is nothing but the real exchange rate and affects the aggregate demand, D, through the trade balance.

Given the fiscal parameters and other assumptions of the model, eqn. A2.1.5 yields the equilibrium price level, and plugging its value in eqn. A2.1.4a, we obtain the amount of domestic money.

The important point to note in this connection is that when B, the central bank's holding of government securities, is an autonomous variable, foreign exchange reserves F emerge as the residual given by the difference between the demand for money balances[3] and the quantity of B. When domestic economic policies remain unchanged over time, there is a persistent increase in B and a corresponding diminution in the country's foreign exchange reserves. Hence, the inevitability of a currency crisis as F approaches zero and the central bank is forced to abandon the peg.

An important insight of the first generation models relates to the timing of the currency crisis. Even before F becomes zero due to increases in B, private economic agents, possessed of perfect foresight, will, at some point, buy up the entire foreign exchange reserves of the central bank and precipitate the crisis. The timing of the speculative attack depends on the value of the shadow exchange rate, S, in relation to the pegged rate, $\bar{E}$. The shadow exchange rate is defined as the exchange rate that will prevail under a free float when the central bank's holding of forex reserves F has been reduced to zero, so that the domestic money supply equals B:

$$M_s = B \qquad (A2.1.6)$$

The interest parity condition under the pure float yields[4]:

$$r = r^* + s \qquad (A2.1.7)$$

where s = expected proportional change in $S = (S^e - S)/S$.

To appreciate what governs S and its variation over time under the Krugman type framework, assume that B increases at a proportionate rate, b, over time and write S in the following form:

$$S = Q.P/P^* \qquad (A2.1.8)$$

where Q =(shadow) real exchange rate = $S.P^*/P$ $\qquad$ (A2.1.9)

The relation between r and other variables in the system are then obtained from eqns A2.1.7– A2.1.9:

$$r = r^* + q + (\pi^e - \pi^{*e}) \qquad (A2.1.10)$$

where q = proportional rate of change in the (shadow) real exchange rate

---

3 Which depends on P, Y and r, all of which are independent of operation of the domestic money market in equilibrium.

4 Check that (eqn A2.1.7) ensures equality of returns on a unit of financial asset invested in the domestic and the foreign market.

$$\cdot = (Q^e - Q)/Q,$$

π^e = expected inflation in the domestic market, and
π^{*e}= expected inflation in the foreign market.

With no change in production, money supply and all in the rest of the world, P^* remains unchanged over time so that:

$$r = r^* + q + \pi^e \qquad\qquad (A2.1.10a)$$

The domestic money market equilibrium condition is then given by:

$$P = \frac{B}{L(Y, r)} = \frac{B}{L(Y, r^* + q + \pi^e)} \qquad (A2.1.11)$$

Remembering that B changes at the proportional rate b over time, the only inflation rate that is consistent with unchanged Y, r^* and q is b. Hence, in equilibrium,

$$\pi^e = b \qquad\qquad (A2.1.12)$$

and $\qquad\qquad r = r^* + q + b \qquad\qquad (A2.1.12a)$

The commodity market equilibrium condition under the free float is given by:

$$D(Y,Y^*,G,R,r - \pi^e,Q) = Y \qquad (A2.1.13)$$

where $r - \pi^e$ is nothing but the real interest rate. Using eqn 2.1.12 and eqn 2.1.10b, eqn 2.1.13 may be written as:

$$D(Y,Y^*,G,R,r^* + q,Q) = Y \qquad (A2.1.13a)$$

Under the Krugman type assumptions, given the expected value of the real shadow exchange rate, eqn 2.1.13a uniquely determines current Q and its proportional rate of change q. Indeed, rational expectations imply that in equilibrium $q = 0^5$, and the real (shadow) exchange rate is given by:

$$D(Y,Y^*,G,R,r^*,Q) = Y \qquad (A2.1.13b)$$

We are now in a position to trace the behaviour of S and other variables over time.

Note that the equilibrium Q, $\hat{Q}$, as obtained from eqn 2.1.13b, depends entirely on the real variables in the system[6], as is to be expected under the neoclassical assumptions of the model. For a given B in any period, other variables, when F is reduced to zero, are then easily obtained:

$$P = \frac{B}{L(Y, r^* + b)} \qquad\qquad (A2.1.14)$$

---

5 If Y, Y^*, G, R and r^* remain unchanged over time, the real exchange rate consistent with equilibrium in the commodity market also remains unchanged over time.

6 Note that r^* entering as an argument in $D(.)$ is the real rate of interest in the rest of the world, since π^{*e} is assumed to be zero. More generally, the argument would be $r^* - \pi^{*e}$.

$$S = \hat{Q}.P/P^* = \hat{Q}.\frac{B}{L(Y, r^* + b)}/P^* \qquad \text{(A2.1.15)}$$

The behaviour of the shadow exchange rate S over time and the point at which the speculative attack is mounted and the switch-over to the flexible exchange rate regime takes place are then easily indicated in Figure A2.1.1.

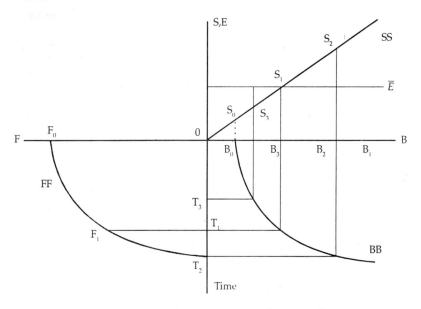

Figure A2.1.1   MOVEMENT TOWARDS CURRENCY CRISIS

Starting from the initial values of B and F at B_0 and F_0 respectively, BB and FF show the values of the two variables over time under the pegged exchange rate system, as B increases at the constant proportional rate b. The shadow exchange rate is given by SS and rises, as may be verified from eqn 2.1.15, proportionately with B. In the absence of any speculative attack, the central bank's foreign exchange reserves are exhausted[7] at time T_2, at which point the exchange rate, left at the mercy of market forces, will jump (from the pegged rate $\bar{E}$) to S_2. However, private economic agents, aware of the time paths of B and S, can make a killing by buying foreign exchange from the central bank immediately before T_2 at the fixed rate and selling the amount after the abandonment of the peg. The scope for making such profits exists at all points between T_1 and T_2 where $S > \bar{E}$. Since each trader knows that others will avail of the opportunity at their earliest possible

7 See the earlier discussion, based on (eqn A2.1.4a).

moment[8], the speculative attack will, in fact, be mounted at T_1 even though the central bank's reserves still stand at (perhaps a healthy) F_1. From T_1 onwards, the economy experiences inflation and (nominal) depreciation of its currency at the rate b (so that the real exchange rate remains unchanged[9] over time).

Though highly simplified, the basic message and some of the conclusions of the canonical model are fairly robust and need to be stressed at this point. The reason behind the collapse of the pegged exchange rate regime, as is obvious from the foregoing exposition, lies in the deviation of the long run equilibrium exchange rate from the rate fixed by the central bank. The focus of the Krugman model on domestic monetary policy as the reason behind the currency crisis is only an illustrative one, and was prompted by the experience of the Latin American countries. It may easily be verified that what matters, among other things, is the relative rates of inflation in the domestic and international markets: a persistently higher π in relation to π^*, it is not difficult to see, cannot but raise the shadow exchange rate above $\bar{E}$ at some point, and hence, trigger off a currency crisis. Nor can the refusal of the central bank to monetize government deficit constitute a solution to the problem. The reason is that, with the rising supply of government bonds, the risk associated with the holding of domestic securities increases over time. Hence, even under a fixed exchange rate system, domestic interest rates need to rise over time with the increase in the risk premium so that prices and the shadow exchange rates exhibit an upward trend and a speculative attack becomes inevitable sooner or later. Again, the shadow rate may also tend to exceed the fixed rate when there is a permanent decline in the demand for the country's exports in the international market or a relative fall in the supply of importables[10]. In other words, persistent overvaluation of a currency, whatever be its sources, will prompt a speculative attack and force the central bank to abandon the peg.

SECOND GENERATION THEORIES

A number of currency crises occuring during the 1980s and early 1990s, especially those faced by the UK and some other members of the European Monetary System (EMS), could not, it was fairly obvious, be explained in terms of the first generation models. The countries forced to devalue or

---

8 Since otherwise the opportunity will be lost, as the exchange rate shoots up to S when the speculators have bought up the entire F.

9 Check also that it will not pay private agents to mount a speculative attack at (say) T_3, before T_1. The reason is that with $S < \bar{E}$, abandonment of the peg will then inflict losses on currency traders.

10 Note that such changes require an increase in $\hat{Q}$ and hence, an increase in S, as may be verified from eqn A2.1.13b and eqn A.2.1.15.

abandon the peg in these episodes did not seem to suffer from any noticeable weakening in their long term fundamentals before the speculative attack; nor did they face any problem in accessing the international capital market in order to replenish their foreign exchange reserves. Indeed, in many cases the exchange rates, after a dip in the wake of the speculative attack, gradually reverted to their pre-crisis levels. These experiences led to a renewed effort at understanding the mechanics of currency crises and to the construction of a series of models (Obstfeld, 1986, 1994, 1996; Agenor, Bhandari and Flood, 1992; Flood and Marion, 1996), under the sobriquet second generation theories. The distinctive features of these theories consist in more realistic modelling of government behaviour than before, in focussing on possibilities of multiple equilibria under a wide array of circumstances, and in highlighting the role of self-fulfilling expectations of currency traders-something which has had no place in Krugman type constructs. A country may experience a currency crisis, the models suggest, even if the government has not been following expansionary policies or the prevailing exchange rate is not grossly overvalued, and the currency peg can prevail indefinitely in the absence of a speculative attack.

Government Behaviour

Unlike the canonical models, the second generation theories recognize that the government's commitment to the currency peg can never be absolute, since there are a number of goals it tries to promote. The implication of multiplicity of policy objectives is that when the currency is under pressure, the decision whether or not to defend the exchange rate is made on the basis of relative payoffs of alternative courses of action. Other things remaining the same, the government prefers a stable exchange rate, since it tends to promote trade and international capital flows. Sticking to the currency peg is of particular importance to countries which have entered into some exchange rate arrangement with other nations[11], and to those which have had a long history of high inflation rates.[12]

Countering a speculative attack is, however, by no means costless. Defence of the exchange rate involves an increase in interest rates[13], which, in its turn, tends to produce a contractionary impact on the domestic

11 This was the case for countries belonging to the European Exchange Rate Mechanism (ERM).

12 Firm commitment to a fixed exchange rate system, if credible, tends to reduce inflationary expectations. This was how many a Latin American country tried to usher in a low inflation regime in their economies. For these countries devaluation or depreciation was always attended with the danger of producing inflationary expectations.

13 So that the incentive for capital outflow is reduced. See the interest rate parity condition, eqn A2.1.7, in this connection.

economy, raises the interest burden of public debt and creates serious difficulties for the banking sector.[14] Hence arises the possibility of self-fulfilling expectations giving rise to a currency crisis: while the pegged exchange rate may be maintained in the absence of a speculative attack, there can be situations where the cost of fending off a concerted onslaught on the currency may be deemed too high by the government.

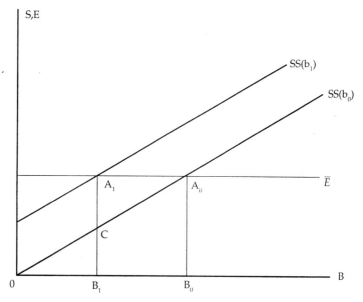

Figure A2.1.2   SELF-FULFILLING SPECULATIVE ATTACK

The second generation models are mostly illustrative and give examples where the speculative attack itself changes the fundamentals and produces a crisis. These examples are based on specific formulations of the government's objective functions, behaviour of private agents, and the way the government reacts to changes in their action in the currency market. In order to indicate the main insights of the new theories and bring out their differences with the canonical models, we consider a variant of the Krugman case, drawing on Obstfeld (1986) and Flood and Marion (1998).

Go back to the first quadrant of Figure A2.1.1 and assume that the growth rate of central bank credit to the government is zero (i.e., $b = 0$)

14 Because of capital losses on bonds held and rise in the incidence of non-performing loans with the reduced demand and enhanced interest charges faced by producers. This could turn out to be a major source of financial upheaval if the banks' balance sheets were not very healthy to begin with.

when the currency is not subjected to any speculative attack. The corresponding shadow exchange rates at different levels of central bank credit to the government (B) are indicated by $SS(b_0)$ in Figure A2.1.2. In this situation[15], the pegged exchange rate E can prevail indefinitely so long as $B \leq B_0$ and there is no speculative attack on the currency. However, if currency traders mount an attack, the central bank may respond by raising the growth rate of credit from zero to (say) b_1. There can be several reasons for such a response. When the size of the public debt is substantial, the increase in interest rates following the speculative attack[16] may force the government to take recourse to seignorage in order to reduce the burden of debt servicing. Alternatively, additional central bank credit to the government may also be required for supporting banks reeling under the impact of high interest rates and the economic squeeze.

The implications of attack-contingent policy changes for the currency market are fairly easy to appreciate in terms of Figure A2.1.2. The increase in the growth rate of B following a speculative attack shifts the shadow exchange rate curve to $SS(b_1)$, the position of which indicates if or when a speculative attack, if mounted, will in fact succeed. Note that for $B \leq B_1$ there is no possibility of a currency crisis since the shadow exchange rate, even in the event of a speculative attack, is then less than $\bar{E}$.[17] At any $B > B_0$, the situation is similar to that discussed in the Krugman model and a currency crisis is inevitable under these circumstances. However, when B lies between B_1 and B_0, a crisis is possible, but not inevitable: without any speculative attack the exchange rate stays put at $\bar{E}$; but when traders launch an attack on the currency, the shadow exchange rate exceeds $\bar{E}$ and there is devaluation or depreciation of the currency. In this case the currency market is characterized by multiple equilibria and possibilities of self-fulfilling expectations. An interesting point to note in this connection is that multiple equilibria are ruled out when the underlying fundamentals are either too strong or too weak: crises do not arise in the former, and are inevitable in the latter.

One can construct a number of other cases of self-fulfilling expectations. Thus, if traders believe that the currency will be devalued following an attack, the attempt to stick to the peg by raising interest rates can take heavy toll of output and employment. With fairly plausible assumptions regarding the government's policy objectives, abandonment of the peg, and thus, validation of traders' expectations may then be preferred to

15 With B and other factors operating in the foreign exchange market remaining unchanged over time.

16 Since the speculative attack is based on expectations that the currency will be devalued, the interest rate has to rise in order to induce investors to hold the country's financial assets. The interest rate can come down and approach the rate prevailing elsewhere only after value of the currency falls and no further devaluation is expected.

17 There is thus no incentive for an attack by knowledgeable currency traders.

adherence to the fixed exchange rate. The most important example of such self-fulfilling crises is said to be the British episode of 1992, when the attack on the pound sterling led to the country's abandonment of the European Exchange Rate Mechanism.

Behaviour of Private Agents: Coordination Problem

The presence of multiple equilibria exemplified above suggests the possibility, but not inevitability, of speculative attacks leading to a currency crisis. One reason for the absence of an attack even when B lies in the zone $B_1 B_0$ (Figure A2.1.2) may be that investors lack adequate information regarding the true state of the economy or the government's objective function. Even when investors have full information in this respect[18], uncertainty faced by an individual investor regarding the behaviour of others may prevent him from taking a short position in the currency market, remembering that a feeble or sporadic attack can easily be warded off and the currency peg will survive. Under these conditions the outcome depends not only on transaction costs, but also on the structure of the currency market. When the market can be swayed by a major player having sufficient funds at his disposal, the outcome in this multiple equilibria case is no longer attended by uncertainty: a speculative attack and abandonment of the peg or devaluation are then inevitable.[19]

However, when no single agent can, on his own, mount a sufficiently large speculative attack, a currency crisis is not guaranteed even if all the traders know that the attack-contingent equilibrium is characterized by $S > \bar{E}$. Game-theoretic considerations suggest that in this case there will be more than one Nash equilibrium, one no-attack and the other attack.[20]

Given the uncertainty of outcome under these conditions, for explaining what actually triggers off currency crises economists have tried to examine how decisions of currency traders may be co-ordinated and the market moves to an attack equilibrium. Of crucial importance in this context are informational problems, since in the absence of these factors multiple

18 i.e., even when investors know that the attack-contingent shadow exchange rate is higher than $\bar{E}$.

19 The 1992 currency crisis faced by Great Britain has widely been attributed to the speculative attack on the part of George Soros. Note that when small traders are aware of such monopoly power that the major players can exercise, there will be a stampede to exit from the currency. In this case the leading player will fail to reap large profits unless he is able to beat the gun. Soros is said to have made millions by attacking the pound sterling by keeping his speculative sale of the currency a well guarded secret for quite a while.

20 The reason is fairly simple. When each trader believes that others will not attack, it is optimal for him not to attack. Hence, a no-attack situation is consistent with the belief and optimal strategy of all traders. Again, since it is optimal for a trader to sell the currency when others are also expected to do so, a speculative attack on the part of everybody is also an equilibrium situation.

equilibriia will not be very important in the currency market. To see why, let the transaction cost[21] of selling short one unit of domestic currency be c. With no uncertainty relating to S, the Bayesian probability of an attack is $1/2$, so that an individual trader will take a short position if and only if

$$\frac{1}{2}[(S/\overline{E})-1]-c-\delta>0 \qquad\qquad (A2.1.6)$$

where δ is the risk premium of the currency trader. Since all currency traders are aware of this rule, eqn A2.1.16 becomes the condition for an economy-wide speculative attack when δ is the same for everybody. In this case the multiple equilibria case collapses into a situation of unique equilibrium with no uncertainty.

However, this result abstracts from a whole host of informational problems traders are confronted with. Apart from the fact that an individual agent has little means of knowing others' δ's, he seldom has the relevant set of information regarding the current state of the economy and the objective function of the government. Again, there are considerable differences across traders regarding the type of information they have. The result is that a typical trader has no firm basis for attaching a numerical value to the probability of the attack contingent an S exceeding $\overline{E}$, to the magnitude of depreciation in case the attack is successful, or to the probability of attack on the part of other traders. A model of currency crises has, thus, to specify a mechanism through which the expectations and actions of private traders are co-ordinated and the economy is pushed into a financial turmoil. In the text we have provided an outline of some alternative models, indicating how traders' expectations or actions may converge and a self-fulfilling speculative attack can come about. However, these models tell only plausible stories and do not seem to possess the hallmark of a robust theory, viz., usefulness for purposes of prediction. This is perhaps the most important weakness of the second generation theories, even though they help to explain some episodes of currency crises which cannot be understood in terms of the canonical models.

The reasons behind the lack of robustness of second generation theories are not very difficult to trace. These theories are built around specific instances where the attack-contingent equilibrium is different from the no-attack equilibrium. Accordingly, they draw attention to a wider array of situations (than in the Krugman type formulations) under which currency crises can take place. However, the fundamentals, weakening of which gives rise to the possibility of multiple equilibria, are so diverse and manifold that in any specific instance it is extremely difficult to be sure

---

[21] Including the cost of arranging for loans.

whether a concerted attack on the currency will succeed or fail. Again, even when the currency market, under the given economic and political environment, is characterized by multiple equilibria, the forces operating in the system may or may not result in a speculative attack. No wonder, the position of an economist professing to predict currency crises is not dissimilar to that of the proverbial captain of a ship navigating a difficult stretch. Having asserted that he knew well the location of all rocks under that part of the sea, the response of the captain as the ship hit a rock was: And this is one of them.

3

Learning and Unlearning from the Thai Currency Crisis

The recent currency turmoil in South East Asian countries has underscored the severe difficulties that even (apparently) robust economies may face under the prevailing system of international finance. Since the mid-1980s the ASEAN countries in general, and Thailand in particular, have been hailed as the newly emerging economic tigers and their macroeconomic performance and policies cited as models for low income countries in the rest of the world. The South East Asian experience illustrates both the opportunities and dangers attendant upon economic liberalization under a globalized financial market and indicates the limitations of conventional wisdom in evaluating macroeconomic scenarios and suggesting policy programmes suited to the present day environment of world trade and finance.

The eye of the storm raging in the ASEAN countries was Thailand and economists generally attribute the pressure on the Malaysian ringgit, the Philippine peso, and the Indonesian rupiah largely to the 'contagion' effect spreading to the economies forming (almost) a free trade zone. The Thai baht was, in fact, the first to come under speculative attack in May, and was finally permitted to float on 2 July 1997. Of the four currencies, the depreciation between 2 July and 30 July was also the largest for the baht. During this month the baht went down against the US dollar by 25 per cent, while the (Philippine) peso fell by 13 per cent, the rupiah by 5.7 per cent and the ringgit by 4.4 per cent. In order to tide over her difficulties

First published in *Money & Finance*, September 1997.

Thailand had also to negotiate a US$ 16.5 billion IMF loan accompanied by onerous conditionalities. It thus appears instructive to focus primarily on the crisis faced by Thailand and see whether we can draw some analytical and policy conclusions relevant for India and other developing countries that have embarked on the course of integrating their domestic financial sector with the rest of the world.

MACROECONOMIC INDICATORS AND POLICIES

Between 1985 and 1995, trends of practically all macroeconomic and social indicators of Thailand, as also her policy programmes, were viewed as highly positive. As far as the policy initiatives were concerned, from the mid-1980s, Thailand switched over from an import-substituting to an export-oriented strategy; undertook measures to step up both public and private saving; effectively tapped the international capital market to supplement domestic saving; invested heavily in infrastructural facilities; and increasingly permitted the free play of market forces in guiding decisions relating to production, investment, and its mode of financing.

Until recently, the performance of Thailand on the economic front was almost picture perfect and all that a developing country could hope for. With an average GDP growth of 9.8 per cent per annum it was the fastest growing country of the world during 1985–95. This growth marked an increase of more than 3 percentage points over that registered in the earlier decade, 1975–84 (see Table 3.1), and was propelled by a quantum jump in domestic investment ratio, from 28.2 per cent in 1985 to 41.0 per cent in 1995[1] (see Table 3.2). The important point to note in connection with this rapid transition from a moderately high to the super high investment regime is that while the inflow of foreign funds was fairly substantial during the reference period, it was domestic rather than foreign saving which financed the major part the growing capital accumulation. Thus the net inflow of capital from abroad constituted 15.3 per cent of gross investment in 1985; but the average share of foreign funds in financing domestic capital formation declined to less than 14 per cent during 1985–95.

1 The corresponding figures for India in the two years were 22.2 per cent and 27.4 per cent respectively.

Table 3.1
AVERAGE ANNUAL GROWTH IN SOME PARAMETERS FOR THAILAND

(%)

	1975–84	1985–95	1992	1993	1994	1995	1996
GDP at Constant Prices	6.6	9.8	8.2	8.5	8.6	8.8	5.5
Private Consumption Expenditure	5.4	8.9	6.9	7.0	8.5	8.5	6.8
Govt Consumption Expenditure	9.6	4.9	6.5	7.8	4.5	2.9	11.9
Gross Domestic Investment	6.6	15.4	6.2	9.7	12.4	12.6	14.6
Import of Goods and Services	7.2	18.9	7.5	15.9	16.6	16.9	-0.9
Export of Goods and Services	9.7	16.8	12.0	19.1	14.6	15.8	-1.8
GDP Deflator		5.0	4.5	3.3	5.3	6.0	6.0
Consumer Prices			4.1	3.6	5.0	5.8	5.9

Source: IMF, *International Financial Statistics*

FISCAL PRUDENCE

No less impressive were the trends of other macroeconomic indicators. Since the mid-1980s the government of Thailand has displayed exemplary fiscal prudence. Between 1975 and 1985, the average annual increase in government consumption (at 9.6 per cent) exceeded the GDP growth by 3 percentage points. There was a sea change in this scenario during 1985–94, when the average increase in public consumption came down to 4.9 per cent per annum while GDP recorded a growth of 9.8 per cent. The strict discipline on the fiscal front was also reflected in the behaviour of the government's current budget balance. The surplus in the revenue account of the government budget (as a ratio of GDP) registered a remarkable improvement, from (–) 0.6 per cent in 1985 to 11.6 per cent in 1995, and attests to the crucial role played by the state in augmenting the domestic sources of capital accumulation. Indeed, in sharp contrast to trends exhibited in most developing countries (including India), the 10.4 percentage point increase in the domestic saving ratio during the period under review, was accounted for by a 12.2 percentage point rise in government savings, more than neutralizing a marginal fall in the private saving ratio. Since the late 1980s, Thailand also enjoyed the rare distinction of consistently generating a fiscal surplus. In 1985 there was, in fact, a fiscal deficit to the tune of 3.7 per cent of GDP. Within three years, however, the deficit had been wiped out and by 1995 the fiscal surplus attained

Table 3.2
KEY MACROECONOMIC RATIOS OF THAILAND

	1975	1985	1990	1992	1993	1994	1995	1996
			as a percentage of GDP					
Gross Domestic Investment	26.7	28.2	41.1	39.6	40.0	41.2	41.0	41.7
Gross National Saving	22.5	23.9	32.4	33.9	34.3	33.2	34.3	35.8
Exports	18.7	23.4	34.1	37.1	37.8	38.8	41.8	38.6
Imports	23.4	26.2	41.9	41.4	42.3	44.0	48.8	45.1
Trade Balance	-4.7	-2.8	-7.8	-4.3	-4.5	-5.2	-7.0	-6.5
Current Account Balance	-4.2	-4.3	-8.7	-5.7	-5.6	-5.5	-7.9	-7.9
Govt's Current Budget Balance	0.0	-0.6	7.4	6.4	6.3	7.4	8.2	7.5
Overall Budget Surplus	0.0	-3.7		2.6	1.9	2.7	3.0	2.4
Total Reserves/Average Import Per Month	0.0	3.6	4.8	5.5	5.9	5.7	5.4	6.2
(reserve incl. gold in million US$)	(2007)	(3003)	(14,258)	(21,183)	(25,439)	(30,279)	(37,027)	(38,645)

Source: IMF *International Financial Statistics;* Asian Development Bank, *Asian Development Outlook.*

the level of 3.0 per cent of GDP. The performance was quite remarkable, even by the ASEAN standard : in the same year the surplus was 0.8 per cent for Indonesia, 0.9 per cent for Malaysia and (–) 0.5 per cent for the Philippines.

TRADE AND EXCHANGE RATE

Until recently, effective monetary and exchange rate management on the part of the Bank of Thailand was also considered to have contributed substantially to the country's rapid growth, along with macroeconomic balance, both internal and external. Between 1985 and 1995 (in fact up to 1 July, 1997) variations in the exchange rate were negligible, the baht being linked to a basket of currencies (with a large weight attached to the US dollar). This policy of maintaining a stable value of the baht was intended to eliminate the exchange risk faced by traders, as also domestic and foreign investors. The credibility of the policy was effectively supported by the track record of fiscal and monetary authorities, including the comfortable foreign exchange reserves maintained by the Bank of Thailand. Even while imports were growing at an average yearly rate of 18.9 per cent during 1985–95, since 1990 forex reserves remained adequate to meet at least 5.5 months' import bill.

The trade and exchange rate regime established since the mid-1980s produced two major effects on the Thai economy. First, the growing inflow of foreign capital enabled the country to raise its investment ratio[2] to an astonishing 41 per cent by 1995. Second, over the reference period Thailand became one of the most open economies in the world. Between 1975 and 1985 the ratio of total trade (exports plus imports) to GDP crawled from 41.4 per cent to 49.1 per cent. In sharp contrast, the trade–GDP ratio in the next

2 We have already noted the important role played by domestic saving behind the phenomenal increase in capital accumulation. Until 1995 the increase in the foreign sources of financing investment was, in fact, not as spectacular as the rise in domestic saving. However, there are reasons to believe that in countries like Thailand, inflow of foreign capital facilitated imports of machinery and equipment and thereby produced a multiplier effect on the scale of domestic investment that could effectively be undertaken. In other words, in the absence of foreign sources of finance, the effective level of domestic saving would have been less through (a) slowing down of GDP growth; and (b) an adverse movement of the terms of trade.

decade shot up from 49.1 per cent to 90.6 per cent. These two factors, conventional economic analysis would suggest[3], must have played an important role in enabling Thailand to enjoy almost a double digit growth rate with no apparent signs of imbalance on the domestic or external front.

MONEY AND FINANCE

The maintenance of an open trade with a stable foreign exchange regime was facilitated by the relatively low domestic rates of inflation. During 1985–95, the GDP deflator and consumer prices rose at an average yearly rate of 5.0 and 4.0 per cent respectively (see Table 3.1). A host of factors contributed to moderate price increases, especially those of consumer goods. Money supply in the broad sense grew at a rate of 18.7 per cent, compared to the GDP growth of 9.8 per cent per annum. In sharp contrast to the trend in almost all developing countries, the absolute quantity of credit (in nominal terms) to the government from both the central and commercial banks registered a fairly steep decline. In 1985, government's indebtedness to the monetary sector totalled Baht 184.5 billion, of which liability to the central bank amounted to Baht 106.9 billion and that to other banks Baht 77.7 billion. By 1995, total bank credit to the government came down by about 63 per cent at Baht 68.2 billion, of which, the shares of the central and other banks' credit were Baht 43.1 billion and Baht 25.1 billion respectively.

The implication of this sharp decline the in government's liability to the banking system was twofold: first, the Bank of Thailand could pursue monetary and exchange rate policies without being constrained by the budgetary requirements of the central government; second, the incremental quantity of bank credit supporting commercial operations exceeded the increase in aggregate finance routed through the monetary system. This enabled banks to pay fairly high returns on bank deposits and thereby intermediate a growing fraction of funds flowing from savers to investors. During

3 Other things remaining the same, a higher investment ratio produces a faster growth in the productive capacity of the economy. Again, a larger trade–GDP ratio suggests a higher degree of specialization on the basis of the country's comparative advantage, and hence, more efficient use of its productive resources. Both the factors contribute to an increase in the growth potential of the economy

the decade under review the real rate of interest[4] on bank deposits averaged more than 6 per cent and the financial intermediation ratio (measured by the broad money to GDP ratio[5]) increased from 56.2 per cent in 1985 to about 79 per cent in 1995. This rapid rise in financial intermediation is generally regarded as an important factor promoting allocative efficiency of the growing volume of investment financed from domestic and foreign sources.

SOCIAL DEVELOPMENT

In recent years, increasing attention has been paid by economists to the magnitude or extent of a country's poverty, sanitation, life expectancy, infant mortality, child malnutrition, or access to safe drinking water. These social indicators (along with conventional economic variables like per capita income or its growth) are now widely used in judging a country's stage of 'development' in the broader sense of the term, and their improvement has come to be recognized as a major policy objective of the government. What is more relevant to note in the present context, there is by now fairly clear evidence that a country's economic growth potential itself is significantly affected by the state of health and the level of skill of its workforce and by the presence or absence of social and political strife. Hence, we need to consider whether the genesis of the current crisis in Thailand can be traced to her poor development on the social front.

As Table 3.3 illustrates, by 1995 Thailand chalked up impressive social development indices which compared very favourably not only with those of India, but with those of East Asian economies as well. The poverty ratio in Thailand was by far the lowest among both lower middle income group countries (to which Thailand belonged) as well as nations in the upper income category. Thailand was one of the very few developing countries with a literacy rate of more than 90 per cent. Also highly positive were her indices of health like life expectancy, infant mortality, child malnutrition, and access to drinking water.

4 Which is nothing but the nominal rate of interest less the rate of inflation. The relevant inflation rate in this case should be the annual increase in prices of consumer goods.

5 Strictly speaking, this expresses intermediation through the banking sector alone.

To sum up, until 1996 the Thai economy appeared extremely healthy and there was practically nothing to suggest that it would be in for trouble in the foreseeable future. Almost all macroeconomic and social sector indices more than satisfied the norms generally used for judging the potential and viability of economic development of a country. Thailand also belonged to the ASEAN group of countries

Table 3.3
SOME SOCIAL INDICATORS: 1995

	Thailand	East Asia	India
Population Growth (%)	1.0	1.3	1.9
Life Expectancy at Birth (years)	69.0	68.0	62.0
Infant Mortality (per 1000 live birth)	35.0	36.0	68.0
Child Malnutrition (% under 5) 1989–95	13.0	17.0	63.0
Access to Safe Water (% of population)	81.0	77.0	63.0
Sanitation (% of population)	87.0	–	29.0
Poverty (% of people living on less than US$ 1 a Day (ppp), 1981–95)	0.1	–	52.5
Adult Illiteracy (%)	6.0	17.0	48.5

Source: World Bank, (1997a); GOI, *Economic Survey 1996–7.*

whose macroeconomic record was way above that of the rest of the world. There was significant policy co-ordination among this group of nations—a crucial condition (World Bank, 1997) for the success of a trading or currency block and for avoiding currency crises. Finally, as an important member of this high performing group Thailand could, in times of trouble, expect speedy succour, not only from her other ASEAN neighbours, but also from Japan which had invested heavily in Thai and other South East Asian economies. There was, thus, little reason to suspect that the baht would, before long, succumb to a speculative attack, or that Thailand would suffer a fate similar to that of Mexico in 1994–5 and of other Latin American countries in the early 1980s.

THE CHINK IN THE THAI ARMOUR

Since the onset of the South East Asian currency turmoil, economists, proverbially adept at explaining why their forecast went wrong, have drawn attention to quite a few sources of crisis in the Thai economy. Some of these relate to relatively long term policies (or their absence) pursued by the Government of Thailand, others to its inability to adjust policies to changing international environment. It will be instructive to make an appraisal of the factors commonly considered to be the most important in impairing the health of the Thai economy and making it vulnerable to a speculative attack on its currency.

CURRENT ACCOUNT DEFICIT

There appears to be a general consensus that large current account deficits in the balance of payments constituted the basic, as also perhaps the proximate, source of the Thai crisis.[6] Between 1991 and 1994, the current account deficit was persistently above 5.5 per cent of GDP and jumped to 8 per cent in 1995 and 1996. Deficit of this order, it is suggested, is unsustainable and cannot but lead to serious balance of payments difficulties. However, before identifying high current account deficit as the villain of the piece, it is useful to consider its interrelation with other macroeconomic variables and the way the deficit can affect the balance of payments viability of an economy.

PERCEPTIONS AND FUNDAMENTALS

There are two (albeit interrelated) ways in which high current account deficits can generate a crisis in the country's external account. First, medium and long term fundamentals of the economy may get distorted as a result of large inflows of foreign funds. Second, even though economic fundamentals remain strong, or even improve, the general perception concerning the deleterious impact of large current account deficits makes a country's currency highly vulnerable to speculative attacks.

THAILAND AND MEXICO BEFORE THE CURRENCY CRISIS

Expectations of balance of payments problems emanating from high deficits in the country's current account are not without empirical

6 The Tarapore Committee (1997) also regards large current account deficits as one of the very few weak elements in "Thailand's approach to CAC" (capital account convertibility). The report was submitted before the outbreak of the Thai crisis. See Reserve Bank of India (1997).

support. Many a currency crisis, including that in Mexico during 1994–5, was preceded by large inflows of foreign funds over a number of years (see Table 3.4). There is, in fact, an interesting parallel between the Mexican and the Thai crises. The currency crises in both countries were preceded by a sudden jump in the current account deficit to GDP ratio, following its maintenance at a fairly steady level over a number of years. However, this does not establish any causal link between current account deficits and weakening of economic fundamentals. Even purely transient factors producing the jump (along with other developments) can generate expectations of an impending balance of payments crisis, induce thereby a speculative attack on the country's currency, and make expectations self-fulfilling.

Table 3.4

SOME MACROECONOMIC INDICES OF MEXICO

(% of GDP)

	1988	1989	1990	1991	1992	1993	1994
GDP (% growth)		3.3	4.5	3.6	2.8	0.7	3.5
Investment	21.1	22.2	22.8	23.4	24.4	23.2	23.5
Saving	19.7	19.4	19.8	18.3	17.1	16.8	15.7
Current Account Balance	−1.4	−2.8	−3.0	−5.1	−7.3	−6.4	−7.8
Exports	21.2	20.3	19.8	17.7	16.6	16.7	18.9
Imports	19.8	20.5	21.0	21.0	22.2	21.1	24.5
Trade Balance	1.4	−0.1	−1.3	−3.2	−5.6	−4.4	−5.6

Source: IMF, *International Financial Statistics.*

Indeed, current account deficits in Thailand, unlike those in Mexico, played a positive role in strengthening rather than impairing the macroeconomic fundamentals of the country. To see how, it is useful to remember that there are three major ways in which large inflow of foreign capital can undermine the balance of payments viability in the long run. First, if borrowing from abroad is used to finance domestic consumption rather than investment, the country will, sooner or later, face difficulties in servicing its debt. Second, even when inflow of external finance adds entirely to domestic capital formation, widespread inefficiency in the use of investible resources may make their returns too low to repay foreign creditors. Third, what is relevant is not productivity of investment in physical terms, but addition to foreign exchange earnings in relation to the requirement for servicing external debt. Thus, it is not enough to add to the productive capacity of the economy unless the additional capacity can be converted into extra earnings in terms of foreign currency. Hence, the need for ensuring that export growth of the country will be enough to discharge interest and repayments obligations on account of foreign borrowing.

On the basis of the criteria noted above, it is easy to indicate the marked difference between the role of current account deficits in the Mexican and the Thai economies. Unlike what happened in Thailand, current account deficits of Mexico during 1989–94 were not accompanied by a commensurate increase in her investment ratio (see Table 3.4). The implication was a fall in national saving which, as a ratio of GDP, showed a declining trend and came down by more than 4 percentage points between 1989 and 1994. In Thailand, on the other hand, the period 1990–5 was characterized by both higher saving and larger domestic investment (see Table 3.1) compared to the earlier period. It is thus clear that while Thailand was supplementing domestic saving with borrowing from the rest of the world to augment her productive capacity, foreign savings flowing into Mexico acted as a substitute for her national saving and primarily provided a boost to domestic consumption.

Deployment of capital was also much more efficient in Thailand than in Mexico. The incremental capital-output ratio[7] (ICOR) in Thailand over the period 1991–5 was close to 4.8 on the average. For Mexico, the average ICOR during 1990–4 was about 7, even if one disregards the dismal GDP growth for 1993. Thus, not only was Thailand using additional resources secured from the rest of world for capital accumulation rather than consumption, but the productivity of capital was also much higher in Thailand than in Mexico.

Finally, GDP growth in Thailand was much more export oriented than in Mexico. Exports grew at a faster rate than GDP in the former, but lagged considerably behind domestic production in the latter. The result was that the export–GDP ratio in Thailand showed a steady growth, from 34.1 per cent in 1990 to 41.8 per cent in 1995.

7 Which denotes additional capital used for producing an extra unit of output. Hence, a lower ICOR generally reflects higher productivity of investment.

In Mexico, on the other hand, the ratio registered a continuous decline from 20.4 per cent in 1989 to 16.7 per cent in 1993, and showed a mild recovery at 18.9 per cent in 1994. Hence, it appears simplistic to bracket the two crises and attribute Thailand's woes to its large scale borrowing from the international capital market.

SCALE OF INDEBTEDNESS

In an era of globalized financial markets a currency crisis, unless induced by purely speculative behaviour, should basically reflect the market perception that the country would not be able to honour its debt obligations. In tracing the genesis of the Thai crisis, we thus need to examine whether Thailand's scale of indebtedness[8] became 'too high' to warrant the loss of confidence in the long term viability of her balance of payments. Even in 1996 none of the usual criteria for measuring the burden of external indebtedness suggested that Thailand would face any problem in servicing her debt. On the basis of this criteria Thailand was placed in the category of 'less indebted countries'. Indeed, between 1985 and 1995, there was a marked decline in all indices of indebtedness, viz., the ratio of total debt to GDP, of total debt to exports, of interest payments to GDP, and of debt service to exports[9] (see Table 3.5).

TRADE DEFICIT

There were, however, some trends on the trading front which may plausibly be interpreted (with the benefit of hindsight) as indicators

8 Note that current account deficits represent yearly increment in foreigners' net claim on the domestic economy while external debt constitutes the stock of accumulated loans in the past, yet to be repaid. Even if a country has not been borrowing in the recent past, for judging her balance of payments viability it is necessary to consider the stock of existing debt, interest at which loans were taken and their repayment schedule—i.e., factors governing the amount and phasing of amortization cum interest payments.

9 The statement was based on figures available in the third quarter of 1997. The Bank of Thailand has recently revised some of these figures and these are placed in brackets below the earlier figures in Table 3.5. The revised estimates for the external debt–GDP ratio for 1995 and 1996 are larger than the older ones; but those for the single most important indicator of the burden of external debt, viz., the ratio of debt-service to exports, are only marginally higher than the earlier figures.

Table 3.5
INDICES OF INDEBTEDNESS OF THAILAND

	1985	1994	1995	1996
Total Debt/GDP	45.1	41.7	42.5 (49.0)	48.8
Total Debt/Exports	171.7	107.0	102.4 (114.2)	123.2
Interest Payments/GDP	2.3	2.5	1.4 (2.5)	2.8
Total Debt Service/Exports	31.9	11.3	11.0 (11.4)	11.1 (12.3)

Source: Central Bank of Thailand.

of weakening of Thailand's economic fundamentals. We have referred to the spectacular increase in Thailand's export–GDP ratio during 1985–95, even while she was enjoying the fastest GDP growth in the world. However, for viability of the balance of payments a country needs to generate an export surplus in the long run, remembering that ultimately it is the excess of export over import earnings which pays off interest plus amortization on external debt. Hence the need to examine the capability of a country to generate a positive trade balance commensurate with its external debt.

Thailand's trade figures during 1992–5 showed a widening gap between imports and exports, with the trade deficit as a ratio of GDP surging from 4.96 per cent in 1992 to 6.8 per cent in 1995. During the same period the debt–GDP ratio of Thailand increased from 35.5 per cent to 42.5 per cent. The increase in the indebtedness ratio, along with the growing trade deficit, may perhaps be viewed as a clear signal of the deteriorating health of the Thai economy over the period. However, such an interpretation of the trends in the two ratios does not appear quite in order.

Note first that the debt–GDP ratio in this period was due in large measure to the fact that from early 1993, when Thai companies were permitted to raise funds offshore, banks and other financial institutions borrowed heavily in foreign currencies to extend domestic credit. However, the large inflow of foreign funds since 1992 had also provided a significant boost to domestic capital formation. The growth rate of domestic investment jumped from 6.2 per cent in 1992 to 9.7 per cent in 1993 and climbed to 12.4 per cent and 12.6 per cent respectively in 1994 and 1995. Larger imports during these years were only a reflection of the use of foreign resources (primarily in the form of imports of capital goods) to build up productive capacity. Exports, it is true, were not rising at a rate commensurate with that of imports. However, given the usual gestation period for most investment projects, an increase in trade deficit over a span of three to four years (after relaxation of controls over borrowing from abroad) should not by itself be regarded as an indication of impairment of the country's economic fundamentals. Until early 1997, international investors were not, in fact, worried about the growing trade deficit and went on pouring substantial funds into Thailand.

Economists have identified two proximate sources of the Thai crisis, one external, the other domestic. The first was stagnation of export earnings over the last 5 to 6 quarters preceding the crisis. This stagnation, against the background of a jump in the current account deficit (from a 5.5 per cent cut in 1994 to nearly 8 per cent in 1995 and 1996) and deceleration of economic growth, came to be perceived as the beginning of the end of the era of Thailand's export led growth. The second factor, inducing widespread belief in bleak prospects of the Thai economy, was the growing manifestation of financial troubles, as non-performing assets of banks and other financial institutions recorded a sharp rise. It is now widely believed that these two developments were due, not simply to cyclical or transitory factors, but to structural weakness of the Thai economy reinforced by policy failures. Let us be specific and see whether the crisis admits of a coherent explanation in terms of these factors.

STAGNATION OF EXPORTS

Between 1985 and 1995, exports from Thailand increased at an average rate of 16.8 per cent per annum, with the export–GDP ratio going up from 23.4 to 41.8 per cent. These aggregate figures do not, however, reveal the growing structural weakness of the economy, especially in the 1990s. Though exports came to occupy such an important constituent of the Thai GDP, the export sector was not sufficiently diversified or upgraded over time to meet international competition or adjust to global demand or supply shocks. Thailand relied heavily on exports of low technology and labour intensive goods like clothing and leather products—a strategy that served her pretty well in rapid absorption of surplus labour and in taking advantage of low wage cost in the earlier phase of development. However, as the wage rate tended to increase with a sharp fall in unemployment, Thai exports became increasingly non-competitive, especially since these industries were footloose and could easily move to other centres with much lower wages than those in Thailand. An indication of the loss of competitive edge of labour intensive and low value added exports from Thailand is underlined by the fact that with unemployment coming down to less than 3 per cent, minimum wages in Thailand have, in recent years, become four to five times higher than those in her regional competitors like China, Indonesia, and Vietnam.[10]

A related structural defect of the Thai economy lay in shortage of skilled labour, and hence, in the difficulty of diversifying in production and export of more sophisticated goods and services. This bottleneck, in its turn, is generally traced to insufficient investment in secondary and higher education. While the literacy rate in Thailand was very high, her secondary and tertiary enrolment as percentage of population in the relevant age group have consistently been much lower than those of not only East Asian countries, but also of the Philippines, Indonesia, Malaysia, and even India. Thus, though Thailand's investment in physical capital as a ratio of GDP has long been one of the highest in the world, not enough resources have been devoted to human capital or skill formation. As a result, Thailand has not been able to develop facilities for the production of relatively sophisticated and value added goods and services.

Indeed, the currency crisis in Thailand came on the heels of the continuing stagnation of exports over the preceding 18 months. The growth rate of Thai merchandise exports (in terms of the US dollar) came down sharply, from 22.2 per cent in 1994 and 24.7 per cent in 1995 to a bare 0.1 per cent in 1996 and did not display any sign of recovery in the current financial year either. The immediate source of trouble on the export front was an adverse external shock which the Thai economy, with its structural imbalance, was unable to absorb. A severe downturn in demand in the world electronic market produced a negative impact on exports from Thailand. What was more important, Thai exports lost out to those from China, which had invested heavily in labour intensive exports and

10 Asian Development Bank (1997).

maintained an undervalued exchange rate in order to utilize the huge excess capacity built up in this sector.[11] The problem was compounded due to the maintenance of a more or less fixed exchange rate between the baht and a basket of currencies where the weight attached to the US dollar was disproportionately large in relation to the importance of Thailand's trade with the USA. As the US dollar appreciated significantly against the yen, mark, and other major currencies, the baht also followed suit. The resulting overvaluation of the baht led to a severe loss of competitiveness of exports from Thailand in major markets.

FINANCIAL FRAGILITY

The second serious weakness of the Thai economy consisted in the malfunctioning of its banks and other financial institutions against the backdrop of large capital inflows in the 1990s. The initial speculative attack on the baht was, in fact, mounted shortly after the collapse of a leading financial house (Finance One) and the revelation that close to two-thirds of the country's 90 finance and securities companies were in serious difficulties. According to the Bank of Thailand, by the end of 1996, about one-seventh of finance company lending, estimated at US$ 6 billion, had turned non-performing. Most financial analysts, however, came up with figures that were about twice the central bank's estimate of non-performing assets.

Subsequent events suggest that the Bank of Thailand did not fully appreciate the gravity of the crisis facing the financial sector. In early 1997 the central bank suspended the operation of 16 financial firms considered to be terminally sick. In the wake of the currency crisis the non-viability of a number of other banks and financial intermediaries became evident and (before seeking loans from the IMF) the Bank of Thailand suspended the operation of 42 more financial companies. The ailment afflicting the financial sector had thus taken a toll of more than 60 per cent of its constituents and is now widely regarded as a (if not *the*) fundamental source of Thailand's currency crisis.

The origin of the woes of the financial sector is traced to the 'overexpansion' of domestic credit in the 1990s, especially since

11 We have subsequently changed our views on the role of Chinese exports in triggering off the Thai crisis. See Chapters 5 and 6.

early 1993, when Thai companies were permitted to borrow from the international capital market. With financial deregulation and unhindered operation of market forces, the major part of credit in this period went to private borrowers. Thus, between 1992 and 1996, there was a quantum jump in loans to the private sector as a ratio of GDP, from 39 per cent to 123 per cent. Overexpansion was most marked in real estate loans, even though by 1993 the property market showed signs of overbuilding and a slowdown in demand. By end 1996 and early 1997, the fall in prices of real estate (which were used as collateral for credit) had landed the majority of the financial firms into serious trouble, thereby undermining international investors' confidence in the Thai economy and inducing a speculative attack on the baht.

The currency crisis in Thailand may be viewed as a vindication of the widely held belief regarding the close connection between the efficiency of financial intermediation in, and viability of balance of payments of, a country when the domestic sector is closely integrated with the global market.[12] Apart from the general weakening of economic fundamentals due to misallocation of resources under an inefficient financial system, in the case of Thailand the nature of the asset–liability structure built up by financial firms played a special role in transforming the troubles faced by these firms into a serious currency crisis. Thai finance companies borrowed on a large scale from the international capital market in order to extend credit to domestic borrowers. Thus, a substantial fraction of liabilities of these companies was denominated in dollars while their assets consisted of loans in terms of bahts. In such a situation a domestic financial crisis leads to the apprehension of reneging on foreign debt, dries up fresh inflow of foreign capital and creates a rush for converting domestic financial assets into foreign currency denominated ones in anticipation of an impending fall in the value of the local currency.

The currency crisis was aggravated, it is now widely held by other features of foreign loans contracted by Thailand. Long used to a more or less fixed rate between the baht and the US dollar, Thai borrowers from the international market did not hedge themselves by entering into forward contracts or ensuring future flow of earnings in terms of foreign currency. The result was that when the downturn

12 See World Bank (1997).

in export earnings led to an expectation of a fall in the exchange rate, the solvency of financial firms was in jeopardy, even if their lending had otherwise been prudent. This, in its turn, threw the financial sector into disarray and deepened the currency crisis.

Second, by early 1997, the structure of Thailand's foreign debt had become highly unbalanced with a preponderance of short term borrowing: out of the outstanding external debt of US$ 90 billion in 1997, as much as US$ 60 billion consisted of short term loans. Thus, even though the Bank of Thailand had foreign exchange reserves to the tune of US$ 40 billion, the amount was insufficient to defend the baht against a concerted attack, irrespective of whether the attack was purely speculative or based on a correct reading of economic fundamentals.

FUNDAMENTALS, SPECULATION, AND CRISIS MANAGEMENT

In examining the roots of the currency crisis faced by Thailand we have closely followed the dominant strands of thought and focused on erosion of export competitiveness and financial fragility as the crucial factors weakening the fundamentals of the Thai economy. However, such identification leaves a number of issues unresolved, and hence, may not be of much use in drawing appropriate policy conclusions for developing countries like India. It appears important in this context to add some caveats to the explanation of the crisis suggested above and go into the role of financial and other policies in aggravating or avoiding such crisis.

EXPORT GROWTH

High wages consequent on low rates of unemployment, it is generally agreed, had led to a loss of competitiveness of Thai exports, the bulk of which consisted of labour intensive products. Attention has also been drawn to external demand shocks of a short term nature to which exports were subject for more than a year preceding the currency turmoil. Thus, shortly before the speculative attack on the baht, the Asian Development Bank (ADB) took a catholic view of the factors causing stagnation of exports from Thailand:[13]

13 Asian Development Bank (1997).

The slowdown in growth is in part a temporary phenomenon resulting from short-term movements in world markets and international prices which reduced trade flows between Thailand and her major trading partners. But there is also a more fundamental economic malaise caused by diminished competitiveness resulting in a loss of international markets. Even if export expansion, as forecast, revives in the near term, innovative ways are needed to improve labour force skills and to encourage the investment needed to support technology.

Note that ADB did not foresee an impending currency crisis. Nor is it simple to explain satisfactorily the emergence of the crisis in terms of the two sets of factors cited above. If the difficulties on the export front are transient (and are perceived to be such), there should be no serious balance of payments problem. Again, recent discussions on the loss of international competitiveness of exports from Thailand appear to ignore both empirical evidence and the economic mechanism through which weakening of economic fundamentals affects the currency market.

Note first that Thailand's growth during 1985–95 was primarily export propelled : with exports rising persistently at a much faster rate than that of domestic production, the export–GDP ratio jumped from 23.4 per cent in 1985 to 41.8 per cent in 1995. The implication is that the rise in wages with the tightening of the labour market itself came about through a phenomenal expansion in exports. Rapid fall in unemployment without upgradation of technology or reallocation of resources in favour of more skill or capital intensive products, no doubt reduces the scope for further expansion of exports. This is precisely what is perceived to have happened in the Thai economy.

However, the emergence and operation of the constraint indicated above should have led to a gradual decline in Thai export growth, not to its abrupt drop. Between 1990 and 1995 growth of exports from Thailand (in terms of the US dollar) did not display any symptom of deceleration. In fact, in spite of relatively high wages and low rates of unemployment, merchandise exports from Thailand (in terms of the US dollar) in 1994 and 1995 registered growth rates of 22.2 per cent and 24.7 per cent respectively. It was only in 1996 that the growth rate plummeted to 0.6 per cent.[14] Such a precipitous fall following a high and accelerated growth cannot be explained in terms of the operation of long-term economic fundamentals.

14 Asian Development Bank (1997)

FLAWED PERCEPTION OF FUNDAMENTALS?

There are more basic issues involved in invoking economic fundamentals like export competitiveness for explaining the currency crisis even when the impact of fundamentals brings export growth to an abrupt end. When operation of these fundamentals is common knowledge, the behaviour of economic agents (including domestic and foreign investors) would be influenced by this knowledge. Such behaviour establishes a close connection between the current exchange rate and the expected competitiveness of exports in future. If there is a widely held belief that Thai exports are going to fall, the current value of the baht will reflect this belief[15] through its impact on the exchange rate expected to prevail in future. The implication is that in the absence of drastic changes in investors' expectations concerning the long-term fundamentals of the economy, exchange rate movements over time should be relatively smooth and not characterized by sharp swings in either direction. If the currency crisis confronting Thailand constituted in fact the consummation of a process of weakening economic fundamentals, investors and other economic agents, it follows, must have been unaware of the growing economic malady—a surmise difficult to sustain in respect of export competitiveness, given the fact that wage increases, shortage of skilled labour and other factors noted in this connection were all in the domain of public knowledge.[16]

FINANCIAL PROBLEMS

Similar difficulties, though on a much smaller scale, arise in focusing on financial fragility as a fundamental source of the Thai currency crisis. Until the first quarter of 1997, foreign investors, let us recall, were willing to pour money into the Thai economy at an ever increasing rate. Meanwhile, the finance companies were operating under a deregulated regime and trying to make the best of the opportunity offered by the gap between the expected return on

15 When exchange control or other measures impeding international flow of goods or capital are not in force.

16 The 1997 speculate attack on the baht, we may note in passing, cannot be explained in terms of the Krugman model (discussed in Chapter 2). The Krugman type explanation would imply that the baht was under-, not overvalued, in the earlier years.

domestic lending and the cost of borrowing from abroad. With earnings of financial firms growing at an annual rate of 25 to 30 per cent until 1996, there was no symptom of reckless lending or of gross inefficiency in financial intermediation.

However, balance sheets and profit-and-loss accounts of financial firms may very often conceal more than they reveal regarding the state of health of these firms, especially under a lax regulatory environment. The Bank of Thailand appears not to have taken its supervisory function very seriously. It was not until late 1995 that some steps were taken to curb lending to property developers, while full disclosure of non-performing loans was required only from October 1996. It is thus possible that there was a general misperception concerning financial fundamentals of the economy and the currency crisis reflected a drastic change in investors' expectations with the removal of this misconception when Finance One collapsed in the first quarter of 1997 and the scale of non-performing assets of other financial firms became public knowledge.

CONFIDENCE AND CRISIS MANAGEMENT

To sum up, the essential feature of a currency crisis consists of the loss of investors' confidence in the balance of payments viability of a country and the consequent apprehension that there is going to be a sharp depreciation of the country's currency in the near future. This loss of confidence may come about due to a drastic revision in investors' perception of the country's fundamentals. What is relevant in this context, we must note, is the perception itself, irrespective of whether it is well or ill founded. In the case of Thailand, several factors (apart from signs of financial fragility) have contributed to this change in perception. Following the widely held notion among economists, the jump in current account deficits in 1995 and 1996 was apparently regarded, as a signal of weakening economic fundamentals and a precursor of the currency crisis. This perception was reinforced by loss of export markets and troubles faced by some financial firms, even though the problems could have been of a short term nature.

Also of crucial significance was the investors' belief in the ability of the authorities to frame and implement the right mix of policies in order to correct the fundamentals or make necessary adjustments to temporary shocks. Confidence in the capability of policy makers, it is widely argued, was rudely shaken by (a) absence of any effective supervision on the part of the Bank of Thailand and the consequent sickness of the large majority of financial firms; (b) maintenance of an overvalued baht; and (c) absence of any attempt to curb 'overexpansion' of bank credit through an increase in interest rate[17] or other devices.

It is, however, a moot point whether the policy measures implied above could have restored investors' confidence and warded off the currency crisis. Effective supervision of banks is, no doubt, extremely important in promoting allocative efficiency and avoiding bank failures in the long run. But the Bank of Thailand's insistence on full disclosure of non-performing assets from the last quarter of 1996 produced a negative impact on investors' confidence and hastened the currency crisis. Regular exercise and nutrious diet help in keeping good health, but can prove fatal for persons who are already sick!

It is also important to recognize that troubles faced by financial firms in 1996–7 was due in no small measure to the slowdown of the economy. The source of this slowdown was an adverse external shock, resulting in a steep fall in export growth[18], and not an overexpansion of domestic credit in earlier years.[19] Under these conditions an increase in interest rates in 1995, *a la* the IMF advice, would have produced a more severe downturn of the economy and deepened the financial crisis in 1996 and 1997.

Commentators on the Thai economy also seem to ignore a basic difficulty confronting the Bank of Thailand in following the IMF advice. Given the high prospective returns on investment in the Thai economy, an increase in domestic interest rates would have induced a larger inflow of foreign funds and added to the troubles on the export front by tending to raise the value of the baht.

The crisis could have been avoided, avers many an analyst, had the Bank of Thailand permitted the baht to depreciate in earlier years. However, there is no hard evidence to suggest that before

17 Thus the IMF has recently revealed that Thailand, Malaysia, and Indonesia did not pay any heed to its advice to raise interest rates during 1995.

18 Exports, let us recall, constituted more than 40 per cent of Thailand's gross domestic product.

19 We have already noted that the inflation rate remained below 6 per cent during 1994 and 1995.

1997 the Bank of Thailand intervened to any significant extent in the currency market in order to maintain an overvalued exchange rate. Throughout 1990–6 foreign exchange reserves of the central bank were worth about 5.5 months' import bill and did not display any declining trend. The central bank intervention in this period, it may reasonably be argued, was directed primarily towards ironing out erratic fluctuations in the exchange rate.

Second, it is far from clear how the market would have reacted to a devaluation of the baht in late 1996 or early 1997. When Mexico announced a 15 per cent devaluation of her currency on 20 December 1994, the International Monetary Fund immediately recorded its approval (on 21 December) with the argument that 'the exchange rate adjustments ... will help reinforce the economic recovery that has been evident since 1994 and secure the viability of Mexico's external position'.[20] The results of the move were, however, disastrous: the speculative attack on the Mexican currency was renewed with such vigour that Mexico had to let the peso float and suffered her worst recession in recent years, as interest rates soared. A devaluation may thus be interpreted as a confirmation of precarious external balance of the country and as a signal of the central bank's weakening resolve (and ability) to defend the value of the currency. Thus, once the country develops some symptoms of external imbalance, the commonly prescribed measures of crisis management may cut both ways and the net outcome is by no means clear.

LESSONS FROM THE THAI CRISIS

It is instructive at this stage to take stock of our analysis of the recent problems facing the Thai economy and see whether we can draw some analytical or policy conclusions. The first two lessons that one can learn from a study of the currency crisis in Thailand (and quite a few other countries) are negative ones. It is generally difficult to explain the crisis in terms of long term fundamentals; nor is it easy to anticipate even an imminent crisis on the basis of actual developments in the short run. The proposition is supported by the experience of both Thailand in 1997 and Mexico in 1994.

20 See G. A. Calvo and E. C. G. Mendonza (1996).

Before the crisis the economic fundamentals of Mexico appeared much weaker on every count than those of Thailand. Yet, until December 1994,

Mexico was hailed as the prime example of success of market-oriented reforms. ... There was debate over the bloated current account deficit and overvalued real exchange rate, and the need for some corrections prior to the 'ascension', but the strength of the country's fundamentals was rarely questioned'.[21]

We have also indicated how only a couple of days before the country was engulfed by the currency crisis, the IMF had foreseen an upswing of the Mexican economy.

Not much dissimilar was the overall perception of the Asian Development Bank (ADB) regarding the Thai economy shortly before the crisis. On the basis of developments in Thailand upto the first quarter of 1997, ADB observed, 'Although the pace of growth is slowing, the economic fundamentals are perceived to be sound', and went on to add: 'action by the authorities (with regard to finance companies) has probably avoided a broader monetary crisis such as that experienced by Mexico in 1994'.[22]

Our earlier discussion also suggests that in a globalized financial market, economic policies of a country, however prudent, may not be enough to avoid a currency crisis when the country is subjected to external shocks. The shock may occur in the form of disruption in trade flows or a sharp rise in interest rates in competing financial centres. Also, as the Latin American and the Thai cases illustrate, when a country faces a currency crisis, other countries belonging to the same region or economic group may suffer from the 'contagion' effect. Given the enormous amount of floating funds in the international financial market[23], and the fact that speculative activity is generally characterized by 'herd' behaviour[24], a country cannot

21 See G. A. Calvo and E. C. G. Mendonza (1996).
22 Asian Development Bank (1997).
23 Some idea of the magnitude of liquid funds is given by the volume of foreign exchange transactions which, in April 1995, averaged US\$ 1,260 billion a day (BIS, 1996).
24 Speculative activity in the currency market reflects expectation of the value of the currency in the near future which, under a free float, cannot generally be predicted on the basis of long term fundamentals or even short term economic factors. Hence, the herd behaviour which consists in following others on the presumption that they know better. Such action is also in

counter a concerted attack on its currency, even though long term fundamentals of the economy remain strong.

The above observations should not be construed to imply that a country can do little in mitigating the impact of a crisis, if not in averting it altogether. For one thing, strengthening of fundamentals supplemented by timely policy adjustments to emerging situations enables a country to limit the damage from adverse external shocks and recover quickly from the depths of the currency crisis. Given the space limitation we propose not to go into all the issues relevant in this connection, but to concentrate on those policies which the Thai crisis appear to highlight.

FINANCIAL POLICY

The proximate source of currency crisis in Thailand was the threat of bankruptcy faced by nearly two-thirds of finance companies, all of which had borrowed heavily from the international market. The policy issues relevant in this context may be grouped under two heads. Under the first are included micro, as also macro measures for avoiding financial crises. Again, since troubles in the financial sector are difficult to avoid altogether in a market driven economy, it is important to take timely steps so that the troubles do not develop into a full blown crisis and undermine investors' confidence in the country's currency.

Absence of disclosure requirement, and of adherence to prudential norms (concerning capital adequacy, asset classification, provisioning, etc.) is universally held responsible for the financial mess in Thailand. However, a closer examination of the Thai experience suggests that the central bank's supervision, along with effective enforcement of these norms, is necessary, but may not be sufficient for avoiding a financial crisis. Lending and borrowing policies of finance companies were, under the deregulated regime, dictated by the profit motive, and until 1996 these policies appeared eminently successful in securing their objective.[25]

---

conformity with Keynes' reading of speculative behaviour: 'Worldly wisdom teaches us that it is better for reputation to fail conventionally than to succeed unconventionally' (Keynes, 1936). This is of special relevance for fund managers of financial firms. For an analysis of herd behaviour see Banerjee (1992).

25 It is interesting to note that despite lax supervision, operation of finance companies in Thailand was not marked by fraudulent practices on a significant scale.

The major source of trouble faced by finance companies lay in overexpansion of loans to property developers. But the malady here is basically macroeconomic and illustrates an inherent difficulty in ensuring optimum allocation of investible resources under the free play of market forces. In any economy undergoing changes there will be shortages in some sectors while others suffer from overcapacity. Higher profits in the former induce larger investment therein, and sectoral imbalances tend to get corrected over time. However, this process of smooth adjustment goes awry when producers act on their own, with everybody rushing to invest in the high profit sectors. The result is a steep fall in profits in this sector as investment elsewhere lags far behind, and hence, does not generate enough demand to ensure capacity utilization of the growing sector. The problem becomes particularly severe in the case of real estate where investment is irreversible and of a long term nature. Such sectoral overinvestment, it is important to emphasize, tends to produce a 'contagion effect' and a downturn of the economy, as investors' sentiment is dampened.

The problem of avoiding such 'coordination failure' is one of the most controversial topics in economics and does not admit to a simple solution. That some restriction on the free play of market forces is necessary to avoid or mitigate financial distress is fairly obvious. The difficulty lies in the choice of instruments and scale of intervention on the part of the monetary or fiscal authorities. One way out may be to limit the exposure of financial firms to particular sectors—a measure that smacks of financial repression and may well stand in the way of efficient allocation of investible funds.

INVESTMENT, FOREIGN BORROWING AND EXPORTS

The Thai crisis appears to highlight another aspect of market failure, viz., unbridled borrowing from abroad to finance expenditure for domestic absorption. As we have already emphasized, for ensuring long term balance of payments viability, not only should inflow of foreign funds be translated into enhanced capital accumulation, but future export earnings need to be large enough to service external borrowing. This does not mean that all funds secured from external sources must be earmarked for investment in the export sector, while finance for enhancing productive capacity to meet domestic demand needs to be raised domestically. The condition for balance of payments viability is a macroeconomic one and concerns the (long run) aggregate flow of debt servicing on the one hand and the flow of current receipts from the rest of the world on the other. Hence, there is nothing wrong if foreign borrowing is used in (say) the power project while finance for investment in the export sector is raised from the domestic capital market. The problem, however, is that when borrowing and investment decisions are driven purely by market forces, the macroeconomic requirement noted above will not generally be satisfied.

The difficulty of ensuring external balance is another manifestation of the 'co-ordination failure' discussed in connection with sectoral over- and under-investment. But here chances of the failure are much greater, since the balance of payments viability of a country depends on the action, not only of its own investors, but also of those in the rest of the world. Future export earnings of a country are crucially affected by the scale (and quality) of investment undertaken in the export sector of competing countries. We have already noted how exports from Thailand were badly hit because of large expansion of capacity on the part of her competitors. More generally, there are so many imponderables in forecasting medium or long run changes in world demand and supply conditions, that well co-ordinated decisions at the national level need not ensure the balance of payments viability of a country.

However, the most serious weakness of the Thai economy, to which almost all commentators have drawn attention, originated from prolonged policy failure at the national level. These weaknesses consist primarily in reliance on labour intensive exports, lack of upgradation of technology, and scarcity of educated and skilled manpower. Part of the problem may be attributed to the lack of foresight of private entrepreneurs[26] who enjoyed almost unfettered freedom in choosing production, investment, and mode of its financing. But the fundamental defect here lay in the lack of public investment in areas which had, for quite some time, been considered crucial for sustained growth, but where private investment would be grossly inadequate in view of large (and positive) externalities.

26 Thus, investment decisions were not apparently based on expectations of rising wages in the future with rapidly declining unemployment.

GUARDING AGAINST CURRENCY CRISES: CONCLUDING OBSERVATIONS

A country with strong economic fundamentals can derive undoubted and substantial advantages by permitting free flow of goods and finance across the national boundary. But as the experience of Thailand suggests, such free flows can also cause severe damage to a country's economy due to the vagaries of international trade and finance— factors over which the country can exercise little control. Thus, a major question that countries, especially those adopting full currency convertibility, have to address is: how can the chances of a currency crisis be minimized when even transient difficulties may result in a loss of confidence?

The answer lies primarily in ensuring against risk of unforeseen changes and having cushions against shocks, even though in the process some growth is sacrificed in the long run.[27] We have observed earlier that large borrowings from abroad do not weaken the economic fundamentals as long as there is a corresponding increase in capital formation in the export sector. However, even if this condition is satisfied, with uncertainties in trends in world demand and supply conditions, larger domestic investment financed through foreign borrowing subjects the country to higher risk of balance of payments problems. Given the (international) investors' aversion to risk, the preponderance of 'herd behaviour' and the difficulty of distinguishing between temporary and permanent shocks, a country is likely to find debt servicing difficult and its currency under attack when its export market is disrupted or its terms of trade decline drastically. Hence the need for discriminating against foreign sources of finance and limiting the scale of the current account deficit, though it is not quite easy to lay down precisely the safe limit for such deficit.[28]

What about policies relating to foreign exchange reserves and the structure of foreign debt in avoiding a currency crisis? It is generally assumed that inadequate foreign exchange reserves in relation to

27 The consideration here is similar to the trade-off between expected return and risk in respect of portfolio choice of investors.

28 It may be noted in this connection that it is the ratio of current account deficit to domestic investment rather than to GDP that appears to be of relevance in this context.

imports and foreign debt make the country prone to a currency crisis. So does, a preponderance of short term debts and bunching of repayments *a la* the Thai experience. These two factors do play a role in the currency crisis, but their importance is more psychological than economic. Large foreign exchange reserves and the fact that the country does not immediately have to seek loans on a significant scale may instil some confidence in its ability to meet current dues in times of trouble on the trading front.

The Indonesian experience, following the contagion effect of the Thai crisis, lends support to the points made above. A number of Indonesian companies had piled up substantial foreign debt before the advent of the South East Asian currency crisis and a major part of this debt had a maturity of less than one year. With the fall of the rupiah and the increase in the domestic rate of interest to prevent any further fall, the firms that had borrowed from abroad incurred heavy losses. No sooner had this information come to light, than there was a massive attack on the rupiah, which added to the woes of the Indonesian economy. The important points to note in this connection are the following:

• First, even if the firms are otherwise efficient, they are likely to incur losses because of the contagion effect, which is extremely difficult to avoid.

• Second, when the currency market is already in a state of flux, the knowledge that there will be a jump in the demand for dollar in the near future by domestic companies generates expectations of an impending fall in the exchange rate, thereby inducing an attack on the currency.

• Third, the process of depreciation (however triggered off), financial troubles of companies burdened with external debt, and (self-fulfilling) expectations of further depreciation can turn out to be cumulative.

All these considerations strongly indicate the necessity of exercising some control over foreign borrowing in general and short term loans in particular.

One should not, however, overemphasize the role of the structure of indebtedness and foreign exchange reserves in affecting the balance of payments viability of a country. Thus, if the troubles are expected to persist for some time, foreign as also domestic investors[29] will take a dim view of the credit-worthiness of the country, so that reliance on relatively long term debt (or foreign direct investment), along with large foreign exchange reserves will fail to ward off the crisis.[30] Thus, while policies concerning foreign reserves and structure of indebtedness are important, the primary focus in the long run has to be on management of risk on the trading front.

There are three major ways of reducing the risk of exposure of a country to forces operating in the sphere of international trade and finance. The extreme solution of eliminating the risk (altogether) is autarkic, but involves too high a cost to merit any serious consideration. However, risk aversion does imply greater weights on investment in sectors producing non-tradables and import-substitutes, though the choice of weights depends on the loss involved in foregoing gains from (international) specialization and capital mobility. The second set of measures consists in diversification of both range and direction of exports, so that gross fluctuations in export earnings are reduced. Such measures are also not costless, remembering that most industries are charac-terized by economies of scale, and that building up of a market in a foreign country requires large initial investment. Third, acquisition of income earning assets abroad (by way of financial or physical investment) by domestic investors is also regarded as an important hedge against unforeseen changes in international trade and finance. However, such hedging, though important for individual investors, is not of much relevance in reducing the risk to which developing countries are exposed, with their domestic absorption (in the form of consumption and investment) exceeding their national income.[31]

Perhaps the most important means of avoiding risk and exploiting opportunities in a changing world is to build up a flexible economic system. Such a system requires, above all, investment in human

29 Note that the Mexican crisis was triggered off largely by the rush for the dollar on the part of the Mexicans, and not so much by foreign investors.

30 Note also that maintenance of larger foreign exchange reserves produces a larger current account deficit (given the gap between interest on foreign debt and earnings from forex reserves).

31 The gap indicates the increase in aggregate net indebtedness to the rest of the world, and hence, is necessarily uncovered by investment abroad.

capital for development of skill, adaptability, and capacity to think up and experiment with new ideas. The distinctive characteristic of this solution is that even a considerable increase in such investment would not involve a trade-off between enhanced economic growth and reduction of risk to international exposure.

SUMMARY

For more than a decade, until 1996, practically all macroeconomic and social indicators, for example, GDP growth, investment and saving ratios, revenue surplus and fiscal surplus, foreign exchange reserves in relation to imports, conventional indices of indebtedness, literacy, life expectations etc., attested to the exceptionally strong fundamentals of the Thai economy. Though current account deficits were high, foreign borrowings supplemented growing domestic saving for investment, and export growth remained far in excess of GDP growth.

Commentators on the Thai crisis have identified two basic weaknesses of the Thai economy: (a) overreliance on low technology and labour intensive exports due to inadequate investment in education and skill formation, and (b) financial fragility.

Outbreak of a currency crisis cannot generally be explained in terms of the operation of economic fundamentals. What matters is the perception of investors who may be guided by fundamentals, purely short term exchange rate expectation, or simply by how fellow investors are behaving, the implication being that economic fundamentals can lead to a currency crisis, only if investors have realized their past mistakes and revised their reading of the fundamentals. In the case of Thailand, it is the stagnation of exports and revelation of the extent of NPAs of finance companies which seem to have led to a change in expectations and triggered off the crisis.

The Thai currency crisis suggests two important policy conclusions. First, neither the strengthening of economic fundamentals nor adoption of precautionary measures in respect of investment and borrowing can be left to the operation of market forces. Second, given the magnitude of floating funds in the international financial system, both prevention and management of the crisis require international co-operation with some organization like the IMF playing a role similar to the one that a central bank plays in the face of (domestic) banking crisis.

4

Crisis, Contagion and Crash
Asian Currency Turmoil

Most of the South East Asian economies are expected to strengthen their performance in 1997 and 1998.

> Asian Development Bank, *Asian Development Outlook 1997* and *1998* (published early second quarter, 1997)

The worst of the Thai crisis is over.

> Managing Director, IMF (24 August 1997)

There are reasons to believe that currency turbulence will eventually wane without greatly damaging the region.

> IMF Report (17 September 1997)

There is no economic reason for what is going on.

> Director, The World Bank, in Jakarta (11 October 1997)

The second half of 1997 saw the most severe crisis ever faced by the high performing economies of East and South East Asia. The problem first surfaced on the ides of May, with a speculative attack on the Thai baht which, though warded off for some time through market intervention, finally forced the Bank of Thailand on July 2 to let the currency float and seek 'technical assistance' from the IMF. Since then the crisis has deepened and widened, spreading not only to other ASEAN countries, but also to almost all emerging markets in the world. In fact, with the mounting financial troubles in the two Asian members of the OECD, viz., Japan and Korea, and the stock

First published in *Money & Finance*, December 1997.

market shocks felt in New York and other major centres, there is a general apprehension of the ASEAN virus seriously afflicting the health of the world economy.

In chapter 3 we discussed in some detail the interplay of factors leading to the currency crisis in Thailand. The present paper focuses on the nature of and the economic process causing the contagion across countries and the policy dilemma confronting the national authorities and international agencies in containing the impact and incidence of the crisis. Our analysis centres around the experience of some selected economies of East and South East Asia, since it is in this region that the contagion has been the most marked and the end of the crisis is not yet in sight. The discussion will be organized as follows. The first section highlights the salient characteristics of the contagion since the fall of the baht and indicates how conventional wisdom concerning measures to avoid the infection or mitigate its impact does not tally with the experience over the last six months. Before analysing the economic forces behind the widening financial turmoil, in the second section, we take a look at the time profile of relevant variables in individual countries and advance a few hypotheses regarding the interrelation among the variables. These hypotheses serve as a background for our discussion on the dynamics of contagion in the third section. In the light of experience of the selected countries, we analyse the role of financial arrangements and policy responses at national and international levels, in reversing or hastening the course of the currency crisis and its contagion. The final section summarizes the main results of the study, both analytical and prescriptive.

WIDENING FINANCIAL TURBULENCE

Before examining the interrelation among economic forces governing the spread and severity of the crisis, it is useful to identify the striking features of the course of financial events in different parts of the world during the second half of 1997. First, by October 1997, the crisis had acquired a global dimension, with practically all economies in the world suffering a meltdown in their share prices or/and exchange rates. Initially, the financial markets of developed countries in Europe and North America shrugged off the ASEAN crisis as no more than a little local

difficulty and their share prices continued to display an upward
trend in tune with their GDP growth in the first two quarters of
1997. However, the Thai troubles did produce (with a time lag) a
negative impact on share prices in Western economies as well—
an impact not fully brought out in Table 4.1, where a comparison
is made of share prices and exchange rates prevailing between 25
June and 3 December 1997. The rising trend of share prices was
arrested and reversed by the second week of August in the USA
and by early October in Western Europe. In spite of this recovery,
by 3 December share price indices registered a fall of 6.5 per cent

Table 4.1

PERCENTAGE CHANGES IN SHARE PRICES AND EXCHANGE RATES BETWEEN 25
JUNE 1997 AND 3 DECEMBER 1997 OF SOME SELECT COUNTRIES

	25 June 1997		3 Dec 1997		% Change over 25 June 1997	
	Share price indices	Exchange rates	Share price indices	Exchange rates	Share price	Exchange rates
Thailand	496.0	25.3	377.4	42.3	–23.9	67.3
Indonesia	712.5	2432.0	399.7	3930.0	–43.9	61.6
Malaysia	1070.0	2.5	548.1	3.7	–48.8	45.2
Philippines	2829.3	26.4	1799.5	35.3	–36.4	33.7
South Korea	705.0	888.0	379.3	1197.0	–46.2	34.8
Japan	20,679.3	114.0	16,585.5	129.0	–19.8	13.2
Singapore	2023.9	1.4	1696.3	1.6	–16.2	12.6
Hong Kong	15,065.0	7.8	11,207.6	7.7	–25.6	–0.1
Taiwan	8956.4	27.9	7902.5	32.3	–11.8	15.8
China	1356.7	8.3	1180.9	8.3	–13.0	0.0
India	4093.6	35.8	3562.4	39.3	–13.0	9.8
Russia	837.3	5765.0	670.1	5940.0	–20.0	3.0
Brazil	13,053.0	1.1	9992.0	1.1	–23.5	2.8
Argentina	820.1	1.0	705.4	1.0	–14.0	0.0
USA	7690.0		8032.0		4.4	
Britain	4640.0	0.6	4970.7	0.6	7.1	0.0
Germany	3798.5	1.7	4082.9	1.8	7.5	2.9
Hungary	6779.6	185.0	6917.7	200.0	2.0	8.1
Mexico	4397.8	7.9	9127.9	8.1	107.6	2.4

Note: Exchange rates refer to the amounts of local currency per US dollar.
Source: *The Economist*, various issues.

in Britain, 7.7 per cent in Germany, and 2.8 per cent in the USA from their respective peaks attained since 2 July 1997.

Second, though the financial crisis originating in Thailand reached a global proportion, it is the economies in Asia, Latin America, and Eastern Europe that have felt its most severe impact. In fact, since the second week of November 1997, share prices in developed Western economies started gaining and recovered much of the lost ground by the first week of December 1997, though it is too early to judge whether the recovery will be transient or long lasting. By contrast, not only has the fall in share prices and/or exchange rates been very steep in other emerging market economies and Japan, but the end of their woes is not yet in sight.

Third, as Tables 4.2–4.3 and Figures 4.1–4.2 suggest, among countries in South East and East Asia, there was a close correspondence between movements in share prices and in exchange rates during the reference period.[1] The correspondence, it is also worth noting, was much closer within the ASEAN economies than between these countries and their more advanced neighbours. Except for Korea, not only were currency depreciation and decline in share prices much more modest in 'the gang of four' and Japan, but also, since the middle of November, there was some recovery in stock markets, along with a perceptible fall in the rate of depreciation of currencies of these economies (see Tables 4.2–4.3, Figures 4.1–4.2).[2] Indeed, since early November the trend in share prices of advanced Asian economies (barring Korea) was similar to that of western countries, though the stock market indices in the former remain considerably lower than those prevailing at the beginning of the Thai crisis.

1 However, there was little depreciation in the Hong Kong dollar or the Chinese yuan, due to the adherence of the two countries to the currency board and fixed exchange rate system respectively. The decline in share prices in China between 2 July and 3 December was also quite negligible. By contrast, the fall in Hong Kong shares was very steep since the third quarter of 1997, irrespective of the base chosen.

2 The decline in share prices in Thailand was, to be sure, less than that in Hong Kong. Note, however, that during July 1997 Thai shares gained 37 per cent before the symptoms of contagion in other South East Asian economies became evident. Again, unlike the Hang Seng, the Bangkok SET did not show any sign of recovery since the middle of November.

Table 4.2
Weekly Exchange Rate Movements With Respect to the US Dollar
Percentage Change Over 25 June 1997

1997	Thailand	Indonesia	Malaysia	Philippines	Japan	Korea	Singapore	Taiwan	Hong Kong
2 Jul	14.62	0.12	0.00	0.00	0.00	0.00	0.00	-0.36	0.65
9 Jul	14.62	0.12	0.00	0.00	-0.88	0.00	0.00	-0.36	0.65
16 Jul	17.79	1.89	2.78	11.74	1.75	0.68	1.40	0.00	0.65
23 Jul	24.90	6.29	4.76	8.71	1.75	0.68	2.80	0.36	0.65
30 Jul	25.30	5.88	4.37	12.88	3.51	0.45	2.80	2.51	0.52
6 Aug	22.53	6.29	4.76	9.47	4.39	0.68	2.80	2.87	0.52
13 Aug	23.72	9.09	9.92	10.98	1.75	0.79	4.90	2.87	0.52
20 Aug	23.72	13.69	10.32	15.15	3.51	1.24	5.59	2.87	0.52
27 Aug	33.99	18.42	12.30	15.53	4.39	1.69	5.59	2.87	0.52
3 Sep	33.99	18.42	12.30	15.53	6.14	1.69	5.59	2.87	0.52
10 Sep	35.18	19.57	15.87	22.35	4.39	2.36	5.59	2.51	0.65
17 Sep	41.90	22.12	19.05	26.89	5.26	2.36	5.59	2.51	0.52
24 Sep	38.74	23.36	21.43	26.89	5.26	2.93	5.59	2.51	0.52
1 Oct	41.90	40.01	33.73	31.44	6.14	2.82	6.99	2.51	0.52
8 Oct	41.50	47.20	25.79	34.47	6.14	3.15	9.09	2.15	0.52
15 Oct	46.25	47.00	25.00	28.41	6.14	3.04	8.39	2.15	0.52
22 Oct	53.75	50.90	34.92	32.58	6.14	3.27	10.49	8.96	0.65
29 Oct	49.80	48.44	34.92	32.95	6.14	8.90	10.49	11.11	0.39
5 Nov	54.90	34.05	30.59	31.82	7.89	9.23	9.79	9.32	0.39
12 Nov	49.80	41.65	30.52	26.52	10.53	11.49	10.49	11.11	0.39
19 Nov	58.10	44.33	38.49	33.33	11.40	16.55	11.89	18.28	0.39
26 Nov	56.92	50.49	39.29	31.82	11.40	25.00	11.89	16.13	0.39
3 Dec	67.31	61.60	45.24	33.71	13.16	34.80	12.85	15.77	0.49
10 Dec	66.80	81.13	45.63	33.71	13.16	76.35	13.29	15.77	0.52

Source: Estimated from data given in *The Economist.*

Table 4.3
WEEKLY SHARE PRICE MOVEMENTS
Percentage Change Over 25 June 1997

1997	Thailand	Indonesia	Malaysia	Philippines	Japan	Korea	Singapore	Taiwan	Hong Kong
2 Jul	14.68	2.48	1.39	-2.28	-2.34	10.26	-2.72	0.45	0.87
9 Jul	28.17	3.59	-3.44	-8.49	-4.75	9.50	-2.02	4.54	-2.40
16 Jul	33.81	1.54	-6.16	-8.55	-1.55	4.92	-5.24	6.57	2.53
23 Jul	27.28	0.80	-3.36	-6.82	-2.65	3.63	-2.43	4.74	4.47
30 Jul	37.00	1.33	-4.23	-8.27	-2.26	3.11	-2.84	11.01	6.09
6 Aug	28.08	-1.77	-11.06	-4.75	-4.73	5.77	-3.23	10.11	9.80
13 Aug	27.56	-7.56	-15.07	-10.68	-8.08	8.18	-7.34	6.70	9.41
20 Aug	18.23	-16.74	-13.12	-14.89	-6.90	5.84	-3.95	10.04	5.25
27 Aug	5.58	-22.04	-20.76	-19.27	-10.82	3.59	-5.33	12.22	3.11
3 Sep	3.65	-28.06	-29.83	-29.52	-9.40	-2.33	-10.06	5.63	-2.33
10 Sep	9.19	-19.30	-19.34	-21.79	-9.55	-1.90	-3.92	2.11	-1.72
17 Sep	4.31	-26.08	-24.20	-26.70	-14.49	-0.75	-5.62	1.46	-4.34
24 Sep	10.28	-22.30	-27.16	-26.59	-10.92	-6.98	-6.1	0.42	-5.71
1 Oct	10.44	-24.63	-25.63	-26.92	-13.72	-8.52	-4.06	-2.92	-0.10
8 Oct	5.77	-27.17	-21.81	-31.19	-14.80	-13.42	-7.01	-7.82	-1.50
15 Oct	7.98	-27.17	-25.10	-27.89	-16.19	-14.23	-8.35	-7.75	-1.16
22 Oct	3.15	-29.09	-31.66	-31.82	-14.47	-14.71	-14.44	-14.11	-2.75
29 Oct	-7.82	-33.74	-38.08	-35.88	-18.48	-28.14	-23.84	-20.84	-28.54
5 Nov	-1.79	-31.09	-31.42	-32.82	-20.46	-21.18	-16	-12.19	-29.10
12 Nov	-5.36	-36.90	-36.03	-34.90	-25.36	-26.60	-16.71	-13.89	-36.22
19 Nov	-12.42	-41.66	-43.60	-33.84	-23.39	-28.71	-16.94	-13.97	-32.60
26 Nov	-18.99	-44.07	-50.83	-36.40	-22.41	-37.77	-18.3	-14.05	-29.70
3 Dec	-23.92	-45.31	-48.78	-36.40	-19.80	-46.20	-16.19	-11.77	-25.61
10 Dec	-21.23	-41.63	-40.52	-30.27	-20.32	-43.28	-15.83	-5.06	-26.83

Source: The Economist.

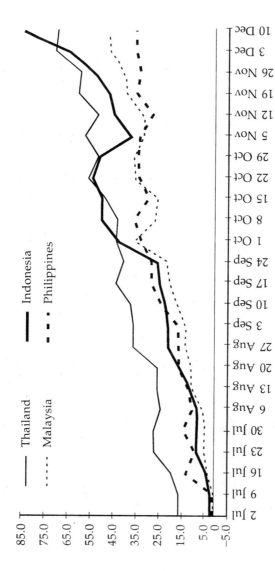

Figure 4.1a: Exchange Rate Movements (Percentage Change over 25 June 1997).

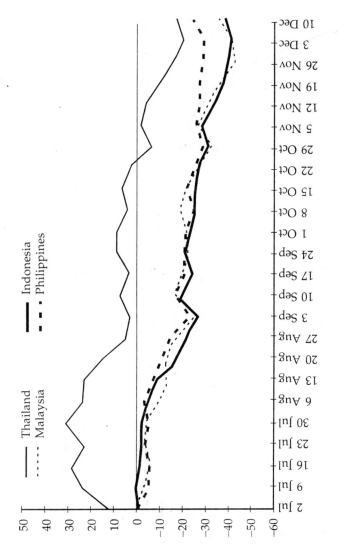

Figure 4.1b: Share Price Movements (Percentage Change over 25 June 1997).

Note: All changes are with respect to US$.

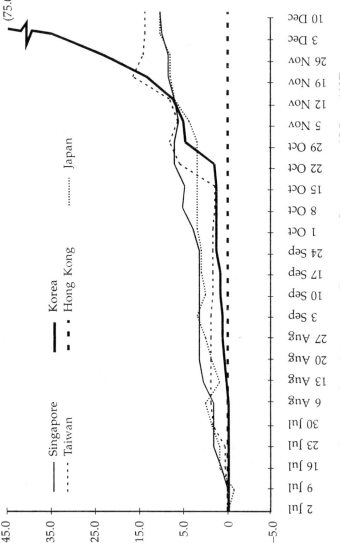

Figure 4.2a: Exchange Rate Movements (Percentage Change over 25 June 1997).

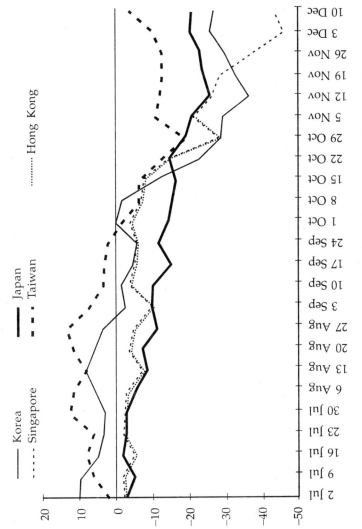

Figure 4.2b: Share Price Movements (Percentage Change over 25 June 1997).

Fourth, the turmoil in currency and stock markets in East and South East Asia has been closely associated with serious troubles faced by banks and other financial firms. As we noted in Chapter 3, the collapse of Finance One, one of the leading finance houses, coming on the heels of the suspension of 16 tottering financial firms by the Bank of Thailand, played no small role in triggering off the currency crisis. The gravity of the problem faced by the financial sector is suggested by the fact that the by 29 July 1997, the day Thailand sought IMF bailout, operation of 58 out of the country's 90 finance companies had to be suspended. There is no indication either that the health of the remaining part of the financial sector had improved over the last four to five months.

The currency and share market contagion has been associated with the loss of confidence in, and the consequent difficulties faced by finance companies of almost all countries in this region. Banking problems surfaced in Indonesia in late September and before approaching the IMF the authorities closed down 16 large banks in the country. No less serious is the state of financial affairs in Japan and Korea. Already there has occurred a string of failures of financial houses in Japan, including Hakaido Takushoku Bank, one of the country's 10 leading money centre banks, and Yamaichi Securities Company, the fourth largest brokerage house. A mountain of bad debt has driven several South Korean banks to the brink of bankruptcy, avoidance of which will require massive infusion of funds. Even where the state of the financial sector is not so rotten, a large number of banks have suffered substantial losses, investors' confidence in their viability has been rudely shaken, and their credit rating downgraded by leading international agencies.

Finally, the current crisis, we need to emphasize, encompasses the financial, as also the real sector.[3] Firms have been forced to cut back production to contain their losses. Employment has shown a downward trend, and so has investment undertaken by companies operating in the afflicted regions. No wonder the ongoing crisis has kept the pundits at various international monetary institutions and elsewhere busy revising downwards their growth forecasts for the East and South East Asian economies.

---

3 Were economic variables like real income, employment or growth not significantly affected in the course of the crisis, we would have dismissed it as being of little relevance for the economic health of nations or their well-being.

PREVENTING CRISES AND CONTAGION: THEORY AND EVIDENCE

The course of economic events during the second half of 1997 provides an almost ideal opportunity for testing the conventional wisdom relating to measures for guarding against a currency crisis and its contagion from elsewhere. Some of the steps suggested are required to be taken by domestic authorities, while others consist in inter-country co-operation, including support from the IMF or other world bodies. In order to assess the efficacy of the recommended programme, we shall focus first on the experience of the five most seriously affected economies, viz., Thailand, Indonesia, Malaysia, the Philippines, and Korea. The key macroeconomic indicators of the five countries are given in the tables of Annexe 4.1 for ready reference. A perusal of Tables A4.1.1–A4.1.5 suggests that neither the emergence of the crisis nor its spread and depth can be reasonably explained in terms of the 'fundamentals' emphasized in the literature. Both in Thailand and other countries the fiscal stance was all that one could hope for. Since 1993, the government budgets have shown a fiscal surplus, an extremely rare phenomenon among modern day nations. Inflation has consistently been at the single digit level, with the 1996 rate at 5.1 per cent for Thailand, 7.9 per cent for Indonesia, 3.5 per cent for Malaysia, 8.4 per cent for the Philippines, and 5 per cent for Korea. Not only have the growth rates of these countries been very high, but the rates showed a rising trend during 1992–5. Even in 1996, when there was a setback due to sharp fall in export earnings[4], GDP growth was still 6.7 per cent in Thailand, 7.8 per cent in Indonesia, 8.8 per cent in Malaysia, 5.5 per cent in the Philippines[5], and 7 per cent in Korea.

Current account deficits did go up over the last couple of years, but remained fairly modest in Korea, Indonesia and the Philippines. Again, a temporary increase in the current account deficit is perfectly in accord with conventional wisdom for preventing a sudden drop in a country's absorption[6] due to transient falls in exports. Note

4 As Tables A4.1.1–A4.1.5 show, between 1995 and 1996, export growth plummeted from 24.7% to 1% in Thailand, 13.1% to 8.8% in Indonesia, 25.9% to 4% in Malaysia, 29.4% to 17.5% in the Philippines and 31.5% to 4% in Korea.

5 Despite the setback on the export front, the GDP growth in the Philippines was higher in 1996 by 0.7 percentage point than that in the earlier year.

6 Consisting of domestic consumption and investment.

also that unlike what happened in other countries (including the USA), current account deficits[7] in the five countries did not crowd out domestic saving, which accounted for the overwhelming part of their capital formation. This, coupled with high GDP growth and the increasing export orientation of their production structure, should have, *a la* widely shared perception, made the countries free from currency crisis and its contagion.

What about the health of the financial sector which is currently viewed as the Achilles' heel of many an Asian giant? There were, to be sure, signs of financial fragility in Thailand and Korea (as also Japan), even before the onset of the currency crisis. In others, however, vulnerability of the banking sector was far from evident. As we shall presently discuss, there are strong grounds for believing that in many cases the chain of causation has run primarily from contagion and crisis to financial fragility, rather than the other way round.

The woes of Thailand are often traced to the policy of keeping the exchange rate fixed between the US dollar and the baht—a policy that made the latter overvalued and Thai exports non-competitive in the world market. While there is some merit in the argument, it is interesting to note that the fall in exports in 1996[8] was a general phenomenon in all Asian economies, irrespective of their exchange rate regime. Indonesia and Malaysia had a much more flexible exchange rate system than Thailand and adjusted their currencies to inflation; even so, between 1995 and 1996, export growth declined from 13.1 per cent to 8.8 per cent in Indonesia and from 25.9 per cent to 4 per cent in Malaysia, and the affliction in the two countries is no less serious than that in Thailand.

The other policy parameter emphasized in this connection is maintenance of 'adequate' foreign exchange reserves. It does appear that low foreign exchange reserves in relation to short term external debts have played a significant part in making the baht, the rupiah, and the won vulnerable to speculative attacks. The key factor here consists in investors' confidence and the role of large foreign exchange reserves lies in boosting this confidence. However, as the case of

7 Which is nothing but foreign saving deployed for domestic consumption or investment.

8 Export growth in Thailand was 22.2 per cent in 1994 and 24.7 per cent in 1995.

Hong Kong dramatically illustrates, once the virus has spread to some countries in a region, maintenance of foreign exchange reserves, however large they may be, does not make the neighbouring nations immune to infection. In spite of reserves worth more than US$80 billion, a long standing currency board system, and full support from China[9], Hong Kong could not avoid the speculative attack on its currency.[10] The Hong Kong dollar, it is true, has not yet been devalued, but only at the cost of a steep fall in share prices and significant slowing down of the economy.

Indeed, recent events across Asia have exposed serious gaps in economists' understanding of the process of contagion and the best way of tackling the problem. At the first sign of the Thai crisis, Indonesia and the Philippines scrupulously followed the measures suggested in mainstream literature on the subject. Unlike Thailand, instead of frittering the foreign exchange reserves away in defence of their currencies, the two countries let their currencies float. As early as 14 July the Philippines secured IMF support worth US$1.2 billion under the recently introduced[11] fast-track regulations. The countries quickly pursued tight monetary policies[12] and announced a cutback in public expenditure, along with an increase in tax rates. At the first symptom of financial troubles, Indonesia also took drastic steps through closure of banks perceived to be non-viable. Alas, all these were of little avail in avoiding contagion or moderating the financial meltdown.[13]

With huge funds floating across global currency and stock markets, an individual country, in spite of doing everything right, may, on its own, fail to stem the tide of financial turmoil. This perception has been strengthened since the onset of the Mexican crisis in 1994–5

9 Whose forex reserves total more than US$120 billion.

10 The investors' loss of confidence in the H K dollar is illustrated by the fact that at one stage the differential between the six-month inter-bank interest rate in Hong Kong and the LIBOR rate for the US dollar was more than 4 percentage points.

11 After the Mexican crisis in 1995.

12 All ASEAN neighbours of Thailand jacked up the interest rates to dizzy heights in order to protect their currencies.

13 Much emphasis has recently been placed on the role of inadequate coverage and lack of transparency of official statistics in spreading the currency crisis. However, the Philippines has regularly been publishing fairly comprehensive data on the economy, including its banking system.

and the massive international intervention needed for its resolution. In the aftermath of this experience, the IMF introduced 'new arrangements to borrow', under which funds could be quickly raised to rescue countries facing a currency crisis. Many East and South East Asian central banks had also entered into agreements to support each other's currencies in the event of a speculative attack.

During the last six months, distressed economies in Asia did receive some succour from their better-off neighbours, but on a quite modest scale. It is the International Monetary Fund that has played the pivotal role in a series of rescue operations. The chronology and scale of these operations make interesting reading. The first to seek financial support from the IMF, 'under new arrangements to borrow', was the Philippines (on 13 July). However, the sum involved (US$1.2 billion) was a pittance compared to the scale of funding in subsequent cases. Thailand asked for IMF bailout on 29 July, Indonesia on 8 October, and Korea on 29 November. For its part, the IMF was fairly quick in arranging for the bailout, the magnitude of assistance going up by leaps and bounds from one case to the next. With the Thai rescue package at US$17.2 billion, the Indonesian at US$40 billion and the Korean at US$57 billion, the total fund for bailouts has already crossed US$115 billion.

The recent rescue operations of the Asian economies, it is worth noting, represent unprecedented financial co-operation at the international level. The IMF has provided the leadership and drawn up the modalities of assistance, but other institutions like the World Bank and the Asian Development Bank, as also Japan, USA, Germany and a few other countries have contributed substantially to the fund to be provided under the IMF programmes, of financial assistance. This is especially so in the case of the Korean programme under which the IMF will provide US$21 billion, World Bank US$10 billion, ADB US$4 billion, while contributions from the USA, Britain, Japan, Germany, France, Canada, and Australia total US$22 billion.

The significance of such co-operation for restoring the health of the global monetary and financial system can hardly be overemphasized. However, the results of the IMF-led international intervention in the Asian crisis have not, so far been very encouraging. Even after nearly six months, the tide of the Asian troubles shows little sign of ebbing. Share prices have been following their downward drift, and so have the currency prices in terms of the US dollar.

A perusal of Table 4.4 suggests that the three economies, that had received large scale infusion of IMF funds, remained seriously problem ridden as of the second week of December 1997. Table 4.4 shows for the three countries the behaviour of the exchange rate and share price movements upto 12 December, from the dates on which the IMF help was sought and the IMF rescue package was announced.[14] The extent of depreciation and decline in share prices remained high from both dates for all the three countries. It is also interesting to note that the weekly fall in currency values and stock indices seems to be directly related to the magnitude of IMF support. For Korea it is too early to judge the efficacy of international rescue operation; but the results in Thailand and Indonesia cast serious doubts on the quality of IMF intervention in dealing with the currency crisis.

For our analysis at a later stage, we draw attention to one interesting feature of market response following the announcement of the IMF bailout. For the country concerned, there was an immediate improvement in stock and currency markets, which generally pulled up markets in neighbouring nations as well. However, the upswing did not last for more than a few days, and soon currencies and share prices tended to resume their downslide. Quite clearly, after a more serious scrutiny, the market recorded its deep disappointment with the IMF packages.

BEHAVIOUR OF FINANCIAL VARIABLES: SOME OBSERVED INTERRELATIONS

The financial variables whose behaviour during the currency crisis we propose to examine are the exchange rate, interest rate and share prices. Not only are the three variables closely connected, but their behaviour mirrors the current and expected movements in the real sector of the economy. Our focus on the financial markets has, we admit, been forced on us: while statistics for short term movements in these markets are more easily available, data for real variables are released with a considerable lag. In the next section we shall try to

14 Recall that in a globalized capital market as of today, not only share prices, but exchange rates too are driven primarily by expectations, which, in their turn, should be affected significantly, among other things, by news regarding the prospects of IMF support and details of the package.

Table 4.4

IMPACT OF THE IMF PROGRAMMES ON CURRENCY AND SHARE PRICES

1	2 Share price and exchange rate on 12 Dec.	3 Date of approach	4 Share price and exchange rate on date of approach	5 Change in share price and exchange rate on 12 Dec. from date of approach (%)	6 Weekly avg of 5 (%)	7 Date of announcement	8 Share price and exchange rate on date of announcement	9 Change in share price and exchange rate on 12 Dec. from date of approach (%)	10 Weekly avg of 9 (%)
Thailand	368.39 45.05	29 Jul 97	679.5 31.7	-45.80 42.10	(19 weeks) -2.41 2.22	11 Aug 97	632.7 31.3	-41.80 43.90	(16.5 weeks) -2.53 2.66
Indonesia	396.08 5120.19	8 Oct 97	518.9 3649.94	-23.70 40.30	(9 weeks) -2.37 4.48	1 Nov 97	472.1 3270.03	-16.10 56.60	(5.5 weeks) -2.93 10.29
S. Korea	359.82 1709.97	21 Nov 97	601.3 1051	-40.20 62.70	(3 weeks) -13.40 20.90	3 Dec 97	379.3 1195.02	-5.10 43.10	(1 week) -5.10 43.10

Note: 1. For Indonesia the share price figure is for 11 Dec 1997 instead of 12 Dec 1997; 2. For Thailand share price index is for 13 Aug instead of 11 Aug; 3. For Indonesia share price index is for 29 Oct instead of 1 Nov; 4. For Korea share price index is for 19 Nov instead of 21 Nov; 5. For Thailand exchange rate is for 13 Aug instead of 11 Aug and 30 Jul instead of 29 Jul; 6. For Indonesia exchange rate is for 3 Nov instead of 1 Nov.

Source: *The Economist*, various issues.

supplement our observations on financial markets, with casual empiricism on the basis of a few fragmentary and qualitative information available for the real sector.

The relation among the three financial variables depends, among other things, on the exchange rate regime and the degree of currency convertibility in force. For more than a decade, Thailand and Hong Kong maintained a more or less fixed exchange rate, while most other countries in the region had a 'dirty float', characterized by central bank intervention to avoid undue volatility in the exchange rate, without hindering its movements in response to economic 'fundamentals'. Over the last six months, barring the Hong Kong dollar, all currencies in the region[15] have practically been on a 'clean float' with little central bank intervention in the foreign exchange market.[16] Again, except for South Korea, other countries chosen for close scrutiny have maintained capital account convertibility for quite some time, though some restrictions on currency transactions were imposed at the onset of the Thai crisis. These features of the exchange rate and currency convertibility regimes are required to be kept in view while studying the relations between movements of interest rates, share prices and exchange rates in the East and South East Asian countries.

Figure 4.3–4.9 present the time profile of the three financial variables during the currency crisis in Japan, Hong Kong, and the five most severely affected countries. A close scrutiny of these charts reveal some interesting correlations among movements in markets for bonds, shares and foreign exchange.

First and the most important, in all the countries currency depreciation[17] went hand in hand with declining share prices, though the period over which the association became strong differs somewhat from one country to another. Thus, Thailand was the first to be hit by the crisis, but the positive relation between share prices and value of the local currency emerges only from August. Similar

15 Except the yuan.

16 However, in some cases 'bands' are in force and these limit the upward and downward movement of a currency *during a day* from the previous day's close.

17 Note that the figure (and tables) give percentage changes in the value of the US dollar in terms of local currencies, so that an upward movement of the exchange rate index implies that the currency is depreciating over time.

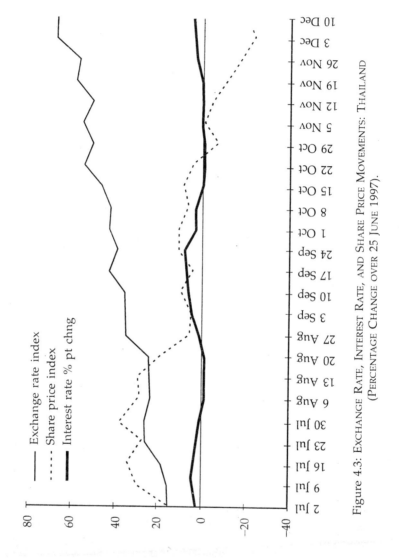

Figure 4.3: Exchange Rate, Interest Rate, and Share Price Movements: Thailand (Percentage Change over 25 June 1997).

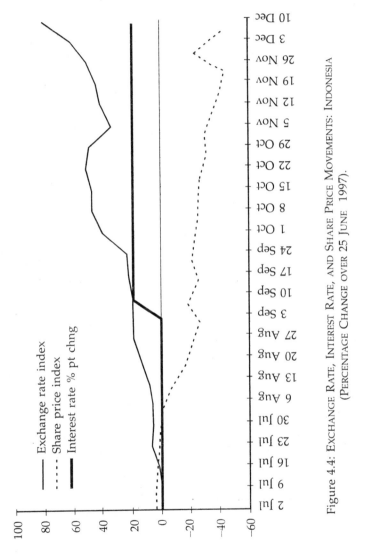

Figure 4.4: EXCHANGE RATE, INTEREST RATE, AND SHARE PRICE MOVEMENTS: INDONESIA (PERCENTAGE CHANGE OVER 25 JUNE 1997).

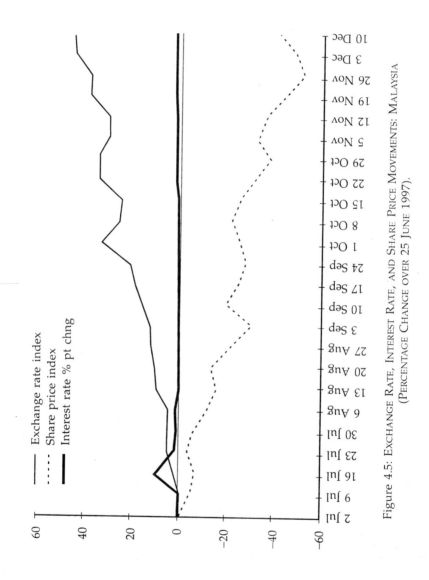

Figure 4.5: EXCHANGE RATE, INTEREST RATE, AND SHARE PRICE MOVEMENTS: MALAYSIA (PERCENTAGE CHANGE OVER 25 JUNE 1997).

Exchange rate index
Share price index
Interest rate % pt chng

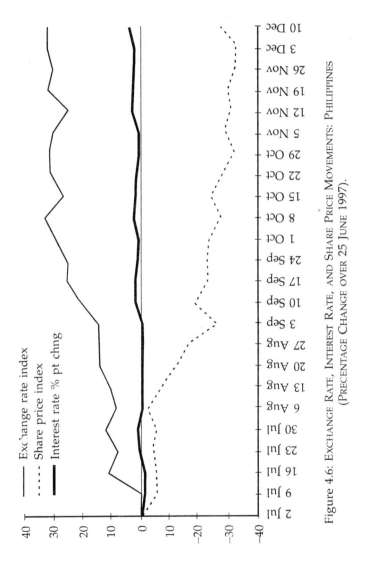

Figure 4.6: EXCHANGE RATE, INTEREST RATE, AND SHARE PRICE MOVEMENTS: PHILIPPINES (PRECENTAGE CHANGE OVER 25 JUNE 1997).

is the experience of the three ASEAN neighbours of Thailand, viz., Indonesia, Malaysia, and the Philippines. Late July to early August may thus be regarded as the period over which the currency troubles originating in Thailand turned into a full fledged financial crisis engulfing the entire group of ASEAN nations.

Interestingly enough, outside the ASEAN group of countries, Japan was the first to show some symptoms of contagion. In fact, a tendency for share prices to slide along with a depreciating yen was apparent since the beginning of August, though the tendency became pronounced only from 20 August. Korean share prices had been falling since the middle of August, but the rate of the won's depreciation was quite minor in the initial phase. It was only from the third week of October that a rapidly depreciating won was accompanied by tumbling share prices. The behaviour of financial variables in Hong Kong stands somewhat apart from that of other Asian countries. With its currency board system, Hong Kong has been able to successfully defend its currency, so that the relation between the exchange rate and share prices observed for other countries does not show up in the case of movements in the Hang Seng index and the Hong Kong dollar.

Second, the relation between the interest rate and the other two financial variables appears less striking than that obtaining between the exchange rate and share prices. Short term interest rates in all the countries except Japan have increased since late June, reflecting the authorities' attempts to arrest currency depreciation. Between 25 June and 3 December, the interest rate went up by 325 basis points in Thailand, 1787 points in Indonesia, 141 points in Malaysia, 324 points in the Philippines, 312 points in South Korea, and 323 points in Hong Kong. This rise in short term interest rates does not fully reflect the extent of the credit crunch effected during the currency crisis. Overnight, interest rates often jumped by 50 to 300 per cent. No less important was the severe rationing of credit faced by corporates and other borrowers in almost all countries. It is, however, clear from Figure 4.3–4.7 that the restrictive monetary measures taken by the central banks could not arrest, let alone reverse, the declining trend in currency values.

Third, the contrast between the experience of Japan and Hong Kong during the currency crisis is worth recording. The interest rate in Japan and the exchange rate in Hong Kong showed little trend between 25 June and 10 December, and this reflects the difference

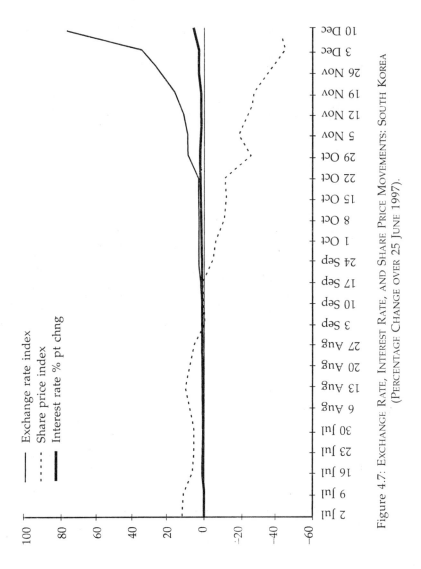

Figure 4.7: Exchange Rate, Interest Rate, and Share Price Movements: South Korea (Percentage Change over 25 June 1997).

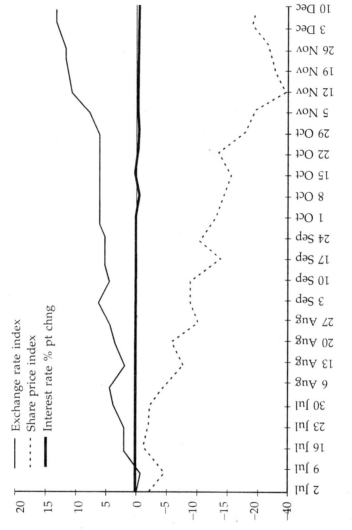

Figure 4.8: Exchange Rate, Interest Rate and Share Price Movements: Japan (Percentage Change over 25 June 1997).

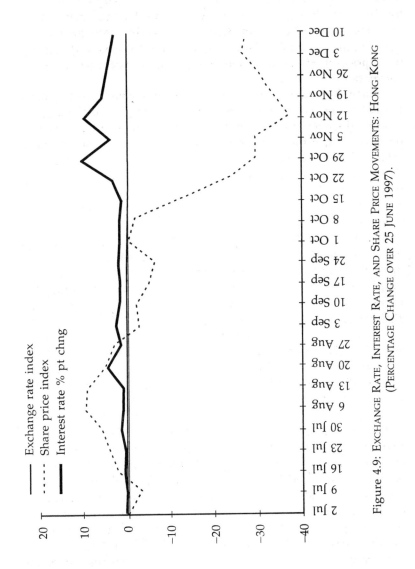

Figure 4.9: Exchange Rate, Interest Rate, and Share Price Movements: Hong Kong (Percentage Change over 25 June 1997).

in the policy stance of monetary authorities in the two countries. No wonder, then, that in Japan the crisis was manifested in the markets for shares and foreign exchange, while the burden of adjustment fell on stock and bond prices in Hong Kong. Again, while the relation between movements in the Nikkei and the yen was fairly strong, bond prices in Hong Kong and Hang Seng did not show any close correlation.

Fourth, behind the overall pattern of movements in the three variables, one can observe some leads and lags, or differences in phasing during the period under review. The most interesting was perhaps the initial adjustment in the Thai financial markets, following the decision of the Bank of Thailand to give up the defence of the baht on 2 July 1997 and adopt a restrictive monetary policy. There was an immediate jump in the baht–dollar exchange rate[18] (by about 15 per cent), along with an increase in the interest rate—developments that make perfect economic sense. However, there was a simultaneous increase in share prices as well. In fact, the main trend observed during the currency crisis was that throughout July a depreciating baht was associated with a fairly rapid rise in share prices. Thus, between 25 June and 30 July, the share price index gained 37 per cent, while the US dollar gained 25.3 per cent against the baht. Again, after a steep fall in August, the Thai share prices remained fairly stable throughout September, even though the baht had been falling all the while. The fall in share prices and the faster rate of currency depreciation in Thailand since early October reflect in large measure the feedback of the Thai malady with the spread of the virus in East and South East Asia.

The Thai crisis spread fairly quickly to the Philippines, though share prices remained stable in July after their fall in the first week by more than 8 per cent. By contrast, during this month the extent of depreciation and fall in share prices were relatively mild in Malaysia and Indonesia. In fact, until the second week of August the Indonesian stock market remained immune to the currency crisis and the depreciation of the rupiah was also quite minor. It is for this reason that the subsequent collapse of Indonesia left everybody groping for a plausible economic explanation of the event. The Indonesian experience becomes more baffling when it is

---

18 Which is the reciprocal of the price of the baht in terms of the US dollar.

noted that the rapid fall of the rupiah since early September has taken place in the face of sharp rise in the interest rate brought about by the monetary authorities.

Korea was the latest to show serious signs of the crisis and suffer the severest crash. The interesting feature about the Korean experience was that though the stock market had shown a declining trend since the middle of August, the fall in share prices remained fairly moderate until the third week of October, when the central bank gave up the defence of the won and permitted it to float. The crash in Indonesia and Korea constituted a qualitative change in the chain of events during the Asian crisis and cannot easily be explained in terms of standard theoretical models.

DYNAMICS OF CRISIS AND CONTAGION: AN INTERPRETATION

We have indicated in the first two sections the main questions required to be addressed in explaining the dynamics of exchange rate, interest rate, and share prices in the course of the currency turmoil in East and South East Asia. It is useful to recapitulate the questions at this stage:

(a) Why did the share prices continue to tumble, even while currencies were depreciating?

(b) Why could not restrictive monetary policies arrest the decline in the exchange rates?

(c) Why was the initial upturn in Thai share prices reversed from the beginning of August, even though by mid July the interest rate had started falling and the exchange rate had become fairly stable?

(d) What accounts for the contagion, even though countries like Indonesia had taken 'appropriate' steps from the very onset of the currency crisis?

(e) How did the contagion spill over from the currency market to the banking sector?

(f) How does one explain the continuing decline in the Nikkei average in the face of persistently low interest rates, large trade balances, and the falling yen?

(g) Why has the series of the IMF sponsored bailout operations failed to resolve the crisis in the region and the countries receiving massive financial support?

It is too early to provide satisfactory answers to the questions raised above. Here, we record no more than our first reading of the turn of events over the last six months—a reading that is seriously hampered by the as yet unsettled state of the region and lack of relevant data, especially of the real sector.

THREE STAGES OF THE CRISIS

Since the questions posed in this connection are closely interrelated and need to be addressed in terms of a coherent analytical framework, we do not take them up separately. A fruitful way of tackling them seems to consist in distinguishing among three phases of the crisis and discussing the nature of relations among the crucial variables within and across the different phases. The reason, the perceptive reader must have realized, is that the interplay and significance of economic forces operating in the system tend to change, often radically, from one phase to another. To motivate the discussion a few words on the basis of our distinction among the phases appear to be in order.

The first phase covers the period during which no significant impact of the Thai crisis was felt by the other countries, ASEAN or non-ASEAN. The second phase was characterized by the spread and deepening of financial troubles in practically all of the ASEAN group of countries. In the final phase, the Thai crisis engulfed the entire East and South East Asia and threatened to undermine the health of the global financial system. This distinction among the three phases, we hasten to admit, is quite rough and ready; but it serves a useful analytical purpose and does not give a seriously distorted picture of the Asian economic scenario during the second half of 1997.

Early Phase of the Crisis

The initial phase of the Thai crisis lasted for about a month, from 2 July (when the Bank of Thailand left the baht floating) to early August 1997. During this period, it is primarily the financial markets in Thailand that showed signs of intense turbulence, while the rest of Asian economies remained relatively unaffected. Between 25 June and 31 July, the baht depreciated by 25 per cent[19], along with

19 Strictly speaking, 25 per cent was the gain of the US dollar against the baht. No harm is done for our purpose if such gains (losses) are referred to as the extent of depreciation (appreciation) of the local currencies.

the Bangkok SET, registering a gain of 37 per cent (Tables 4.2–4.3 and Figure 4.2–4.3). The depreciation was 5.9 per cent in Indonesia and 4.4 per cent in Malaysia, with share prices registering a marginal gain of 1.3 per cent in the former, and a loss of 3.4 per cent in the latter. Only in the Philippines were movements in the exchange rate and share prices relatively large: during this period the Philippine peso lost nearly 12.9 per cent, while the fall in the Manila Composite amounted to 8.3 per cent.

Outside the ASEAN block, the time profiles of the financial variables did not display any marked or systematic movements. Except for the yen (which fell by 3.5 per cent), depreciation in other currencies were negligible. So far as the share prices were concerned, while the key Nikkei average lost 2.3 per cent, and the Straits Times (Singapore) 2.3 per cent, stock markets in South Korea, Taiwan, and Hong Kong gained 3.1, 11, and 6.1 per cent respectively. The order of the changes and absence of a systematic pattern of movements in the financial sector elsewhere suggest that countries contracting the Thai virus were passing through an incubation period of a month or so.

What is no less interesting is that since mid-July there were indications of containment and blowing over of the crisis originating in Thailand. All ASEAN foreign exchange markets displayed remarkable stability for three to four weeks. After its initial jump in mid-July, the Philippine peso moved within a narrow band, up to almost the middle of August. The other three ASEAN currencies lagged behind the peso by about a week in attaining stability for various lengths of time. Curiously enough, the baht remained stable for nearly five weeks, while the stability of the ringgit and the rupiah lasted for around three weeks.

The other point worth noting is that in all the three ASEAN neighbours of Thailand, share prices remained quiet over a period of three to four weeks and the stability in the share market preceded that in the foreign exchange market by about one week. Only the Bangkok SET showed a fair degree of volatility after mid-July. However, even in this case, the sharp rise in share prices during the first half of July was absent in the second half, with fluctuations occurring around a mildly upward trend.

The end of the first phase of the Asian troubles and beginning of the second occurred in August, though the precise line of demarcation is somewhat blurred. From the beginning of August, share prices started falling in all the ASEAN countries, but exchange rates remained stable for a while. It is only since the second to the third week of the month that ASEAN currencies other than the baht have started depreciating more or less relentlessly. By the fourth week of August[20] the baht also resumed its downward drift and the overall scenario in the region left little doubt concerning the serious contagion caused by the Thai crisis.

Given the observed behaviour of the exchange rates and other variables in different countries during the first phase of the currency crisis, we shall concentrate primarily on the experience of Thailand and touch on the economic forces operating elsewhere only to the extent that they significantly affect the Thai financial markets. The most important and puzzling aspect of the dynamics of currency crisis during July was the increase in the Bangkok SET, along with the depreciation of the baht, irrespective of whether the interest rate was moving up or down. There was also some difference in the behaviour of the financial sector between the first and the second half of July. It is useful to start with this difference in order to isolate the economic forces operating during the first phase of the crisis.

Strange Correlations: In the face of an increase in the interest rate by 375 basis points during the first half of July, there was, contrary to text-book results, a rise in share prices along with a fall in the baht. Particularly impressive was the performance of the Bangkok SET, which gained 34 per cent over the sub-period. By contrast, share price increases were quite minor in the second half of July, even though the interest rate recorded a fairly steep fall. In trying to make economic sense of the somewhat bizarre behaviour of financial markets, we need to extend the text-book models of open economy macroeconomics in a number of ways.

First, it is necessary to differentiate between bonds and shares, and examine how the two assets cease to be close substitutes in times of crises. Second, the three financial markets we have been focusing on clear instantaneously, but adjustments in production, income or trade balance tend to be relatively long drawn. Hence, the short run movements in interest rates, share prices, and exchange

20 Hence arises the problem of drawing a clear line of demarcation between the first and the second phase. Quite clearly, the line separating the two phases will depend on our assessment regarding the relative importance of the stock and the foreign exchange market as barometers for recording financial turbulence.

rates will, in the main, be expectations driven. However, these expectations are generally formed on the basis of the perceived behaviour of the real sector and the way it is linked to the financial sector of the economy. Third, in the course of the crisis, expectations tend to change with both the actual experience of the domestic and the international economy, as also with policy responses of governments and global organizations like the IMF.

On the face of it, the behaviour of economic variables during the initial phase of the crisis defies economic logic. However, once we step outside the confines of mainstream models, where all bonds and shares are clubbed into a single financial asset[21], it is not very difficult to see that an expected boost to the activity of the real sector will tend to raise current share prices, as also interest rates.[22] Again, in a booming economy, a moderately restrictive monetary policy will generally fail to rein in rising share prices, nor will an easy money policy arrest the downslide of the share market when expectations have turned adverse. In other words, share and bond prices[23] may change in the same or in the opposite direction, depending upon the nature and magnitude of forces propelling the economic system.

So far as the Thai crisis is concerned, recall that before 2 July the baht-dollar exchange rate was kept fixed, even though for quite some time the US dollar had been gaining against the yen and a number of other Asian currencies. This, together with higher wages in Thailand, compared to those prevailing in other ASEAN countries and China, was widely perceived to have made the baht overvalued and contributed significantly to Thailand's large balance of trade deficit in 1996. The sharp fall in the baht, with the immediate changeover to a flexible exchange rate regime on 2 July was thus expected to have an expansionary effect on the economy similar to that of devaluation under a fixed exchange rate system.

The magnitude of the boost to expected profits, and hence, to the Bangkok SET in the first half of July may be attributed to four factors. First, the fall in the baht made Thai exports cheaper and imports dearer by 15 to 20 per cent[24] within a few days following

21 See Rakshit (1997, 1997a) for an alternative approach to modelling of the financial sector.

22 As both profits and interest rates are expected to go up in the future.

23 Recall the inverse relationship between bond prices and interest rates.

24 See fn. 21 for the slight inaccuracy involved.

the change-over of the exchange rate regime. Second, given the relatively low record of inflation in Thailand, the export competitiveness attained overnight was expected to last long enough to make its impact felt on the balance of trade. Third, partly because the fallout of the Thai troubles on other economies was expected to be minor, and partly since speculative attacks on the currencies of neighbouring regions were countered with market intervention[25], the crowding-out effect[26], it was felt at this stage, would be negligible. Fourth, with the volume of trade amounting to around 90 per cent of Thailand's gross domestic product, the expansionary forces unleashed through an improvement in trade balance were expected to be exceptionally strong. The positive association among share prices, interest rates, and depreciation is not, thus, as bizarre as it may appear at first sight.

After its initial fall on 2 July, the baht remained fairly stable for about a fortnight, with no major depreciation elsewhere. The second substantial decline of the baht took place between 16 and 23 July, and was clearly associated with the slide in other ASEAN currencies as well. Note also that the depreciation in the Philippine peso, the Malaysian ringgit, and the Indonesian rupiah took place between 9 and 23 July and was preceded in each case by a decline in share prices.[27] This lead in the share price downturn was due to the adoption of somewhat restrictive monetary policies and the sharp fall in the baht, so that there was downward pressure on other currencies as well.[28] The second half of July, especially its last week, may indeed be regarded as the period over which the South East Asian financial markets attained temporary equilibrium, with exchange rates, interest rates, and share prices adjusting to the initial shock imparted by the Thai crisis (see Tables 4.2–4.3, Figures 4.1–4.2). No wonder the Bangkok SET recorded only a minor

25 On 11 July central banks of the Philippines and Indonesia permitted their currencies to move within much wider bands. The peso registered a decline almost immediately, but the rupiah's fall was both minor and delayed (see Table 4.2).

26 Operating through depreciation of other currencies.

27 The initial stickiness of these currencies was due, in part, to market intervention on the part of the central banks.

28 Partly because the central banks gave up defence of their currencies and expectations of a slowing down of the economies dampened the sentiment of international investors.

improvement during this (sub) phase, and that too was due in part to the easing of monetary stringency with a perceptible petering out of the baht's decline.

Second Phase—Contagion in South East Asia

The second phase of the currency crisis was marked by a sharp decline in both share prices and exchange rates over the entire ASEAN block of countries and lasted for about two months, from early August[29] to late September or early October (see Tables 4.2–4.3, Figures 4.1–4.2). Before discussing the salient features of this phase, we need to examine why the quietude marking the South East Asian financial markets during late July turned out to be no more than a lull before the storm.

An integral part of our explanation of the process of transition from the first to the second phase consists in recognizing the fragility of the financial equilibrium attained towards the later part of the first phase. The equilibrium, as we have already emphasized, was expectational and very short run, with no firm basis as yet for economic agents to assess the short and medium term behaviour of the domestic and the international economy. In such a situation participants in the market tend to be highly risk averse, and their expectations revised disproportionately in response to new information or policy pronouncements. Moreover, lacking the faculty of the three witches in *Macbeth* to '... look into the wombs of time/ And say which grains will grow and which will not', the large majority of investors tend to follow market leaders, become unduly influenced by credit ratings or prognosis of financial 'experts', and displayed 'herd behaviour'. All these tend to make the expectational equilibrium highly fragile and generate movements of a cumulative nature, once the equilibrium is disturbed by some unforeseen events or new information.

For the moment, we shall focus only on hard evidence for changes in expectations and abstract from herd behaviour, which, though intermittently operative at different stages of the crisis, became a major factor only in the third phase. Perhaps, the most important shock disturbing the expectational equilibrium came from the knowledge concerning the threat of bankruptcy that a host of Thai finance companies had been facing. Already, in the first quarter of

29 See our earlier comments on the dividing line between the first and the second phase.

1997, 16 financial firms considered to be seriously sick were asked to suspend their operation. Before seeking the IMF bailout on 29 July 1997, the Bank of Thailand again took a similar measure, but this time the number of financial intermediaries involved was as large as 42. The revelation that 58 out of a total of 90 finance companies were terminally sick could not, but have rudely jolted the investors' confidence in the health of the rest of the financial firms, and hence, of the economy as a whole.

Second, the IMF rescue package, it was well known, would be attached with the all too familiar conditionalities like higher taxes, cuts in government expenditure, and restructuring of the economy including closure of distressed banks—measures that could not but produce an adverse impact on the real sector, and hence, on profits, at least in the short and the medium run. Even before the IMF gave some details of the bailout package (on 11 August), the government of Thailand had announced a series of austerity measures for tackling the financial crisis on 5 August.

In the light of the factors mentioned above, it is not very difficult to see why the Bangkok SET shed 7 per cent between 30 July and 6 August. There was an immediate fall in share markets of other ASEAN countries as well, and the reasons are not too far to seek. Given the already fragile state of investors' expectations, conditions were ripe for quick contagion in stock markets in South East Asia. Matters were not helped by stringent monetary measures adopted by central banks in a bid to prevent a currency meltdown. The severest were the steps taken in August by the Bank of Indonesia at the first serious threat to its currency. Not only were interest rates raised, but the state enterprises and pension funds were directed to transfer their deposits from commercial banks to the central bank. Such measures could not but lead to apprehensions of a serious squeeze on economic activity and profit.

Leads and Lags in Financial Markets: An interesting feature of the dynamics of financial markets during the second phase of the currency crisis was that though share prices everywhere had started falling from the very beginning of August, there was a lag before the downward pressure became perceptible in currency markets. 13 August marks the beginning of a more or less continuous decline in the rupiah, the ringgit, and the Philippine peso (see Figure 4.1); and this decline was triggered off by a renewal of speculative attack on that day. Remarkably enough, for about a month from the fourth week of July, the baht remained stable, and only since late August did it join the other ASEAN currencies in their downward trend.

The main reason for the baht's stability, both absolute and relative, may be traced to expectations of the IMF bailout[30] and the announcement (on 11 August) that US\$17.2 billion would be available to Thailand to tackle the currency crisis. The market apparently considered the sum sufficient to tide over the payments problems, before the already attained depreciation of the baht, together with the measures required under the IMF rescue package, helped to produce the salutary impact on trade balance, strengthen the domestic financial structure, and restore the confidence of international investors.[31]

The renewed downward pressure on the baht from the fourth week of August may be traced to two factors, one minor, the other major. From around the second week of the month, ASEAN currencies other than the baht showed a declining trend and this trend became sharper when the central banks gave way in the face of the speculative attack on 13 August. The much steeper fall of the baht between 20 August and 27 August was partly due to quick adjustment required to restore the relative exchange rate between the baht and other currencies of the region.

Much more important in initiating the renewed fall of the baht was the information relating to the scale and structure of external indebtedness vis-à-vis the foreign exchange reserves of Thailand. Between mid-May and end-June, the Bank of Thailand had already used up a part of its US\$40 billion foreign exchange reserves held at the beginning of the currency crisis. What was much more serious was that out of the total external debt estimated at US\$90 billion, no less than two-thirds consisted of short term borrowing. The economic logic behind the resumption of the baht's downslide despite the IMF support is then not too difficult to appreciate. When this information came to light, traders in the foreign exchange market knew (for certain) that there would shortly be a jump in the demand for the dollar with the maturity of short tern (external)

30 Recall that Thailand formally approached the IMF for financial support on 29 July.

31 Such expectations were fostered by the experience of Mexico which, with IMF support, did not take too long to recover from the 1994–5 crisis.

loans. Even with the proposed financial support from the IMF, this augmented demand for dollar could not be met unless additional foreign exchange was available from other sources. Second, given the bleak prospects of domestic firms and the general state of uncertainty, international investors, it was reasonable to surmise, would not renew loans or extend new credit.

Finally, even with the baht's substantial depreciation against the dollar, no significant succour could be expected from the balance of trade account in the near future. Thailand ended 1996 with a trade deficit of nearly US$11 billion, and the short term prospects of the deficit declining sharply, let alone turning into a surplus because of depreciation, did not appear too encouraging. It is well known that the improvement in trade balance from the fall in value of a country's currency occurs only with a considerable time lag.[32] Moreover, depreciation of other ASEAN currencies was expected to erode much of the trade related advantage of the fall of the baht. Meanwhile, Japan, one of the most important trading partners of Thailand, had started showing signs of distress and relapsing into economic downturn. Under these conditions a rational economic agent would expect a payments crisis and the consequent currency meltdown in the near future, and this expectation, in its turn, was bound to put a downward pressure on the current exchange rate as well.

Some distinctions between the first and the second stage of the crisis are worth mentioning at this juncture. We have already noted how the baht and the Bangkok SET moved in opposite directions during the initial phase of the Thai turmoil. Even Indonesian shares did not register any net loss during July, though they did undergo a mildly downward adjustment in the second week after some gains in the first. By contrast, during the second phase of the crisis, both currencies and share prices followed a declining trend in all ASEAN countries, with some leads and lags, as noted earlier.

However, while the declining trend of exchange rates did not display any tendency to flatten out, towards the end of the second phase, the fall in ASEAN share prices had shown some signs of deceleration until, throughout East and South East Asia, both the stock and foreign exchange markets started falling rapidly during the final phase of the crisis.[33] Even before the final phase, some East

32 A relationship economists call the 'J curve'.
33 We have already mentioned the currency board system of Hong Kong and the relative insulation of China.

Asian financial markets were subjected to downward pressure of varying degrees (see Tables 4.2–4.3, Figure 4.1–4.2). Exchange rate declines were as yet minor, but since the first or second week of August, share markets in Japan, Korea, and Hong Kong were on a downward course.

In order to appreciate the mechanism behind the downward trend in share prices and exchange rates and the transition from the second to the third phase of the crisis, it is necessary to indicate, in the Asian context, why some of the commonly held views on relations among financial variables and policy requirements involve gross fallacies, once the crisis has run its course for some time and seriously dented investors' confidence. This will also enable us to see why the IMF sponsored policy packages, as also measures adopted by countries which did not seek IMF support, not only failed to resolve the crisis, but played no mean a role in its deepening and widening.

Financial Mechanism Under a Crisis: The failure of conventional wisdom, not to make a mystery of it, arises primarily from two sources. First, there is a basic difference in the behaviour of the economic system under normal conditions, and that in a state of flux or gloom. Second, the temporal behaviour of financial variables in a country depends significantly on whether markets elsewhere are undergoing similar experiences or not. The main point to note in this context is that in the course of the crisis, currency depreciation and stock market slump tend to become mutually reinforcing, and financial markets respond in a seemingly perverse manner to fiscal and monetary measures generally recommended to contain the crisis.

Consider first the impact of tight money policy, which all countries followed in order to counter speculative attacks on their currencies. Under the textbook scenario, such measures provide a boost to the domestic currency in two ways; the first is immediate, the second somewhat delayed. As the interest rate goes up, investors find domestic financial assets more attractive than those of other countries. The result is an inflow of foreign funds and a tendency for appreciation of domestic currency. Again, a tight money (as also fiscal) policy produces a deflationary impact, and hence tends to improve the balance of trade. This improvement in the balance of trade involves a lag, but the expectation of such improvements should normally strengthen the domestic currency without much delay.

So far as the Asian experience is concerned, note that hardening of interest rates everywhere could hardly be expected to induce inflow of foreign funds, unless the global fund managers were to reallocate their portfolios in favour of Asia at the expense of other markets. The reason for the absence of such a switch is not difficult to discern. When the debtor is already facing difficulties in honouring his obligations, willingness to pay higher interest rates does not help in securing loans. Under these conditions, higher interest rates undermine lenders' confidence in the viability of both the economy and specific projects to be financed.[34]

What is no less relevant is that in the South East Asian economies and Korea an overwhelming part of the foreign debt was incurred by private corporates or financial firms. Under these conditions, a contractionary policy could not but induce serious doubts regarding the ability of borrowers to service their debt in future.

Indeed, pursuit of such policies adversely affected the health of the financial sector in all countries, including those where banks were not initially burdened with large non-performing assets. The stock market meltdown and sharp decline in prices of real estate threatened the viability of banks which had provided substantial loans against these assets. Even production loans tended to turn non-performing, with a slowing down of the economy and a steep rise in interest costs. The resulting failure or threat of bankruptcy of financial firms further undermined the confidence of domestic, as also international investors. The story fits especially well the process of Indonesia's collapse from a seemingly robust position in the initial stage of the crisis.[35]

With all countries simultaneously following restrictive monetary or fiscal policies, transmission of contractionary forces across national frontiers played an important role in reinforcing the downward

---

34 A rational investor cannot but be wary of the negative impact of high interest rates on the health of the economy, as we shall see in a moment. Again, higher interest rates induce borrowers to undertake riskier projects, or give rise to what is called the problem of moral hazard (see Stiglitz and Weiss, 1981).

35 We have already referred to the stringent monetary measures adopted by the Bank of Indonesia to ward off speculation against the rupiah.

tendency in stock (and hence currency) markets.[36] The South East Asian countries accounted for a substantial part of overseas investment and foreign trade of Japan. It is no wonder then that the Japanese share markets came to feel some downward pressure, almost from the beginning of the currency crisis. When the other big economy in the region, viz., Korea, also showed signs of cracking up, inter-country interaction pushed practically all financial markets of the East and South East Asia into a severe maelstrom.

Transmission From Currency to Stock Markets: The final part of the mechanism reinforcing the financial crisis consists in the transmission of forces from the foreign exchange market to the rest of the economy, including the stock market. We have already noted that for a depreciating currency to provide a boost to the real sector, other things, especially the exchange rates in competing countries, need to remain the same. To be more specific, the presumption that depreciation will have a salutary impact involves a fallacy of composition, when other currencies are also drifting downwards. Second, not only in ASEAN countries, but in Japan and Korea also, the import content of major items of exports was fairly large. Hence, even in the absence of competitive depreciation, the advantage from a falling currency would be unlikely to be substantial. Moreover, a rational economic agent would expect a tighter monetary policy with a rise in domestic prices[37] and a consequent dampening of economic activity.

In a number of Asian countries, especially in Thailand, Malaysia, and Korea, there were special factors which made currency depreciation a bane to domestic banks and corporates. Taking advantage of the interest rate differential between loans from domestic and foreign sources, banks and other companies had borrowed heavily from the international money market. Moreover, the loans were often without any forward cover and mostly short term.[38] Given this situation, a depreciating currency tended to

36 Recall that worsening economic prospects tend to scare foreign investors away and create a downward pressure in the currency market as well.

37 Through depreciation.

38 The reason was that for more than a decade exchange rates had moved within an extremely narrow band, and banks' lending was also short-term.

inflict heavy losses to domestic finance companies and raise the bugbear of bankruptcy or financial chaos. Even when it was the manufacturing companies that had taken foreign loans, their inability to service debt to domestic banks in the face of mounting losses also led to serious financial distress. Hence the transmission of troubles from the currency to stock markets.

The Final Phase

In the light of the financial mechanism discussed above, the transition from the second to the third phase of the Asian crisis, as also its dynamics during this phase, may now be indicated briefly. While both currency and share prices in the ASEAN countries were experiencing a downslide in the second phase, share prices in the rest of East Asia also started showing some downward drift. However, currencies of the latter group of nations more or less held their ground during this period because of the lag in contagion, central bank intervention, and the perception that their external payments position was not as vulnerable as that of the ASEAN countries.[39]

The process of transition was hastened by the sharp fall of the rupiah as the government of Indonesia announced large cuts in expenditure, serious banking troubles surfaced, a few leading banks were suspended and the central bank came out with the expected decision to seek IMF bailout.[40] Since then trends in stock and currency markets in Asia have been sharply downward sloping, with occasional bouts of the slide accelerating or slowing down. The first bout of acceleration occurred following the speculative attack on the Hong Kong dollar from the second week of October. The attack was successfully resisted[41], but the sharp rise in Hong Kong interest rates, along with the depressionary forces operating in the entire region, made the Hang Seng plummet by more than 35 per cent between early October and mid-November, triggering off a global meltdown in share prices and strengthening the forces pulling down financial markets in Asia.

39 The magnitude of Korea's short term indebtedness in relation to her exchange reserves was yet to come to light.

40 These factors, as we have seen, put a downward pressure on both the exchange rate and share prices.

41 Foreign exchange reserves worth US$80 billion helped in keeping the exchange rate fixed, but not in preventing stock market meltdown.

The second and perhaps the most serious stage in the process of financial slide in Asia was reached in the third week of October, when the Korean economy showed palpable signs of an impending banking and payments crisis. A string of actual and anticipated corporate failures, large external debts (amounting to US$110 billion) of which two-thirds were short term, quite inadequate and rapidly declining foreign exchange reserves[42]—all these factors undermined confidence in the viability of the Korean economy. The apprehension that the payments problem would be serious enough to force Korea as well to approach the IMF was vindicated about a month later. Meanwhile, the downward trend in both the yen and the Nikkei average had been persisting since the second week of August, and by October there was a general perception that a number of Japanese banks and finance companies would incur huge losses, if not turn bankrupt. With two of the largest economies and trading nations of the world[43], viz., Japan and Korea, facing serious troubles, there developed a near unanimity regarding bleak economic prospects of Asia, and perhaps of the entire world. In the pervading gloom all positive information was discounted, anything negative was accorded undue credence[44], and the agony of Asian economies continued unabated.

Policy Response and Financial Crisis: As we have already noted, policies of individual countries to tackle their financial troubles, as also the series of IMF-led rescue operations, have failed miserably to contain the Asian crisis. Indeed, the crisis appears to have become deeper with the widening scale of IMF intervention and vigorous pursuit of conventional policies by all countries, including those which did not seek IMF support. The ineffectiveness of these measures is attested by the uninterrupted fall in stock and currency prices everywhere during the third phase of the crisis. Not only

42 By end October, foreign exchange reserves were of the order of US$30 billion.

43 Korea is the 11th largest in terms of GDP and 6th in terms of foreign trade.

44 Thus, the ringgit fell in October following downgrading of the Malaysian banks by Moody's, even though the latest figures showed an export surplus of US$1.2 billion. Note that the high rating on the part of international agencies had in earlier years played no small role in inducing large flow of funds to the emerging markets in Asia.

have market participants taken a dim view of the policy programmes, but international agencies too have made their assessment clear through downgrading of the ratings of Thai, Korean, Japanese, and other banks in the region, even after the announcement of huge financial support for Korea.

In terms of our earlier analysis, the sources of the policy failure at the national and international level may be traced to two factors. The first consists in the failure to distinguish between long term policies and measures required for crisis management. Thus, enforcement of strict prudential norms and closure of non-viable banks when the economy is booming promote financial efficiency, but may be instrumental in hastening or deepening the currency crisis when it looms large or has surfaced. Second, there has been an utter lack of appreciation of the spillover effects of domestic polices on other countries and the reinforcing mechanism operating in the course of the currency crisis. To illustrate, consider the package of measures under the IMF bailout programmes:

- cuts in government expenditure, increase in taxes, and reduction of fiscal deficit;
- tight money policy;
- closing down of ailing banks;
- financial liberalization with removal of restrictions on entry of foreign banks; and
- removal of trade barriers.

Thailand has closed down 56 out of 58 suspended finance companies, initiated moves towards financial liberalization, followed a restrictive monetary policy, and adopted measures to reduce government expenditure. Malaysia and the Philippines have also adopted austerity programmes in their budgets. Even Japan has started following policies very similar to those advocated by the IMF. In a bid to reduce the fiscal deficit to less than 3 per cent of GDP, Japan raised tax rates, announced substantial cuts in public expenditure, and adopted a reform programme with deregulation as one of its principal components.

We have already seen why adoption of these measures by a group of countries, whose economies are closely interrelated, tends to deepen the crisis and trigger off a chain reaction with a strong feedback. The reinforcing mechanism, to recapitulate, runs from the set of measures to the significant slowing down of the real sector, high interest rates with severe credit rationing, cutbacks in investment, production and employment, sharp falls in profitability with a meltdown in stock and currency markets, a jump in non-performing assets of banks or finance companies, loss of investors' confidence, and so on.

That the above is not simply a theoretical curiosum is amply illustrated by the Asian experience over the last few months. GDP growth rates in all countries in the region are expected to fall steeply and become negative in quite a few.[45] Corporates have postponed or drastically reduced their investment plans. Consumers' confidence has been severely jolted. Countries face large scale mass redundancies. And what is most relevant, problems faced by banks and other financial intermediaries in all countries have become more severe and intractable in the course of the crisis. With the chaos following the suspension and closure of nearly two-thirds of finance companies, the still functioning financial firms in Thailand are reportedly faced with growing troubles, with more and more loans turning non-performing. Banking sectors in other countries have also been thrown into a quagmire of bad debt and loss of confidence.

KOREA AND JAPAN

Of special significance in this context are the policies being pursued in Korea and Japan—countries whose health has a crucial bearing on the performance of all economies in the region. In recent months, much has been written about the inefficiency of the Korean conglomerates, misallocation of credit due to directed credit programmes and restrictions on trade, the consequent sickness of the financial sector, and hence, the need for measures *a la* the IMF package. Even if one ignores, for the moment, the deleterious impact of these measures on other countries, the widely touted diagnosis and prescription for the Korean ills are not supported by the country's macroeconomic scenario. Between 1992 and 1995, there was a progressive decline in Korea's incremental capital–output ratio from 7.3 to 4.1.[46] During the same period, export growth jumped from 8 per cent to 31.5 per cent. What is more,

---

[45] Under the IMF programme, Korea has been asked to reduce its targetted growth rate from 6 to 3 per cent.

46 Calculated from Table A4.1.5 in Annexe 4.1.

before 1996 Korea consistently ran a fiscal surplus of about 3 per cent, and her current account deficit hovered around 1 to 2 per cent of GDP (see Table A4.1..5). By all standards, these figures do not suggest either structural inefficiency or an ill-conceived macro-economic policy stance. With its accelerating export growth and high credit rating, Korea (unlike China and Hong Kong) did not feel the necessity of holding large international reserves (see Table A4.1..5). What is more important, the central bank did not recognize the increasing risk and vulnerability associated with external borrowing in general, and short term borrowing in particular.

It was only from 1996 that the Korean economy started facing troubles. However, these troubles emanated primarily from external shocks, manifested in a sharp drop in export growth, to 4.1 per cent from 31.5 per cent in the previous year. Even so, in 1996 the GDP growth was 7 per cent and current account deficit was below 5 per cent. On the heels of the external shock to which all ASEAN economies were also subject, came the Thai crisis and its spread elsewhere. There were primarily two structural defects in the Korean economy, which aggravated the problem: one internal, the other external. With the very high debt–equity ratio, the Korean conglomerates started suffering heavy losses with the economic downturn and this, in its turn, seriously affected the viability of the banking sector. Under these conditions, stringent monetary and fiscal policies (along with removal of restrictions on imports) could not but aggravate the banking crisis. The second structural defect perhaps prevented the pursuit of an expansionary policy and forced Korea to solicit IMF support. This defect consisted in low foreign exchange reserves in relation to the scale of short term borrowing.

The interesting point to note in this connection is that Korea's external debt, estimated at US$110 billion is negligible in relation to her productive capacity and economic potential. In fact, Korea's was primarily a liquidity problem, which, thanks to domestic policies and the IMF intervention, may be transformed into an organic and long term one.

The case of Japan defies any rational economic explanation. Japan has throughout had a substantial surplus in her balance of trade. Her external reserves at the end of September was US$225 billion. Her economic slowdown is due entirely to the decline in domestic demand, to which contractionary fiscal policy has made no mean contribution. In fact, the slowing down of the Japanese economy has started since April, when the higher sales tax became effective. Since then recessionary tendencies have become stronger and pessimism deepened with cuts in government expenditure and increase in taxes. One cannot help asking: Is Japan bent on economic harakiri and damaging her neighbours seriously?

AN OVERVIEW

The Thai currency crisis, surfacing in mid-May, spread over the second half of 1997, to the entire East and South East Asia. In the first phase of the crisis, lasting till July, the major casualty was Thailand, which had to ask for substantial IMF support. Though currency markets in other ASEAN countries too were subjected to some downward pressure, the impact during this phase was of a minor order. It was in the second phase that all ASEAN economies showed serious signs of contagion and deepening financial troubles. Since the first week of October, there has been a qualitative change in the character of the crisis with its rapid spread to other countries in Asia and massive IMF funding, solicited first by Indonesia and then Korea.

The crisis has been marked by meltdown in stock and currency markets everywhere, as also by growing redundancies and scaling down of investment by private firms. The other important feature of the crisis consists in the string of bankruptcies of banks and other financial intermediaries, and serious troubles faced by units that are still in operation. Policies adopted by afflicted countries and large scale rescue operations mounted by the IMF in association with a number of industrialized countries and other global institutions have failed to arrest the tide of deepening troubles in Asia.

For an understanding of the course of the crisis and reasons for policy failure, three interrelated factors are required to be kept in view. First, with the globalization of financial markets, the behaviour of exchange rates is governed, not so much by export or import flows, but more by transactions in the market for financial assets. The implication is that not only share prices, but exchange rates also are driven by expectations and these may have little to do with economic 'fundamentals'. Second, the relation among financial variables like bond prices, exchange rates, and share prices tend to change drastically with the spread of the currency crisis. Third, policies adopted by a country to resolve its crisis may be effective if other countries are not pursuing similar sets of measures. But if all countries go in for contractionary policies along with sharp depreciation in their currencies, the effect cannot but be deepening economic gloom, with an increase in the downward pressure on stock and foreign exchange markets.

Our analysis indicates two sets of policy conclusions,[47] one at the national and the other at the international level. The Asian experience suggests that strengthening the fundamentals is no guarantee against currency crisis when the scale of movement of capital across nations is so large and the movement primarily expectations driven. Hence the necessity of developing a diversified production structure, even at the cost of departing somewhat from the principle of comparative advantage. It is also quite clear that leaving the scale and structure of external borrowing entirely to market forces makes a country highly vulnerable to currency crises. The implication is that an individual country needs to impose some curbs on inflow of foreign capital in general, and short term borrowing in particular. In the light of the growing troubles faced by banks in all countries in the region, it appears that in normal conditions financial reforms may be necessary to improve a country's economic fundamentals, but pursuit of such policies in times of crisis can only help its deepening. Finally, the failure of the IMF operations suggests strongly the need for abandoning preconceived ideas on working of economies, irrespective of their specific conditions and for having an integrated, rather than a country by country approach in dealing with currency crises and their contagion.

47 See Chapter 3 for a discussion of some of the points made here.

ANNEXE 4.1   MACROECONOMIC INDICATORS OF CRISIS COUNTRIES

Table A4.1.1

KEY MACROECONOMIC INDICATORS: THAILAND

	1989	1990	1991	1992	1993	1994	1995	1996	1997	1998
GDP (% growth)	12.2	11.6	8.4	7.9	8.2	8.9	8.7	6.7 (5.5)	(6.1) -1.3	(6.6) -9.4
GNP (% growth)	12.6	11.7	8.1	7.6	8.6	8.6	8.3	6.40	(5.7) -1.9	(6.2) -10.8
Gross domestic investment (% of GNP)	35.5	41.6	42.8	40.4	40.5	42.0	44.2	43.8 36.1	(44.1) 42.7	(44.0) 25.3
Gross national saving (% of GNP)	32.0	33.0	35.1	34.6	34.75	35.2	35.0	35.3 (34.57)	(35.6) 33.93	(35.0) 37.2
Merchandise exports (% growth)	25.7	15.0	23.8	13.7	13.4	22.2	24.7	0.1 (-1.9)	(4.5) 3.8	(8.0) -6.8
Merchandise imports (% growth)	27.1	28.0	13.9	8.3	13.3	18.5	31.6	4.1 (0.6)	(4.5) -13.4	(7.2) -33.8
Current account balance (% of GNP)	-3.5	-8.6	-7.8	-5.8	-5.7	-5.8	-8.3	-8.10	(-7.3) -2.06	(-7.4) 13.3
International reserves (million US$)	9515.0	13305.0	17517.0	20359.0	24473.0	29332.0	35982.0	37731.0	26179.0	28825.0
Import cover (months)	4.4	4.8	5.6	6.0	6.4	6.5	5.9	6.2	4.9	7.9
Net fiscal balance (% of GNP)	3.0	4.6	4.8	2.9	2.1	1.9	3.1	2.5	-0.9	-2.6
Revenue surplus (% of GNP)	2.8	4.5	4.7	3.0	2.1	2.0	8.3	8.4	7.2	4.7
Inflation rate (CPI)	5.4	5.9	5.7	4.1	3.4	5.1	5.8	5.9	(5.0) 5.6	(4.8) 8.1

(Contd.)

Table A4.1.1 Contd.

	1989	1990	1991	1992	1993	1994	1995	1996	1997	1998
Debt-service ratio (% of export)	16.3	16.9	13.0	13.7	18.5	11.3	11.0 (12.3)	11.1 15.6	(11.0) 21.3	(11.0)

Note: Figures in brackets for 1997 and 98 are ADB forecast; For other years figures in brackets are revised ones.

Source: Asian Development Bank, *Asian Development Outlook 1997–8, 1999, 1999(Update); International Monetary Fund, International Financial Statistics Yearbook* 1996 and 1999; *World Bank, World Development Reports;* Central Bank Thailand.

Table A4.1.2
KEY MACROECONOMIC INDICATORS: INDONESIA

	1989	1990	1991	1992	1993	1994	1995	1996	1997	1998
GDP (% growth)	7.5	7.2	7.0	6.5	6.5	7.5	8.2	7.8	(8.0) 4.9	(7.9) −13.2
GNP (% growth)	7.4	7.2	7.1	6.4	7.6	7.5	8.2	7.8	(8.0) 4.4	(7.9) −14.8
Gross domestic investment (% of GNP)	37.0	38.0	32.3	37.7	34.5	33.7	34.8	37.7 (33.41)	(39.2) 34.4	(40.0) 19.0
Gross national saving (% of GNP)	35.7	35.1	33.5	35.4	33.2	31.9	31.4	33.7 (29.7)	(36.7) 32.9	(35.2) 20.1
Merchandise exports (% growth)	17.8	16.7	10.6	14.0	8.3	9.9	13.1	8.80	(10.8) 7.9	(12.0) −14.0

(Contd.)

Table A4.1.2 Contd.

	1989	1990	1991	1992	1993	1994	1995	1996	1997	1998
Merchandise imports (% growth)	23.5	33.5	18.5	5.5	3.8	13.9	23.0	11.8 (10.4)	(11.3) -6.8	(10.2) -28.2
Current account balance (% of GNP)	-1.2	-3.0	-3.8	-2.3	-1.4	-1.7	-3.6	-4.1	(-4.0) -1.5	(-3.3) 4.7
International reserves (million US$)	5454.0	7459.0	9258.0	10449.0	11263.0	12133.0	13708.0	18251.0	16587.0	22713.0
Import cover (months)	4.0	4.1	4.3	4.6	4.8	4.6	4.0	5.0	4.6	9.8
Net fiscal balance (% of GNP)	-2.1	0.4	0.5	-0.4	0.6	0.6	0.7	0.2	0.0	-5.0
Revenue surplus (% of GNP)	-2.2	0.5	0.5	-0.6	0.4	7.2	7.6	9.0	9.1	4.8
Inflation rate (CPI)	6.4	7.8	9.4	7.6	9.6	8.5	9.4	7.9	(7.5) 6.6	(8.0) 64.7
Debt–service ratio (% of export)	38.0	31.5	34.0	31.6	33.8	30.7	30.9	33.7 (34.2)	(32.9) 39.5	(32.3) 36.0

Note: Figures in brackets for 1997 and 1998 are ADB forecast; for other years figures in brackets are revised ones.
Source: Asian Development Bank, *Asian Development Outlook* 1997–8, 1999, 1999 (update); International Monetary Fund, *International Financial Statistics Yearbook* 1996 and 1999; World Bank, *World Development Reports*; Central Bank Indonesia.

Table A4.1.3
KEY MACROECONOMIC INDICATORS: MALAYSIA

	1989	1990	1991	1992	1993	1994	1995	1996	1997	1998
GDP (% growth)	9.2	9.7	8.7	7.8	8.3	9.1	10.1	8.8	(8.5) 7.7	(8.5) -7.5
GNP (% growth)	9.2	11.1	7.7	7.6	8.7	9.1	9.3	8.5	(7.8) 7.2	(7.9) -5.2
Gross domestic investment (% of GNP)	30.3	32.8	37.9	35.4	36.9	42.5	45.4	45.1	(45.6) 45.4	(45.8) 28.1
Gross national saving (% of GNP)	31.2	30.7	28.5	31.4	32.2	35.5	36.4	38.8	(41.2) 39.5	(41.6) 41.8
Merchandise exports (% growth)	18.1	16.3	17.0	18.1	16.1	23.1	25.9	4.0 (7.3)	(7.9) 6.0	(15.0) -7.8
Merchandise imports (% growth)	35.9	30.2	25.4	8.6	14.6	28.1	29.4	1.3 (1.7)	(5.2) 7.0	(14.9) -26.8
Current account balance (% of GNP)	0.9	-2.1	-9.4	-4.0	-4.7	-6.0	-9.0	-6.3 (-5.3)	(-4.7) -5.6	(-4.2) -1.9
International reserves (million US$)	7783.0	9754.0	10886.0	17228.0	27249.0	25423.0	23774.0	27009.0	20788.0	25559.0
Import cover (months)	4.2	4.0	3.6	5.2	7.2	5.1	3.7	4.0	6.0	5.1
Net fiscal balance (% of GNP)	-5.4	-5.0	-4.6	-4.5	-5.6	2.4	0.9	0.7	1.9	-3.6
Revenue surplus (% of GNP)	-5.8	-6.1	-4.7	-4.6	-5.5	2.4	6.9	7.6	8.5	8.2

(Contd.)

Tabel A4.1.3 Contd.

	1989	1990	1991	1992	1993	1994	1995	1996	1997	1998
Inflation rate (CPI)	5.4	5.9	5.7	4.1	3.4	3.7	3.4	3.5	(3.7) 4.0	(3.8) 5.3
Debt–service ratio (% of export)	15.1	10.3	7.7	6.6	7.8	4.9	6.2	5.9 (6.9)	(5.1) 6.2	(4.9) 0.9

Note: Figures in brackets for 1997 and 1998 are ADB forecast; For other years figures in brackets are revised ones.
Source: Asian Development Bank, Asian Development Outlook 1997–8, 1999, 1999 (update); International Monetary Fund, *International Financial Statistics Yearbook* 1996 and 1999; World Bank, *World Development Reports*; Central Bank Malaysia.

Table A4.1.4
KEY MACROECONOMIC INDICATORS: PHILIPPINES

	1989	1990	1991	1992	1993	1994	1995	1996	1997	1998
GDP (% growth)	6.2	3.0	-0.5	0.3	2.1	4.4	4.8	5.5	(6.0)	(6.5)
								(5.8)	5.2	-0.5
GNP (% growth)	5.6	3.9	0.6	1.5	2.2	5.3	5.0	6.8	(7.0)	(7.0)
								(7.2)	5.3	0.4
Gross domestic investment	21.9	24.3	20.1	21.0	23.6	23.5	21.6	23.9	(25.5)	(26.5)
(% of GNP)								(22.2)	22.8	18.4
Gross national saving	18.5	18.2	17.9	19.1	18.2	19.0	19.0	20.5	(21.0)	(22.0)
(% of GNP)								(17.8)	19.5	19.1
Merchandise exports	4.7	8.0	11.1	15.8	18.5	18.5	29.4	17.5	(22.0)	(24.0)
(% growth)								(17.7)	22.8	16.9
Merchandise imports	17.0	-1.7	20.1	22.2	19.8	21.2	23.7	25.0	(20.0)	(18.0)
(% growth)								(20.8)	14.0	-18.8
Current account balance	-3.4	-6.1	-2.3	-1.9	-5.5	-4.5	-3.3	-4.1	(-4.5)	(-4.5)
(% of GNP)								(-4.5)	-5.1	1.91
International reserves	1417.0	924.0	3246.0	4403.0	4676.0	6017.0	6372.0	10030.0	7266.0	9226.0
(million US$)										
Import cover (months)	1.5	0.9	3.0	3.4	3.0	3.2	2.6	3.5	2.2	3.6
Net fiscal balance	-2.2	-3.5	-2.1	-1.2	-1.5	1.1	0.5	0.3	0.1	-1.8
(% of GNP)										
Revenue surplus	-1.7	-3.1	-1.7	-1.8	-0.9	1.5	5.4	3.2	2.6	2.6
(% of GNP)										
Inflation rate (CPI)	12.2	14.2	18.7	8.9	7.6	9.0	8.10	8.4	(7.0)	(7.0)
								(9.1)	6.0	9.7

(Contd.)

Table A4.1.4 Contd.

	1989	1990	1991	1992	1993	1994	1995	1996	1997	1998
Debt–service ratio (% of export)	25.4	27.0	23.0	24.4	25.5	17.4	16.00	12.5 (12.7)	(12.0) 11.7	(12.0) 11.9

Note: Figures in brackets for 1997 and 1998 are ADB forecast; For other years figures in brackets are revised ones.

Source: Asian Development Bank, *Asian Development Outlook* 1997–8, 1999, 1999 (update); International Monetary Fund, *International Financial Statistics Yearbook* 1996 and 1999; World Bank, *World Development Reports*; Central Bank of Philippines.

Table A4.1.5
KEY MACROECONOMIC INDICATORS: SOUTH KOREA

	1989	1990	1991	1992	1993	1994	1995	1996	1997	1998
GDP (% growth)	6.38	9.51	9.13	5.06	5.75	8.60	9.00	7.10	(6.3)	(6.9)
									5.5	-5.8
GNP (% growth)	6.92	9.65	9.16	5.03	5.88	8.40	8.70	6.70	(6.1)	(6.7)
									4.8	-6.3
Gross domestic investment (% of GNP)	33.91	37.19	39.17	36.84	35.29	36.30	37.40	36.5	(36.2)	(35.3)
								(38.7)	35.4	29.4
Gross national saving (% of GNP)	36.35	36.50	36.33	35.55	35.60	35.20	36.20	35.4	(34.7)	(34.7)
								(33.9)	33.5	42.9
Merchandise exports (% growth)	2.95	2.79	10.23	8.03	7.69	15.70	31.50	(4.3)	(8.6)	(16.2)
								4.1	6.7	-4.9
Merchandise imports (% growth)	18.63	13.63	16.72	0.31	2.48	22.40	32.10	12.20	(4.7)	(12.3)
									-2.2	-36.1
Current account balance (% of GNP)	2.44	-0.69	-2.84	-1.29	0.31	-1.00	-1.80	-4.90	(-3.7)	(-2.8)
									-1.8	12.7
International reserves (million US$)	15214.0	14793.0	13701.0	17121.0	20228.0	25639.0	32678.0	34037.0	20368.0	31974.0
Import cover (months)	2.97	2.54	2.02	2.51	2.90	3.01	2.90	2.65	1.63	6.68
Net fiscal balance (% of GNP)	0.19	-0.68	-1.63	-0.50	0.64	2.36	1.97	0.50	-1.40	-5.10
Revenue surplus (% of GNP)	1.48	1.73	0.56	1.27	2.16	0.32	-0.24	6.96	6.88	6.39
Inflation rate (CPI)	5.74	8.58	9.30	6.22	4.82	6.20	4.50	5.00	4.5	7.5
								(4.7)	(4.6)	

(Contd.)

Table A4.1.5 Contd.

	1989	1990	1991	1992	1993	1994	1995	1996	1997	1998
Debt–service ratio (% of export)	11.80	10.70	7.10	7.60	9.20	6.80	–	–	–	–

Note: Figures in brackets for 1997 and 1998 are ADB forecast; for other years figures in brackets are revised ones.

Source: Asian Development Bank, *Asian Development Outlook* 1997–8, 1999, 1999 (update); International Monetary Fund, *International Financial Statistics Yearbook* 1996 and 1999; World Bank, *World Development Reports*; Central Bank, South Korea.

5

Retracing the Roots of Asian Troubles: 1996–7
Some Analytical Issues and Empirical Evidence

Hotspur   . . . . Were it good
To set the exact wealth of our states
All at one cast? To set so high a main
On the nice hazard of one doubtful hour?
It were not good; for therein should we read
The very bottom and the soul of hope,
The very list, the very utmost bound
Of all our fortunes.

Shakespeare,[1] Henry IV, 4,1,45–52

With the East and South East Asian financial markets showing, since the second/third week of January 1998, some signs of stabilizing, if not of robust recovery, it is an opportune moment to take stock of the major issues that the Asian currency turmoil has brought to the fore. In Chapter 3, the focus was on the genesis of the Thai crisis[1], while in Chapter 4, we discussed the dynamics of the contagion that made some of the conventional policy instruments lose their cutting edge, or even counterproductive. In the present

First published in *Money & Finance,* April 1998.

1 The Thai baht, let us recall, was the first to be subjected to a speculative attack in mid-May 1997 and the turmoil started engulfing the rest of the region after the fall of the baht in early July.

paper we propose to reconsider the distinguishing features of the Asian crisis and examine the validity of its alternative explanations advanced in the course of the debate over the last nine months.

SOURCES OF ASIAN TROUBLES

By now, economists have agreed that the nature of the Asian financial turmoil is quite different from the earlier currency crises faced by Mexico, Brazil, Argentina, and other Latin American economies. The troubles in these countries originated primarily in fiscal profligacy. The chain of causation generally ran from large fiscal and monetized deficits to high or hyperinflation, and hence to overvalued exchange rates with growing trade deficit. The resulting run on foreign reserves and expectations of an impending fall in the exchange rate led to flight of domestic capital, along with speculative attack on the currency by foreign investors. Thus, though the proximate cause of the crisis was loss of confidence of domestic and international investors, the adverse expectations were grounded on accumulated evidence over time concerning the unsustainability of the current exchange rate in the none–too–distant future.[2]

As we have already noted in our earlier papers, most of the signals preceding the Latin American crises had been conspicuous by their absence in the Asian economies before they started suffering from severe meltdown in their currency and share prices from the middle of 1997. For a number of years, until 1997, government accounts in Thailand, the Philippines, Malaysia, and Korea showed a succession of surplus budgets. Indonesia, it is true, often ran a fiscal deficit, but the deficit was in the range of 0.2 to 0.4 per cent of gross domestic product. In the absence of monetized deficit, the growth rate of broad money in all these countries was quite modest, and so was the rate of inflation.[3]

2 We have already emphasized in Chapter 3 that this loss of confidence necessarily implies a drastic revision of investors' expectations and their failure, so far to judge correctly the country's weakening fundamentals on the balance of payments front. It is also not very difficult to see that economic theory may help in identifying signals of weakening fundamentals, but not generally in forecasting the timing of the crisis.

3 See Tables A5.2.1–A5.2.7 in Annexe 5.2 for major macroeconomic indicators of the East and South East Asian economies. See also Rakshit

In the context of high growth, large domestic saving, exemplary fiscal prudence, and low rate of inflation in the region, two major hypotheses have been advanced for explaining the Asian woes, the first by Professor L Summers and the IMF, the second by Professor P. Krugman[4] (1998). While Krugman identifies bank loans for speculative investment as the villain of the piece, the first hypothesis focuses on the unsustainability of large and persistent current account deficits, along with the maintenance of fixed exchange rates in the face of changing domestic and international economic environment. In Chapter 3 we recorded our initial reading of the possible sources of the Thai crisis, including the ones highlighted in the two theses mentioned above. With the unfolding of events and churning of ideas over the last nine months, it appears worthwhile to re-examine the basic problems taking account of the important similarities and differences in the operation of economic forces across the East and South East Asian economies.

CURRENT ACCOUNT DEFICITS WITH PEGGED EXCHANGE RATES

In assessing the role of current account balance in causing the Asian currency crisis, note first, that before 1996 the balance of payments of all afflicted economies did not display large and persistent deficits in the current account. Between 1992 and 1996, the deficit as a ratio of gross domestic product was relatively large for Thailand, Malaysia, and the Philippines[5], but quite modest for Indonesia, and negligible for Korea (see Table 5.1). The balance of payments of all other major economies in the region, viz., Japan, China, Taiwan, Singapore, and Hong Kong[6], registered moderate to massive surpluses in their current account over successive years. The financial turbulence of some of these countries was, to be sure, due to contagion operating

---

(1997b, 1997c) for some details of the genesis of the Asian crisis in general, and Thai troubles in particular.

4 Unlike the Krugman diagnosis, the Summers–IMF thesis is somewhat loose and catholic, cataloguing as it does a conjunction of factors leading up to the crisis.

5 However, after its jump to 5.5 per cent in 1993, the current account deficit of the Philippines came down to around 4.5 per cent during 1994–6.

6 The current account balance of Hong Kong turned negative in 1995, but was too small to be of any consequence.

Table 5.1

CURRENT ACCOUNT BALANCE AND DEBT SERVICE IN ASIAN ECONOMIES

Year	Thailand		Indonesia		Malaysia		Philippines		Korea	
	Current account balance as % of GDP	Debt service as % of exports	Current account balance as % of GDP	Debt service as % of exports	Current account balance as % of GDP	Debt service as % of exports	Current account balance as % of GDP	Debt service as % of exports	Current account balance as % of GDP	Debt service as % of exports
1989		16.3		38		15.1	-3.42	25.4		11.8
1990	-8.3	16.9	-2.8	31.5	-2.1	10.3	-6.1	27	-0.9	10.7
1991	-7.7	13	-3.4	34	-8.8	7.7	-2.3	23	-3	7.1
1992	-5.6	13.7	-2.2	31.6	-3.8	6.6	-1.6	24.4	-1.5	7.6
1993	-5	18.5	-1.5	33.8	-4.8	7.8	-5.55	25.5	0.1	9.2
1994	-5.6	15.6	-1.7	30	-7.8	7.7	-4.6	18.5	-1.2	6.8
1995	-8	11.8	-3.3		-10	6.8	-4.4	18	-2	
1996	-7.9		-3.3		-4.9		-4.7		-4.9	
1997	-3.9		-2.9		-5.8		-4.5		-2.9	

Source: World Bank, *World Debt Tables;* IMF, *World Economic Outlook,* December 1997.

through interdependence of regional economies reinforced by 'herd behaviour' on the part of international investors (Chapter 3 and 4); but the problems faced by Indonesia, Korea or Japan defy satisfactory explanation in terms of pure contagion. In the light of the experience of these countries we need to search for factors other than current account deficits for explaining the emergence and depth of the Asian crisis.

Even in the case of countries which ran large deficits in their current account, it is important to appreciate the nature and economic implications of the net inflow of foreign funds for financing domestic absorption[7] (see Box 5.1). Contrary to the the Latin American experience, in Thailand, Malaysia, and the Philippines the current account imbalance was not driven by mounting budgetary deficit or associated with a decline in domestic saving (see Tables A5.2.1,

---

Box 5.1
CURRENT ACCOUNT DEFICIT AND BALANCE OF PAYMENTS VIABILITY

To appreciate the role of current account deficit in causing currency crises, it is useful to consider the economic significance of the deficit and its relation with major macroeconomic variables. Note first that:

Current account deficit (CAD) in the balance of payments
= (Payments on current account) − (Receipts on current account)
= [Imports of goods and services (M)]−[Exports of goods and services (X) + *Net* factor incomes including net transfer receipts from abroad (NFIA)].   (5.1.1)

Remembering that:

Gross national product (GNP) = Private consumption (C) + Government consumption (G) + Investment (I) + X − M + NFIA,   (5.1.2)

and that: Aggregate saving (S) = GNP-Aggregate consumption
$$= GNP - (C + G),   (5.1.3)$$

the relation between current account deficit, investment, and saving is given by:

$$CAD = (M) - [X + NFIA]$$
$$= I - [GNP - (C + G)]$$
$$= I - S   (5.1.4)$$

(Contd.)

---

7 By way of private and public consumption and investment.

Box 5.1 Contd.

Again, the gap between current payments and receipts in the balance of payments necessarily equals net inflow of foreign funds, implying that:

CAD = Increase in net liability of the country to the rest of the world.   (5.1.5)

In other words, when a country runs CAD, net claims of foreigners on the domestic economy grows over time. This need not necessarily be a bad thing, provided the growing external liability is matched by the country's enhanced capacity for earning from international transactions. To be more specific, viability of balance of payments requires that in the long run the country should be able to generate an excess of exports over imports, sufficient to pay for charges on account of interest or dividend on foreign capital.[1]

It is thus not very difficult to see that large and persistent current account deficits tend to undermine the balance of payments viability if:

- inflow of foreign capital finances domestic consumption rather than investment;
- productivity of investment is low in relation to the interest on foreign loans;
- the country faces a (relatively) shrinking international market for its exportables; or
- the supply conditions of the country's imports tend to deteriorate over time.

1 We are ruling out Ponzi game which permits an economic agent to run into ever increasing debt in relation to its income by continuously using capital receipts for making payments on current account.

A5.2.3 and A5.2.4). Quite clearly, the growing liability on the external account of these countries was matched by the addition of productive assets in the domestic sector, so that current account deficits could not, on their own, have produced a crisis on the balance of payments front.[8] There are other considerations which cast serious doubts on the hypothesis relating to the role of current account deficits behind the financial upheaval in the ASEAN–4[9] and Korea.

8 Box 5.1 lists the factors affecting the balance of payments viability when part of domestic absorption is financed through inflow of foreign funds.
9 Comprising Thailand, Indonesia, Malaysia and the Philippines.

First, in all these countries there was very little accumulation of external debt on the part of the government. The net capital inflow, reflected in the current account deficit, was driven almost entirely by market forces, representing the demand for external funds by private borrowers in the domestic economy and the supply of finance by foreign banks and fund managers. The market solution to the problem of determining the extent to which foreign sources of finance should be tapped to facilitate domestic absorption appeared highly efficient until 1996. During the period 1990–5, the yearly export growth in dollar terms averaged around 20 per cent in Thailand and Malaysia, 18 per cent in the Philippines, and 15 per cent in Korea. Even the Indonesian export growth, at 12 per cent, was fairly decent, if not spectacular. What is no less relevant to note is that the growth of export earnings in all the five seriously affected economies displayed a sharply rising trend since 1992, when restrictions on inflow of foreign funds were relaxed.

Second, we should recognize that large current account deficits[10] following moves towards capital account convertibility is not only natural, but constitutes an important characteristic of the optimal process of adjustment of capital stock over time. With the removal of impediments to free flow of capital across national boundaries, capital should, *a la* the mainstream economic theory, tend to move from low to high productivity regions in the world. In a static world with perfect foresight, the consummation of this adjustment process consists in convergence of returns on capital in different regions, with the marginal productivity of capital declining over time in capital importing countries and rising in capital exporting ones. The important point to appreciate in this connection is that in the initial stages of the adjustment process[11], in high productivity countries the magnitude of net inflow of foreign capital (represented by the current account deficit) should be larger than that in later stages. Hence, large current account deficits of Thailand and other ASEAN economies following relaxation of control on capital account cannot be regarded as an important factor undermining their balance of payments viability.

Third, large current account deficits in Thailand and Malaysia were, in no small measure, a reflection of the 'flying geese' pattern

10 Or surplus, in the case of capital abundant economies.
11 When the differential in returns on capital between the two groups is higher than that in the later stage.

of investment[12] characterizing the East and South East Asian economies. By the early 1990s the wages in Thailand and Malaysia still lagged far behind those in the 'gang of four' and Japan, but had become much higher than the wages prevailing in Indonesia and China. This caused a significant shift in the pattern of investment across this group of countries. While labour intensive enterprises were being set up in the low wage economies, Thailand and Malaysia started attracting investment in relatively more capital intensive lines of production. In Thailand, for example, large automobile manufacturing units were set up through Japanese FDI and this involved substantial imports of heavy machinery and equipment. The consequent increase in current account deficit may thus be viewed as an integral part of the optimal response to changes in relative factor prices in the East and South East Asian economies.

Finally for the balance of payments problems that large current account deficits are perceived to produce.[13] As we have already observed, in a static world with perfect foresight, inflow of foreign funds in capital scarce economies, even if substantial in relation to their GDP, is no cause for concern and constitutes an optimal process of allocation of global capital across different countries. The real world is, however, always in a state of flux and characterized by uncertainties. In such a world, unforeseen shocks may be quite severe, prove past investment decisions wrong, and make the borrowing economy's external balance vulnerable to the vagaries of changing market conditions, external or internal. But what is relevant in this context is not the net inflows of foreign capital[14], but the

12 The flying geese pattern of investment refers to movement of industries across the East and South East Asian economies in response to changes in factor prices. The initial stage of industrialization of the East Asian economies was marked by setting up of labour intensive industries to take advantage of cheap and abundant supply of labour. As wages rose with rapid absorption of labour in these countries, investment in more capital intensive activities took place and there was a movement of labour intensive industries to (the low wage) ASEAN economies and China.

13 Current account deficits, let us remember, necessarily indicate foreigners' willingness to invest in the domestic economy, and hence, do not produce any balance of payments problem in the current year. The deficits are regarded as a potential source of trouble in the future when the external debt has to be serviced.

14 i.e., the current account deficit, which is a flow.

burden of external liability of the country. There are a number of indicators of this burden, of which the most useful is the ratio of external debt service to exports.[15] Judged by this criterion, the burden of external indebtedness was negligible in Thailand, Malaysia, and Korea, and moderate in the Philippines and Indonesia (see Table 5.1). It is also interesting to note that in all these economies the debt service to export ratio displayed a declining trend during the 1990s. There had, thus, been no signal until 1996 that current account deficits were unsustainable, or that the countries were heading towards an external debt trap.

PEGGED EXCHANGE RATES

A common refrain of most commentaries on the ASEAN currency crisis has been that the maintenance of pegged exchange rates to a basket of currencies with a disproportionately large weight attached to the US dollar played an important role in eroding the competitiveness of exports from this region and creating problems on the external front. Two specific reasons for balance of payments difficulties faced by Thailand and her neighbours are advanced in this connection. First, by far the most important trading partner of the South East Asian countries was Japan, not the United States. With the US dollar gaining against the yen by 11.5 per cent during 1996, and a further 9.5 per cent in the course of the first four months of 1997, under the then prevailing exchange rate system, the ASEAN currencies also recorded significant appreciation vis-à-vis the yen. Second, there was a sharp decline in the export competitiveness of this group of countries following the massive devaluation of the yuan in 1994. The two factors, it is suggested, caused sharp deterioration in the trade balances of the countries under consideration, especially since China had built up a huge productive capacity in goods that were close substitutes of these countries' exportables.

15 The 'burden' in this context, let us make it clear, refers to the vulnerability of the balance of payments to unanticipated shocks. Given this focus, the external debt service to GDP ratio, though useful for other purposes, is not a very good indicator of the debt burden. Of the two countries having the same debt–GDP ratio, the balance of payments vulnerability of the one with the larger ratio of debt service to exports will be greater. Our conclusion in the text does not however, depend on which of the relevant ratios we choose as the crucial indicator of the debt burden for the ASEAN economies.

While assessing the significance of pegged exchange rates (along with large current account deficits) in causing the currency crisis, the following observations appear to be in order. First, for South Korea, not only had the current account deficit been fairly small, but the won was also permitted to depreciate in response to a fall in the demand for Korean exports. During 1996, the rise in dollar against the won was to the tune of 8.9 per cent, and by the end of June 1997, the depreciation of the won was larger than that of the yen.[16] The IMF hypothesis, thus, does not seem to fit in with the Korean experience.

Second, a careful sifting of evidence suggests that the role of the Chinese devaluation on the ASEAN exports was, at best, marginal. Since the devaluation was coupled with the virtual elimination of large subsidies hitherto enjoyed by exporters (mostly in the form of a substantial premium on export earnings over the official exchange rate), the actual decline in prices of Chinese goods in the international market was much smaller than the fall in the official value of the yuan in 1994. Indeed, during 1993–5 the export growth of the ASEAN–4 was quite high and showed a rising trend, contrary to what one would expect on the basis of changes in the nominal value of the yuan vis-à-vis the baht, the ringgit, the (Philippine) peso or the rupiah (see Tables A5.2.1a–A5.2.4a). It is also worth noting that the Chinese export growth registered a sharp increase in 1994, but declined thereafter (see Table A5.2.7a). It was in 1996, two years after the Chinese devaluation, that the ASEAN exports suffered a severe slump. However, in China too, export growth came down sharply, from 24.9 per cent in 1995 to 1.5 per cent in 1996. Indeed, during 1996 substantial slowing down of export growth was a common experience of all emerging market economies as well as of Korea and Japan (see Tables A5.2.1a–5.2.7a). The explanation of the problems facing the South East Asian countries should not, thus, be sought in the 1994 Chinese devaluation or in the 'inappropriate' trade and exchange rate policies pursued by these countries.

Third, it is important to recognize in this connection that, given the nature of goods supplied by developing economies in the world market, the demand for exportables from an individual country may be elastic, but that from all these countries taken

16 Note that the Korean and Japanese exports are close substitutes in the international market.

together is not very sensitive to changes in prices. Hence, a competitive devaluation among ASEAN economies (and China[17]) in the face of a sharp downturn in world demand during 1996 would, in all probability, have resulted in a steeper fall in their export earnings and have hastened rather than staved off the currency crisis.[18]

Finally, in tracing the roots of the troubles in Thailand and other ASEAN economies to their exchange rate regime, the IMF-type hypothesis ignores some important policy issues, as well as the way these countries managed their exchange rates upto the beginning of 1997. During 1993–6, the ratio of Thai official reserves to average imports per month[19] was practically unchanged at 5.5 months. This suggests that market intervention on the part of the Bank of Thailand was directed primarily toward ironing out of day-to-day fluctuations in the exchange rate, rather than propping up the value of the baht against the free play of market forces.[20] This was also largely true of the other ASEAN–4 countries.

The market-driven exchange rate may, it is possible, be itself 'overvalued' in the sense that the rate fails to adjust in response to a fall in the competitiveness of the country's exports or in the long term productivity of domestic investment. Such failures in the South East and East Asian foreign exchange market, if any, arose primarily from the (unwarranted) positive perception of international investors regarding the economic outlook of Thailand and other economies, prompted largely by their past record of high growth, low inflation, and stable exchange rate. The implication of this line of reasoning is that for avoiding the currency crisis the central banks should have tried to push down the exchange rate through an

17 Which account for a substantial share of labour intensive exports in the international market.

18 World demand for goods comprising exports from Korea and Japan was much more elastic than that from the ASEAN–4; even so, in 1996 the Korean and Japanese exports suffered a serious setback in spite of a slide in the won and the yen.

19 The ratio indicates the number of months for which the import bill can be financed from official reserves.

20 Had the central bank tried to raise the exchange rate against the operation of market forces, there would have been a depletion of foreign exchange reserves. Between 1995 and 1996 foreign exchange reserves of the Bank of Thailand, we may note, went up by nearly US$2 billion.

interest rate cut or expansionary monetary policy.[21] However, for Thailand and other ASEAN economies such a course of action was generally viewed as counterproductive, since it would have contributed toward 'overexpansion' of domestic credit for financing speculative investment. It thus appears that the IMF-type explanation has too many gaps to make it reasonably satisfactory in the context of the course of economic events preceding the Asian currency crisis.

BANKING CRISIS AND CURRENCY CRISIS

A highly interesting explanation of the currency turmoil in Asia has been put forward by Professor Paul Krugman (1998). The Asian problem, Krugman suggests, had in fact very little to do with the currency market *per se*, but owed its origin primarily to failure in financial intermediation. The hypothesis is advanced on the basis of the common and most striking feature of the five most seriously afflicted economies in the region. Though the ASEAN–4 and Korea differed significantly in their stages of development, economic structure, and pattern of trade, the banking systems in all these countries were bedevilled by bad loans, advanced for financing highly speculative ventures. It is this banking crisis that, the hypothesis suggests, had spilled over to the currency market and set in motion a mutually reinforcing mechanism, under which exchange rates and share prices were dragged down relentlessly during the second half of 1997 and the first quarter of 1998.

HIGH RISK LENDING UNDER MORAL HAZARD

That severe and systemic banking troubles can trigger off a currency crisis is not very difficult to appreciate.[22] The importance of the Krugman hypothesis lies in its identification of the crucial factor behind the preponderance of non-performing loans plaguing the

21 Such a policy would have reduced the inflow of foreign funds (as returns on domestic financial assets become less attractive) and led to a decline in the exchange rate.

22 We shall presently indicate the major routes through which problems in the banking sector affect the market for foreign exchange, directly or indirectly.

financial intermediaries of the five major victims of the currency crisis. The source of the banking troubles in these economies is traced to large scale extension of credit for financing risky investment and, such lending, in its turn, is attributed to 'moral hazard'[23] under government guarantee of deposits with banks and non-bank finance companies. It is useful to summarize the salient features of the Krugman model before we discuss its relevance in the Asian context.

If the depositors know (or feel) that they will be paid back in full from the government coffers in case of bank failure, there is little incentive for them to keep track of the health of banks or to withdraw deposits, even in the face of palpable signs of their insolvency. When such guarantee (explicit or implicit) is coupled with little supervision of banks and no penalty to their managers (owners) in the event of losses or bankruptcy, conditions are ripe for financing high risk investments on the Panglossian presumption[24] that all will be for the best in the best of all possible worlds. The following, simple illustration suggests why such lending decisions are quite natural with moral hazard looming large.

Consider a banker who can borrow from domestic or international sources at a fixed rate of interest any amount he likes[25]—a fairly reasonable assumption under the government guarantee of deposits. In Period 0, let there be two alternative investment projects, A and B, each costing Rs 100 and yielding their entire return in Period 1. Assume further that (a) in Period 1 there can be only two states of nature[26], 1 and 2, both of which

23 Moral hazard refers to rash, imprudent, or socially undesirable course of actions induced by guarantees or insurance. Thus, a person having health or car insurance may not take good care of his health or may be inclined to careless driving.

24 *a la* Dr. Pangloss in the Voltaire fiction, *Candide.*

25 This will also be true of all bankers taken together when the country's borrowing from abroad is negligible in relation to the global supply of funds.

26 States of nature are (in this case) possible conjunctions of events that determine the outcome of the projects. Thus, for investment in HYV seeds by a farmer, a state of nature consists in the extent of rainfall, price of the crop, and other factors relevant for the return on such investment. If there are two alternative investment projects, states of nature will be the unions of the sets of possible events that govern the yield on the two projects.

are equally probable[27]; and (b) under 1, gross returns on investments in A and B will be Rs 110 and Rs 130 respectively, while the corresponding returns under state 2 will be Rs 110 and Rs 40.

The gross expected return[28] on A, $E(A)$, is given by

(1) $E(A) = \frac{1}{2} \times (110–100) + \frac{1}{2} \times (110–100) = 10$ per cent, and that on B by

(2) $E(B) = \frac{1}{2} \times (130–100) + \frac{1}{2} \times (40–100) = minus$ 15 per cent.

It is clear that with no moral hazard problem, A will be chosen, since it is perfectly safe and yields a higher return than that on B. In fact, in the example given above, an (risk neutral)[29] investor will invest in A, so long as the interest rate is less than 10 per cent, but will not touch B with a barge pole unless depositors (or the government) pay him at least 15 per cent on the sum borrowed and invested!

Now consider the banker's behaviour when (a) there is government guarantee of deposits (and interest obligations); and (b) he can go scot free if the investment fails. Under these conditions the gross return to the banker from the safe investment is still the same as before, viz., 10 per cent. However, if the banker chooses B, his gross return under State 1 is Rs 30; but under 2, even though there is a loss of Rs 60 on the capital invested, the return to the banker is zero, since the loss is borne entirely by the government. The implications is that the expected return to the banker from B under moral hazard[30], $ER_m(B)$, is

27 i.e., the probability of the occurrence of both 1 and 2 is 1/2. These assumptions, as we shall presently note, are only for simplicity, and not crucial for the Krugman conclusions.

28 Before interest payments on deposits.

29 An investor is said to be risk neutral when his decision is based only on expected returns on alternative projects; (b) risk averse when the expected return on the riskier project (characterized by larger dispersion of possible yields) needs to be higher to induce him to choose the project; and (c) a gambler or risk lover if he enjoys taking risk and hence likes to invest in riskier ventures even when their expected payoffs are not larger than those on safer investments.

30 The return on A under moral hazard, $ER_m(A)$, is 10 per cent, as we have noted.

(3) $ER_m(B) = \frac{1}{2} \times 30 + \frac{1}{2} \times 0 = 15$ per cent.

Clearly, the bank now chooses B rather than A, even though from the social viewpoint the return on the former is negative[31] (*minus* 15 per cent).

The interesting point to note in this connection is that $ER_m(B)$ is not the highest interest rate the banker will be willing to pay on deposits. The maximum, as shown in Annexe 5.1, is in fact, the Pangloss return, R_p, which obtains under the best of all possible circumstances and equals 30 per cent in the example chosen. To see why the banker will borrow even when the deposit rate is 30 per cent for investing in B, consider any lower rate of interest, say 25 per cent. If the state of nature turns out to be 2 in Period 1, there is a loss of 60 per cent, but this does not hurt the banker. If, on the other hand, state 1 prevails, his net gain is 5 per cent after paying 25 per cent to depositors. Hence, it is the Pangloss return rather than $ER_m(B)$, that determines whether borrowing by the bank will be worthwhile or not.

OVERINVESTMENT, RESOURCE MISALLOCATION AND FINANCIAL FRAGILITY

In terms of the example given above, it is easy to see how moral hazard problems undermine the health of the banking system and necessarily culminate in a financial crisis. The simplest way of analyzing the problem is to focus on the distortionary effects produced with government guarantee of deposits when banks use their deposits (as in Krugman (1998)) for acquiring real, rather than financial assets. A more detailed account of some of the effects is given in Box 5.2.

Note first that banks' choice of assets on the basis of the Pangloss outcome[32] necessarily leads to misallocation of resources, with the diversion of funds from projects having higher expected returns to those yielding low, or even negative returns on the average. Such misallocation has a deleterious impact, not only on the financial

---

31 The reason is that when 2 occurs, the loss of Rs 60 is borne by tax payers or depositors (in case the implicit guarantee is not fulfilled)

32 Relating to return on investment or price of the asset, depending on whether it is the supply of asset or deposit that is perfectly elastic. For details see Annexe 5.1.

Box 5.2
MORAL HAZARD AND BANKING CRISIS
Some Macroeconomic Perspectives

Without losing any essential element of the problem, the overall impact of investors' behaviour under moral hazard can be indicated through a simple extension of traditional analysis.

Consider an economy with full employment of resources, a competitive banking system and perfectly flexible interest rates. In Figure B.5.2.1 SS denotes saving, corresponding to different interest rates and II the undistorted investment demand indicating the expected values or the internal rates of return on investment.[1] With no inflow or outflow of foreign capital, the level of domestic investment (and saving) will be I_0 (or S_0), and the interest rate i_0 equals the expected return on I_0, so that (on average) the return on capital accumulation (just) suffices the cost of borrowing.[2] If the country can borrow any amount it wants to at an interest rate of i_w from the international financial market, full capital account convertibility raises domestic investment to I^* and generates a current account deficit[3] of S^*I^*. Note however, that in this case also the expected return on investment equals the cost of borrowing, suggesting that the country (and banks) will not on the whole face any problem in servicing its (their) external (and internal) debt.

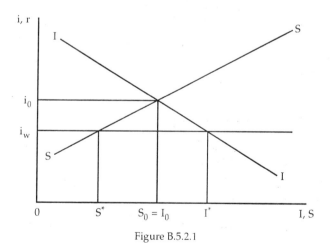

Figure B.5.2.1

1 Assuming that investors are risk neutral. See fn. 29 of the text in this connection.
2 This equality is a characteristic of the competitive banking system.
3 Gap between investment and saving. See Box 5.1.

(Contd.)

Box 5.2 Contd.

Figure B.5.2.2 summarizes the macroeconomic behaviour of the system, where investment is driven, not by expected, but by Pangloss returns, shown by I_pI_p. Recalling that the Pangloss return corresponds to the best possible outcome, I_pI_p lies above II. However, a decision based on Pangloss outcome implies distorted choice of investment projects, so that for any given level of investment the expected return on the Pangloss package, indicated by E_pE_p in Figure B.5.2.2, must be less than that on the undistorted package (underlying II). Note also that since the most favourable state of nature generating the Pangloss outcome also implies a favourable exchange rate, the cost of external borrowing under the Pangloss outcome, c_w, will be less than the expected cost of borrowing, i_w, under undistorted decision making. With no capital account convertibility whatsoever, aggregate investment in the economy due to moral hazard will be I_p^0 (=S_p^0), rather than I_0. Thus, moral hazard leads to an increase in domestic investment and saving; however, now the expected return on investment, (e_p^0), falls short of the cost of borrowing i_p so that a financial crisis becomes inevitable sooner or later. The crisis is aggravated by capital account convertibility. Investment driven by Pangloss return is now I_p^* (Figure B.5.2.2) and the excess of expected cost of borrowing over the expected return on investment $i_we_p^*$. Not only is there an 'overinvestment', but there is also a higher current account deficit, a lower level of domestic saving, and a heavier burden of external borrowing. The country cannot, thus, escape a systemic banking problem as also a balance of payments crisis.

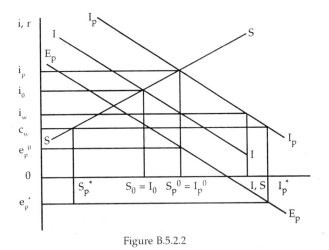

Figure B.5.2.2

system, but on the country's growth potential or economic fundamentals as well.

Second, even with no external inflow of funds, moral hazard leads to overinvestment since

(a) the Pangloss return governing banks' decision is higher than the expected yield on investment chosen under the undistorted regime; and

(b) saving is generally positively related to interest rates.

Third, when banks can borrow from the international capital market, the extent of overinvestment will be larger. Indeed, availability of external funds reduces domestic saving and results in larger current account deficits than net borrowing from abroad under undistorted financial decision making.

Finally, the Pangloss value based investment cannot be sustained, as banks incur mounting losses over time and the cost of their (repeated) bailouts becomes prohibitive. The result is withdrawal or non-fulfilment of government guarantee of deposits, which, in its turn, sets off a banking crisis. The outcome will be the same when banks' investment consists of acquisition of non-reproducible assets like land since the Pangloss value (or return) at which such assets are bought is larger than their expected value.[33]

FROM BANKING CRISIS TO CURRENCY CRISIS

The chain of causation from the domestic banking crisis to currency crisis is not very difficult to discern. The impact of financial fragility on the balance of payments is the greatest and the most direct when banks have borrowed from the international market on a large scale. As in other cases, in this case also, the crisis is set off by a reversal of expectations. Under the conditions considered above, it is the actual or impending failure of explicit or implicit guarantee (under which loans were contracted on the basis of their Pangloss returns) that causes foreign investors[34] to take a dim view of the expected returns on their loans to financial firms. The result is non-renewal of loans as they mature and drying up of new inflow of external funds. Since the balance of payments and the exchange rate have so far been buttressed by external borrowing (under explicit or

33 See Annexe 5.1.
34 As also domestic investors.

implicit guarantee), the reversal of the flow of foreign funds cannot but cause a balance of payments crisis and drive down the value of the domestic currency.

The problem is compounded by the fact that as investors anticipate an outflow of funds due to the impending banking crisis, they would expect the exchange rate to depreciate. The resulting attempt to liquidate domestic in exchange for foreign financial assets makes the expectation self-fulfilling.

Even when the external indebtedness of banks is negligible, large scale troubles in the domestic financial sector produce an adverse effect on the balance of payments through two routes.[35] First, irrespective of its roots, a banking crisis induces not only foreign but domestic depositors also to park their funds in countries where the financial system is considered healthy. Such substitution of foreign for domestic monetary assets aggravates the run on banks and produces self-fulfilling expectations of currency depreciation.

Second, a banking crisis is invariably attended with a severe contraction of credit. When a bank fails, it takes considerable time before its regular customers can meet their borrowing requirements from other banks. Even when banks do not actually go bankrupt, there is a severe decline in their capacity to extend credit due to cash drain from the banking system and the consequent fall in the money multiplier.[36] At the same time, the rise in non-performing assets induces banks to invest in government bonds at the expense of commercial loans. The result is a credit crunch for firms and a cutback in their production and investment. Such effects cannot but cause a deterioration in the country's economic prospects or creditworthiness (as perceived by domestic and foreign investors) and may well trigger off a currency turmoil with its reinforcing mechanism.[37]

---

35 These two routes of transmission, needless to say, are present, irrespective of whether bank borrowing is from domestic or external sources.

36 Which is nothing but the ratio of aggregate supply of money (which approximates the aggregate credit extended by the central and commercial banks) and the reserve or high power money in the system.

37 For a discussion of the reinforcing mechanism and the feedback from the foreign exchange market to the financial sector see Chapter 4.

THEORY AND EVIDENCE

The Krugman thesis on the roots of the Asian crisis is neat and seems to fit in with the banking troubles plaguing the East and South East Asian economies. However, a closer examination of the model and empirical evidence suggests quite a few gaps, some of which Krugman himself is acutely aware of (see Krugman, 1998). In evaluating the Krugman hypothesis, we shall focus on both the critical assumptions of the model and the discrepancy between its predictions, and the actual behaviour of the economies under examination.

The central feature of the Krugman model is the moral hazard problem causing investments to be undertaken on the basis of their Pangloss rather than expected returns. The source of the moral hazard is the explicit or implicit guarantee of bank deposits by the government. The model's outcome relating to investment, it is important to note, follows from the fact that in case the investment decision turns out to be wrong, not only is depositors' money (along with interest accrued) paid back in full, but bankers and investors[38] (using bank loans) also do not incur any cost whatsoever. Absence of penalty for a wrong decision is, however, possible only if:

(a) bankers and investors do not employ any funds of their own; and

(b) their future earnings as managers of financial firms or companies remain unimpaired, even though they have driven their firms to bankruptcy.

It is difficult to visualize a situation where (b) will hold. Neither did (a) hold in the Asian economies that have been facing financial turmoil. Apart from the fact that a part of the funds at the disposal of banks was owned by shareholders, bank loans to property developers and other investors in Thailand did not meet their financial requirements in full. In Malaysia (and Japan) loans were often obtained against shares, so that borrowers were automatically subject to substantial costs if the investment proved unproductive. The major part of bank loan in Korea was cornered by the

---

38 In the Krugman model bankers themselves are the final users of funds. If so, they are no longer financial intermediaries and 'bank' deposits do not enjoy government guarantee. Hence, the need to distinguish between banks and investors.

conglomerates[39], in which the stakes of the controlling families were very high.[40] Thus, the assumptions underlying the Krugman model are not quite in conformity with the conditions prevailing in the East and South Asian financial markets.

The relevance of a theory should, one may argue *a la* Friedman, be judged more by its predictive power than by the realism of its assumptions.[41] Following this criterion, we focus on the two most important results of the Krugman model. First, all investment should be routed through banks since they offer (under competitive conditions) the Pangloss return to their depositors. Second, not only would there be a tendency for investments to be concentrated in highly risky ventures, but their returns would also, on the average, be quite low, if not negative. Such investments cannot but make the performance of the economy volatile and produce an adverse impact on factor productivity and growth.

The two most important predictions of the model are not borne out by the Asian experience. As Krugman himself admits, substantial foreign direct and institutional investment had continued to pour into the Asian economies before the crisis surfaced in the first/ second quarter of 1997. What is more significant, upto 1996 these countries enjoyed a prolonged spell of high and sustained growth with little volatility[42] (see Tables A5.2.1a–A5.2.5a). Investment driven by Pangloss returns could not have produced such macroeconomic performance of the countries under review.

Financial intermediaries did, to be sure, indulge in speculative investment in real estate and shares. However, the quantitative significance of such funding in relation to total investment was quite minor. In Thailand, for example, there was no significant increase in bank lending to property developers since 1993[43] when

39 Especially after financial sector liberalization in the late 1980s. See Amsden and Euh (1990).

40 Since the overwhelming part of the shares of the conglomerates were owned by the controlling families, the high debt–equity ratios of Korean companies do not adequately reflect managers' stakes.

41 Which may well be simplifying rather than critical.

42 Even in 1996, growth rates of the five most seriously affected economies ranged from 5.7 per cent to 8.6 per cent.

43 In fact, by 1993 the boom in land prices appeared to have run its course and this could be due, among other things, to slackening of bank advances against real estates.

banks were permitted to borrow from external sources. It is also noteworthy that until 1996, earnings of Thai financial firms grew at an annual rate of 25 to 30 per cent per annum (see ADB, 1997). This does not support the view that bank investments in Thailand were highly distorted.

While earnings reported in profit and loss accounts of banks may be taken with a pinch of salt, evidence from the behaviour of the real sector is quite conclusive against the Krugman hypothesis. During 1985–96 not only was Thailand the fastest growing economy in the world, but her total factor productivity grew at an astonishing 3.25 per cent per annum. What is no less relevant is the fact that there was very little year-to-year fluctuation in the growth rate, contrary to what one would expect from the Krugman diagnosis. Neither does the diagnosis appear correct for other Asian economies. In Korea, for example, loans were used primarily for extension of productive capacity of the chaebol and until 1996–7 there was no evidence that such investment was of an unproductive nature. Indeed, over the five year period from 1992 to 1996, there was a marked improvement in the overall productivity of Korean investment, with the GDP growth running ahead of growth in capital accumulation by about 2.3 per cent per annum.

Finally, until 1996, the export growth rate of the Asian economies, as noted earlier, was not only high, but also displayed a rising trend. Given the already high export–GDP ratio the countries had attained by the late 1980s, such performance on the export front would have been impossible without substantial gains in productivity and their competitive strength in the international market.

MORAL HAZARD AND IRRATIONAL EXPECTATIONS

In spite of its analytical elegance, the Krugman model suffers from a serious theoretical flaw which considerably undermines the relevance of its results. Investment on the basis of the Pangloss return, as we have seen, presumes that the government will always bail out financial firms in case of trouble. However, even if the government is willing, its ability to fulfil the guarantee of the deposits depends on the scale of bad debt and losses piled up by the banks. Recall that investment *à la* the Krugman framework inevitably leads to widespread losses of firms and large scale banking crisis of an endemic nature. Hence, any rational economic agent should harbour serious doubts regarding the viability of the financial system and the ability of the government to meet the depositors' claim or to rescue banks going bankrupt.[44]

To be more specific, a rational depositor should not take seriously even explicit guarantee of deposits if he is reasonably certain (as he should be under the Krugman framework) of the emergence of a systemic banking crisis in the none-too-distant future. One can make sense of the domestic and foreign lenders entrusting funds with financial firms beset by moral hazard only if depositors (a) do not know that all (or a large number of) banks and investors are guided by the Pangloss rather than expected returns on investments; or (b) cannot work out the macroeconomic outcome of investment decisions driven by moral hazard.

The moral hazard problems induced by guarantee of deposits and the way the typical banker and investor behave under these conditions are fairly well known.[45] Nor is it difficult to comprehend the macroeconomic consequences of large scale investment in high risk ventures. Hence, the behaviour of depositors, *a la*, the Krugman model, cannot be explained in terms of rational expectations.

Indeed, until 1997, both domestic and foreign lenders displayed strong faith in the fundamentals of the East and South East Asian economies.[46] This is attested by two sets of factors. First, these countries attracted a large inflow of funds by way of FDI and FII, which carried no government guarantee whatsoever. Second, until the crisis broke out, neither the international credit rating agencies, nor the global fund managers with all the information and highly trained manpower at their disposal had any inkling of the impending trouble.[47] The perception that investment in the East and South East Asian countries was concentrated in high risk areas with low

44 With firms and banks going bankrupt, depositors' claims may well exceed the country's GDP. Even when the claim is not so large, administrative and political constraints do not generally permit the raising of substantial funds required for bailing out banks.

45 Especially to big lenders like foreign banks or fund managers.

46 There was no apprehension that a major part of investment in these economies was highly speculative.

47 Indeed, even in July/August 1997, international agencies expected the crisis to blow over fairly soon, without any serious damage to Thailand and other economies. See the quotations in Chapter 4. Similar views were expressed by the research staff of Goldman Sachs and other fund managers.

expected returns was thus not shared by keen observers and economic agents who had substantial stakes in these economies.

BANKING CRISIS: CHAIN OF CAUSATION

There are other features of Asian economies which go against the Krugman conclusion concerning the chain of causation running from the banking crisis to the currency crisis. Malaysian banks, for example, were highly capitalized and their non-performing assets at end of September 1997 amounted to a tiny 3.7 per cent of total bank lending. Still, the country was drawn into the vortex of currency crisis which, in its turn, led to a substantial increase in bad debt of banks.

Again, exposure of Indonesian banks to real estates and shares was quite limited. Serious banking troubles in Indonesia were, in fact, witnessed only after the currency crisis had set in and the central bank had started using conventional tools for tackling the crisis. Following the slide of the rupiah in August 1997, the Bank of Indonesia not only raised interest rates to exorbitant levels, but also directed state enterprises and pension funds[48] to shift their deposits from commercial banks to the central bank.[49] The result was a severe credit crunch, a sharp fall in business activity and investors' confidence, and rapid accumulation of non-performing assets by banks.

Banks in Korea first reported losses in 1996 and this (with the benefit of hindsight) could indeed be attributed to 'excessive' investment in automobile, steel, and memory chips by Korean conglomerates.[50] In the next section we shall consider the Korean experience to identify the source of the trouble; it appears fairly clear, however, that investments in Korea might have been 'imprudent'[51], but not 'speculative' in the usual sense.

Note finally, that banking troubles in China were on a much larger scale than those in the ASEAN–4 or Korea. In 1997, bad loans of the Chinese banks were estimated to be at least 30 per cent of the

---

48 Which accounted for a substantial part of total bank deposits.

49 Such a shift causes a one-to-one decline in reserve (or high power) money and reduces the bank's ability to extend credit by a multiple of the decline (*a la* the money multiplier analysis).

50 In 1996 there was a fall of 80 per cent in prices of computer chips in the world market.

51 Though hardly anybody thought so at the time they were undertaken.

country's gross domestic product, as compared with 12.7 per cent in Korea and about 15 per cent in the South East Asian countries in November 1997.[52] Yet China escaped from the Asian crisis relatively unscathed.

GENESIS OF THE CURRENCY TURMOIL: AN ALTERNATIVE HYPOTHESIS

In trying to unravel the tangled sources of the Asian woes, it appears useful to identify the factors that were common to the five most afflicted economies—factors which could *a priori* cause a crisis of confidence among domestic and international investors. All these countries, a perusal of Tables A5.2.1–5.2.5 suggests, started facing troubles on the macroeconomic front only from 1996. Hence, we need to take a close look at what went wrong since 1995 and how the problems surfacing in 1996 culminated in a currency crisis with a lag of about a year.

Note first that 1996 witnessed a precipitous drop in the export growth of the ASEAN-4 and Korea. As compared to the figures for 1995, the fall in the export growth rate recorded in 1996 amounted to 24.6 percentage points in Thailand, 21.8 points in Malaysia, 11.9 points in the Philippines, and 27.4 points in Korea. Only in Indonesia was the fall relatively moderate, at 4.3 percentage points. Apart from its immediate impact on the countries' macroeconomic performance in general, and balance of payments in particular, the crucial significance of the decline lay in two important features of the miracle economies. First, such sharp deceleration in export growth rates had not occurred for a long time[53] and marked a serious break from the steeply rising trends in export growth these countries had enjoyed since 1990. This could not but make the investors wonder whether the golden era of export-led growth of the Asian tiger economies had come to an end.

---

52 By the last quarter of 1997, NPAs in the ASEAN countries and Korea had increased by leaps and bounds due to the currency crisis and inappropriate monetary and fiscal measures (see Chapter 4).

53 Except in the Philippines. However, during 1990–5 even the Philippine export growth rate showed a steeply upward trend.

Second, the shake-up in investors' confidence was due in no small measure to the high degree of openness of these economies. The quantitative significance of the external sources of demand for their domestically produced goods is indicated by the fact that in 1995 the export–GDP ratio was 42.5 per cent in Thailand, 22.9 per cent in Indonesia (for 1994), 97.7 per cent in Malaysia, 36.2 per cent in the Philippines, and 32.8 per cent in Korea.

With exports constituting such a high proportion of aggregate demand, it is natural that a sharp downturn in their growth should lead to, and be compounded by, a fall in the growth rate of capital accumulation as well.[54] Until 1996, high GDP growth in the Asian tiger economies was propelled by export industries, and their track record over more than a decade had induced firms, including the Japanese multinationals, to set up production facilities to cater to rising external and domestic demand. The relation between export and investment was most marked in Thailand. As export growth crashed from 24.7 per cent in 1995 to 0.1 per cent in 1996, growth in domestic capital accumulation came down from 13.5 to 3.1 per cent between the two years, and plunged further to *minus* 12.4 per cent in 1997. Similar was the experience of other countries in the region.[55] It was this combination of sluggishness in export and investment that acted as a severe brake on the real sector, inflicted heavy losses upon producers and banks, and caused a reversal of expectations[56] of domestic and foreign lenders, regarding the countries' short and medium run prospects in general, and sustainability of their exchange rates in particular.

SOURCES OF ADVERSE SHOCK

Before examining the link between the adverse shock, the real sector was subjected to in 1996–7, and the outbreak of the currency crisis,

54 In the Philippines, investment growth fell with a time lag in 1997.

55 Thanks to her refusal to heed the IMF advice of adopting a severely contractionery monetary and fiscal policy, Malaysia enjoyed a recovery of investment in 1997. This was not strong enough to prevent the contagion or meltdown in share and currency prices; but GDP growth in Malaysia in 1997 was a fairly healthy 7 per cent compared to the growth of 0.6 per cent in Thailand, 5 per cent in Indonesia, 4.3 per cent in the Phillipines, and 6 per cent in Korea.

56 This, as we have emphasized repeatedly, is a necessary condition for speculative attack on a country's currency.

a few words on the nature of the shock are in order. We have already indicated why the slowdown in export growth in the ASEAN–4 and Korea cannot be attributed to their exchange rate policies[57] or to the 1994 devaluation of the yuan. During 1996, the growth rate of Chinese exports itself plummeted to 1.5 per cent, from 24.9 per cent in the earlier year. Japanese exports fared no better: in spite of a depreciating yen over 1996, exports from Japan recorded a negative growth of 6.6 per cent during the year, compared to an increase of 11.2 per cent attained in 1995. The fall in export earnings was thus a common feature of the East and South East Asian economies[58], and not confined to only Thailand or other members of the ASEAN–4.

With export growth of practically all emerging market economies recording a significant fall in 1996, it is reasonable to conclude that cyclical factors must have played some part in causing the slowdown. In the Asian tiger economies, one can discern other and more potent forces at work. During 1985–95, increase in exports from these economies far exceeded the growth, not only of aggregate world trade, but also of trade in items the countries had specialized in. This was possible only through a rising share of the international market that the Asian economies gained at the expense of their rivals. However, with the increase in market share, export growth rate of the East and South East Asian countries could not but decelerate at some stage[59] and fall in line with the rate of increase in world demand for their exportables.

Perhaps the most important reason for the Asian countries' trouble on the export front, lay in large scale investment in their exportables and development of global 'oversupply' of these goods. Rapid accumulation of capital in the ASEAN–4 and Korea was

57 Characterized by pegging of currencies to the US dollar, which had started appreciating against the yen since 1995.

58 In fact, almost all emerging market economies suffered a setback on their export front in 1996.

59 Such a decline can be prevented only if the countries continually branch out into newer items of exports at the expense of their existing suppliers in the world market. Note also that growth in export earnings from 'not-traditional' items should be high enough to counter the slowdown in export growth in traditional products, both because of the rising share of the countries and a shift of comparative advantage away from traditional exports with changes in factor prices.

driven by investors' confidence in the sustainability of growth in export demand the countries had enjoyed so far. Meanwhile, other emerging economies, including China, had also built up huge productive capacity in labour and low-skill intensive goods which formed the bulk of ASEAN exports. Substantial investment was also undertaken in computer products and automobiles in Thailand. These items, along with steel, ship building, and consumer electronics constitute the principal sources of Korean export earnings. The extent of global 'oversupply' in major exportables of the East and South East Asia was estimated to be at least 30 to 35 per cent in most cases.

The undue exuberance of investors in export industries, it is interesting to note, is an instance of co-ordination failure under the free play of market forces. With all investors acting on their own and expecting to cash in on the projected growth in export demand, a disproportionality crisis at the world level, *a la* Marx[60], was not an unnatural phenomenon. When investment on a large scale is concentrated in a small range of exportables, growth in domestic demand alone will be quite inadequate to permit full capacity utilization or avoid substantial losses to investors. Hence, viability of such investment requires a sharp rise in world demand for the goods countries export and their enhanced competitiveness in the world market. The major part of the rise in demand for ASEAN and Korean exports could come only from Japan[61] and other high income countries. However, at the best of times, the GDP growth of these countries was around 3 per cent, so that the increase in world demand for goods entering the East Asian export basket lagged behind their rising supply in the global market.[62]

DOWNTURN IN EXPORT DEMAND AND CURRENCY CRISIS

We have already indicated why, with their high degree of openness and rapid accumulation of investment in the export sector, the

60 Marx considered a closed economy while advancing his thesis. The thesis is echoed in the idea behind the theory of 'balanced growth', which suggests that large investment in one sector can be viable only if there is an increase in productive capacity elsewhere.

61 Japan was also a major competitor of Korea in the world market.

62 To sustain a demand growth of 15 per cent or more, the income elasticity would then have to be at least 5—a requirement too demanding to be fulfilled in the medium, let alone the long run.

Asian economies were especially vulnerable to an adverse shock on their foreign exchange earnings. The shock was immediately transmitted to domestic investment and aggregate demand, and to earnings of firms and banks. The problems facing the banks were aggravated in no small measure by the high debt–equity ratio producers maintained[63] on the expectation of sustained growth in their profits, uninterrupted by cyclical downturns or random shocks. Thus, it was overoptimism based on past trends that magnified the impact of the shocks and created conditions for speculative attacks on the countries' currencies.

However, as the Chinese experience suggests, a sharp slowdown in export growth or widespread losses of firms, coupled with a banking crisis, need not necessarily culminate in a currency crisis. It is instructive in this connection to isolate the factors that distinguished China from her troubled neighbours, in order to appreciate how an adverse demand shock originating in the export sector can be transmitted to markets for financial assets and foreign exchange, and cause a meltdown in currency and share prices.

By 1996, the export orientation of China had become high, but was still considerably less than that of other economies in the region. What is more significant, the economic (and institutional) structure of China prevented a sharp decline in domestic demand, even while exporters were faced with serious troubles. Note first that state-owned enterprises, which accounted for a fair share of total employment in China, are notorious for their inefficiency; but their maintenance of the payroll in the face of mounting losses helped considerably in softening the impact of the fall in demand from external sources.

Second, with the government still playing a substantial role in capital formation, in 1996 the fall in export demand was neutralized to some extent by a step up in domestic investment. Third, the size of the Chinese domestic absorption was huge, and its constituents were fairly close substitutes of goods entering the export basket. Under these conditions, it was not difficult for China to pursue policies for preventing a slide in domestic economic activity. With the dominance of private enterprises in their economies, the negative impact of the adverse external shock could not but have been larger in other countries in the region; nor were they in a position, given

---

63 With the concurrence of banks.

the importance of firms catering to the international market, to adopt effective steps to counter the recessionary tendencies.

In the context of the currency crisis, the most important difference between China and the five countries under scrutiny consisted in the nature of transactions on the capital account. Domestic economic agents in China could not invest in the international capital market. Short term external borrowing by firms and banks and foreign portfolio investment in the Chinese capital market were not permitted. The overwhelming part of the external inflow of funds in China was in the form of foreign direct investment. The result was that there was little scope for speculative attack on the yuan, or the emergence of a payments crisis at short notice. Even so, China had built up a foreign exchange reserve of more than US$120 billion, which was far in excess of the requirement for managing transactions on current account and for absorbing shocks on the external front.

Conditions in Korea and the ASEAN–4 were radically different. Korea[64] had already been forced to open up her capital account as a pre-condition for joining OECD. By 1992–3, Thailand and her neighbours had considerably relaxed controls on transactions on the capital account. There was substantial inflow of funds by way of foreign institutional investments—funds which could be withdrawn at a moment's notice if the exchange rate or share prices were expected to fall. Companies and banks availed of short term external loans in order to finance investment of a long term nature. What was no less imprudent, firms and banks taking external loans denominated in foreign currency did not care to hedge against exchange rate fluctuations.[65]

The factors noted above made the countries' balance of payments highly vulnerable and their currencies prone to speculative attack. Judged against such contingencies, the foreign exchange reserves of the countries were woefully inadequate.[66] In the case of Thailand,

64 And Mexico.

65 The reliance on short term loans and absence of forward cover for foreign borrowing were both cost-cutting devices which would have made perfect economic sense, had there been no possibility of (a) a downgrading of the country's and firms' credit rating; and (b) abandonment of the pegged exchange rate system. Clearly, in this respect also banks' and investors' exuberance, born out of past trends, was at work.

66 This in its turn made the currencies prime targets of speculative attack even when the countries' difficulties could be transient. For a

Korea, and Indonesia, the reserves, in fact, fell considerably short of external loans shortly to mature (and commitment of central banks concerning the forward sale of foreign currencies). Such information could not but make the domestic currency an easy prey of speculative predators, especially since the exchange rate had so far been propped up by large inflows of foreign funds.

CONCLUSION

A careful analysis of theoretical foundations and sifting of empirical evidence bring out serious inadequacies of the two major hypotheses advanced for explaining the Asian currency crisis, the first focussing on large current account deficits, along with pegged exchange rates, the second on the banking crisis arising out of moral hazard under explicit or implicit government guarantee of deposits. Our own explanation of the crisis centres round a combination of external shock and some important features of the ASEAN–4 and Korea that magnified the impact of the shock and caused a drastic revision in investors' expectations regarding the short and medium term outlook of these countries.

While the Krugman theory concerning the pivotal role of moral hazard does not appear correct, there is little doubt that investment decisions were driven by undue exuberance, based as they were on extrapolation of past trends into the future, especially in respect of export demand. Such high levels of export oriented investment in emerging economies in general, and the East and South East Asian economies in particular, reflected co-ordination failure, characteristic of the free market solution, and paved the way for deceleration of export growth in high performing economies in Asia. The deceleration would not have driven the countries into a currency crisis, had they not permitted large scale financing of long term investments with short term external loans without any forward cover, allowed substantial foreign funds to flow into their capital markets, and maintained foreign exchange reserves totally inadequate in relation to international 'hot money' held in the domestic financial system.

---

discussion of the basis of investors' expectations, herd behaviour and currency crises see Chapters 3 and 4.

The most important point to note in connection with the Asian experience is that, under capital account convertibility and free play of market forces, strong fundamentals do not necessarily make a country immune to currency crises. On the basis of their performance upto 1995[67] there can be little doubt regarding the inherent strength of the tiger economies in Asia, their overall efficiency in resource use, or their long term growth potential. The external liabilities of these economies, let us remember, were negligible in relation to both their productive capacity and average export earnings. The problem, however, is that a currency crisis aggravated through inept handling can drag the real sector down for a considerable period[68] and seriously undermine the long term fundamentals themselves.[69]

ANNEXE 5.1   SOME NOTES ON BANK INVESTMENT UNDER MORAL HAZARD[1]

In the text the analysis of banks' behaviour under moral hazard was conducted under the simplifying assumption that there were only two possible states of nature, 1 and 2, and that banks' choice lay between two investment options, *A* and *B*. It is fairly straightforward to generalize the results and draw conclusions regarding the choice of investment when the banking system is competitive.

BEHAVIOUR OF AN INDIVIDUAL BANKER

Let us retain the two key assumptions of the Krugman model relating to government guarantee of deposits and zero penalty of the bank's failure to discharge debt obligations. Assume that

(a) a bank can borrow any amount it likes at the deposit rate *d*;

67 Even in 1996, the GDP growth of the afflicted economies, ranging from 5.7 per cent (in the Philippines) to 8.6 per cent (in Malaysia), would have been considered highly commendable in any other part of the world.
68 See Chapters 3 and 4 for a discussion of currency crisis, policy responses, and operation of the real sector.
69 Prolonged and large scale unemployment, decimation of domestic financial infrastructure, precipitous fall in fixed capital formation, massive cutbacks in investment in human resource development—all erode the long term economic fundamentals of a country.

1 Readers not interested in technicalities may read only the concluding section of the annexe.

(b) there are k alternative investment projects, each costing Re 1 and n possible states of nature, with p_i denoting the probability of the occurrence of the ith state, and

(c) the banker himself undertakes the investment project.

Let R_{ji} refer to the gross return to the banker on project j when the ith state of nature occurs. After interest payment the net return to the banker is then $[R_{ji} - (1 + d)]$. Under moral hazard the net return on j to the banker, $r_m(j)$, shoud then be given by:

$$r_m(j) = \sum_{i=1}^{n} p_i (R_{ji} - (1+d)) \qquad (A5.1.1)$$

for all i's such that $R_{ji} - (1 + d) \geq 0$

Quite clearly, among the k projects the banker will choose the project f for which

$$r_m(f) \geq r_m(j), j = 1......k \qquad (A5.1.2)$$

PANGLOSSIAN CHOICE UNDER COMPETITIVE BANKING

Now, for the outcome under a competitive banking system. Consider first the situation where supply of investment goods (or assets) is perfectly elastic and the gross returns on them remain unaffected by the scale of aggregate investment. When $r_m(f)$ is positive, there will be a scramble for funds among banks, so that the deposit rate goes up until the net return r_m is reduced to zero.[2]

The interesting thing to note in this connection is that as the deposit rate goes up, some $(R_{fi}-(1+d))$'s of project f, which were previously positive, now become negative and hence, drop out in calculating $r_m(f)$. Thus, competition should raise $1+d$ to the point where it equals the largest among gross returns on alternative investment projects under all possible states of nature. In other words, the equilibrium deposit rate d^* equals the Pangloss return R_p-1:

$$d^* = Max(R_{ji}-1) \text{ for } j=1..k;i=1,...n. \qquad (A5.1.3)$$
$$= R_p-1$$

where R_p is the highest return under the best of all possible worlds.[3] The important point to note in this connection is that in the choice of projects and determination of the interest rate, among $k \times n$ possible outcomes only the best possible one matters, however low its probability might be.

2 Perfectly elastic supply of funds cannot thus go hand in hand with perfectly elastic supply of investible assets.

3 Note that the project chosen for a given d, such that $0 < d < d^*$ will generally be different from that chosen with $d = d^*$.

DISTORTED AND UNDISTORTED CHOICE OF INVESTMENT: A SUMMARY

The way moral hazard distorts investment and interest rates can be summarized in following terms. Table A5.1.1 gives the matrix of gross returns on k investment projects corresponding to n states of nature. Under competitive conditions with no moral hazard, that investment project will be chosen which yields the largest expected return and the equilibrium interest rate r^* will be given by

$$r^*=Max[E(1),E(2),...E(k)]-1 \qquad (A5.1.4)$$

Under moral hazard the choice will fall on the project with the highest Pangloss return and the corresponding interest rate d^* will be

$$d^*=Max[R_p(1),R_p(2),...R_p(k)]-1=R_p-1 \qquad (A5.1.5)$$

Table A5.1.1
MATRIX OF GROSS RETURNS

Investment projects	States of nature 1	2	...n	Expected return	Pangloss return
1	R_{11}	R_{12} ...	R_{1n}	$E(1) = \sum_{i=1}^{n} p_i R_{1i}$	$R_p(1) = Max(R_{21}, R_{22}, ...R_{1n})$
2	R_{21}	R_{22} ...	R_{2n}	$E(2) = \sum_{i=1}^{n} p_i R_{2i}$	$R_p(1) = Max(R_{21}, R_{22}, ...R_{2n})$
–	–	–	–	– – –	– – – –
–	–	–	–	– – –	– – – –
–	–	–	–	– – –	– – – –
k	R_{k1}	R_{k2} ...	R_{kn}	$E(k) = \sum_{i=1}^{n} p_{ki} R_{ki}$	$R_p(k) = Max(R_{k1}, R_{k2}, ...R_{kn})$

EXCHANGE RATES AND EXTERNAL BORROWING

One of the interesting aspects of the moral hazard problem having an important bearing on the Asian crisis is the banks' tendency not to hedge against exchange rate movements when they take foreign currency loans. In the model considered above, among the events constituting a state of nature one will be the exchange rate prevailing in Period 1. In terms of the earlier analysis it is clear that with government guarantee of deposits and no penalty for imprudent decisions, the risk of exchange rate movements will be borne (!) by the banker[4], i.e., he will not take any forward cover. The best of all possible states of nature producing the Pangloss outcome will be characterized by the exchange rate which along with other elements of the state yields the largest value among the $k \times n$ possible R_{ji}'s.

INELASTIC SUPPLY OF ASSETS

Consider now the other extreme case where bankers can get any amount of fund at a fixed interest rate, but the supply of investible assets is perfectly inelastic. In this case competition among banks will determine the asset price rather than the deposit rate. If the price of acquiring one unit of the asset j is P_j, the net return to an individual banker of investing in j is given by

$$r_m(j) = \frac{1}{P_j} \times \sum_{i=1}^{n} p_i [R_{ji} - P_j(1+d)] \qquad (A5.1.6)$$

for all i's such that $R_{ji} \geq P_j (1+d)$.

The banker will choose the asset with the highest r_m. However, so long as r_m is positive, competition among bankers will raise the price of the asset until the net return is driven down to zero. Since increases in P_j's pushes more $[R_{ji} - P_j(1+d)]$'s below zero, the equilibrium will once again be Panglossian with the asset chosen and its market price, Vp, given by

$$Vp = \frac{Max(R_{ji} - 1)}{1+d} \qquad j = 1,....k; i = 1,.....n \qquad (A5.1.7)$$

CONCLUSION

The following results under moral hazard driven investment decisions are fairly obvious.

• Under competition among banks the choice of investment projects depends entirely on the highest possible outcome under the best of all possible states of nature, irrespective of the numerical value of its probability.[5]

• The type of investment chosen is the same whether market forces drive (a) deposit rates with perfectly elastic supply of assets to banks; or (b) prices of assets the supply of which is perfectly inelastic.

---

4 Assuming that the government guarantee is for all deposits. Otherwise foreign lenders' decision will be influenced by the risk of possible changes in the exchange rate.
5 So long as it is not zero.

• When the country can borrow at a fixed rate of interest from the rest of the world, there is no incentive for banks to hedge against exchange rate movements. In this case the interest rate on domestic deposit d^* equals the interest rate on foreign deposit d_f minus the rate of appreciation of the currency under the Panglossian state of nature:

$$d^* = [(d_f.e_p)/e] - (e - e_p)/e \qquad (A5.1.8)$$

Where d_f is the (fixed) interest rate on foreign loans, e the current exchange rate (domestic currency per unit of foreign currency) and e_p the possible exchange rate in Period 1 under the state of nature yielding the Pangloss solution.[6] In other words, under moral hazard the cost of foreign borrowing relevant for bankers may well be less than the interest rate prevailing in the international capital market.

• In general, for all bankers taken together the supply of (even) reproducible assets (like capital goods) may not be perfectly elastic. Again, larger aggregate investment in their chosen field should also cause bankers to revise R_{ji}'s downward. Both these factors limit the scale of borrowing by banks, even when moral hazard problems loom large and the supply of external finance is perfectly elastic.

• Purchase of assets at their Pangloss value by financial intermediaries cannot be sustained over time since the cost of successive bailouts by the government becomes prohibitive when a major part of aggregate investment is routed through financial intermediaries.

6 Since under this state e_p can be significantly smaller than e, we have not used approximation in A5.1.8.

ANNEXE 5.2   MACROECONOMIC PROFILES OF EAST ASIAN ECONOMIES

Table A5.2.1a

AVERAGE ANNUAL GROWTH IN SOME ECONOMIC PARAMETERS FOR THAILAND

(%)

	1989	1990	1991	1992	1993	1994	1995	1996	1997	1998
GDP at constant prices	12.2	11.6	8.4	7.9	8.2	8.9	8.7	5.5	-1.3	-9.4
Pvt consumption expenditure	9.8	12.3	6.6	6.9	7.9	8.9	8.5	6.2	-6.6	-9.5
Govt consumption expenditure	6.4	10.7	6.3	15.3	9.0	6.1	10.5	6.9	-0.6	-3.2
Gross domestic investment	20.8	30.7	13.4	0.6	8.5	10.5	13.5	3.1	-16.9	-41.2
Fixed capital formation			11.9	2.0	9.1	10.3	13.9	4.2	-24.1	-28.5
M2		26.7	19.8	15.6	18.4	12.9	17.0	12.6	16.4	9.6
Domestic credit		26.8	15.5	18.0	22.7	28.9	23.1	14.0	17.1	-1.4
Merchandise imports ($)	27.1	28.0	13.9	8.3	13.3	18.5	31.6	-8.1	-7.3	-7.4
Merchandise exports ($)	25.7	15.0	23.8	13.7	13.4	22.2	24.7	4.1	4.5	7.2
GDP deflator	6.1	5.7	6.1	4.1	3.4	4.6	4.6	6.0	0.1	9.6
Consumer prices	5.4	5.9	5.7	4.1	3.4	5.1	5.8	5.9	5.6	8.1

Source: ADB, *Asian Development Outlook*, 1997, 1999 and 1999 (update); IMF, *International Financial Statistics*, 1996, 1999; IMF, *World Economic Outlook*, December 1997.

Table A5.2.1b
KEY MACROECONOMIC RATIOS OF THAILAND

(% of GDP)

	1989	1990	1991	1992	1993	1994	1995	1996	1997	1998
Gross domestic investment		40.9	42.9	39.9	39.9	40.5	42.3	41.7	35.0	24.4
Gross national saving		32.6	35.2	34.3	34.9	34.9	34.3	33.7	32.9	35.9
Current account balance		-8.3	-7.7	-5.6	-5.0	-5.6	-8.0	-7.9	-2.0	12.8
Fixed capital formation		40.2	41.6	39.2	39.4	39.9	41.8	40.8	31.3	26.5
Foreign liabilities of banks		6.4	6.0	6.9	11.7	20.3	24.3	26.6	46.5	31.9
External debt service		3.8	4.0	4.3	4.4	4.8	5.0	4.7	7.3	
Exports + services	35.0	34.1	36.0	36.5	37.4	39.1	42.5	38.6	47.1	
Imports	35.7	38.5	38.1	36.5	36.8	38.0	43.9	39.0	40.9	38.4
Trade balance	-0.7	-4.4	-2.1	0.0	0.7	1.1	-1.4	-5.1	1.0	14.5
Net fiscal balance	3.0	4.5	4.7	2.8	2.1	1.9	2.9	2.4	-0.9	-2.5
Revenue surplus	17.1	18.5	19.1	17.9	17.9	18.5	18.7			
Official reserves/imports (in months)	4.4	4.5	5.0	5.2	5.5	5.5	5.3	6.2	4.9	7.9

Source: ADB, *Asian Development Outlook*, 1997, 1999 and 1999 (update); IMF, *International Financial Statistics*, 1996, 1999; IMF, *World Economic Outlook*, December 1997.

Table A5.2.2a

AVERAGE ANNUAL GROWTH IN SOME ECONOMIC PARAMETERS FOR INDONESIA

(%)

	1989	1990	1991	1992	1993	1994	1995	1996	1997	1998
GDP at constant prices	7.5	9.0	8.9	7.2	7.3	7.5	8.2	7.8	4.9	-13.2
Pvt consumption expenditure	0.0	9.8	8.2	1.2	19.2	6.5	16.9	9.9	9.7	11.2
Govt consumption expenditure	12.3	2.7	8.8	10.8	1.0	-2.6	11.4	4.9	-0.1	-28.1
Gross domestic investment	19.8	10.2	13.9	-1.5	19.7	1.0	13.1	6.2	11.2	-49.5
Fixed capital formation			3.9	2.4	9.4	12.8	11.3	6.9	-1.0	
M2		44.6	17.5	19.8	20.2	20.0	27.2	26.7	52.7	62.3
Domestic credit		58.3	18.9	14.1	21.0	22.9	21.7	22.7	25.7	53.7
Merchandise imports ($)		31.5	15.7	7.8	6.0	13.9	23.0	10.4	-6.8	-28.2
Merchandise exports ($)		16.7	10.5	14.0	8.3	9.9	13.1	9.0	7.9	-14.0
GDP deflator	9.6	9.1	8.7	7.4	19.1	7.1	10.1	8.5	12.0	83.3
Consumer prices	6.4	7.8	9.4	7.6	9.6	8.5	9.4	7.9	6.6	64.7

Source: ADB, Asian Development Outlook, 1997, 1999 and 1999 (update); IMF, International Financial Statistics, 1996, 1999; IMF, World Economic Outlook, December 1997.

Table A5.2.2b

KEY MACROECONOMIC RATIOS OF INDONESIA

(% of GDP)

	1989	1990	1991	1992	1993	1994	1995	1996	1997	1998
Gross domestic investment		30.7	32.1	29.5	32.9	30.9	32.3	30.7	31.3	18
Gross national saving		27.9	28.7	27.3	31.4	29.2	29	27.3	29.9	19.1
Current account balance		-2.8	-3.4	-2.2	-1.5	-1.7	-3.3	-3.4	-1.4	4.5
Fixed capital formation		28.3	27.0	25.8	26.3	27.6	28.4	30.7	31.3	18.5
Foreign liabilities of banks		11.0	8.6	10.3	10.9	10.9	9.6	5.6	13.8	20.0
External debt service		8.3	8.4	8.7	8.4	8.0	8.5	9.0	11.6	20.0
Exports + services	26.3	27.6	27.8	29.0	25.8	22.9	26.2	25.0	29.4	55.5
Imports	17.3	20.6	22.2	21.3	17.9	18.4	20.1	18.9	19.4	27.7
Trade balance	9.0	7.0	5.6	7.7	7.8	4.5	1.4	1.1	1.6	1.9
Net fiscal balance	-2.1	0.4	0.5	-0.6	0.4	0.5	0.6	0.2	0.0	-4.7
Revenue surplus	-2.0	0.4	0.4	-0.4	0.6					
Official reserves/imports (in months)	4.0	4.1	5.7	6.6	7.5	6.2	5.05.5	5	4.6	9.8

Source: ADB, Asian Development Outlook, 1997, 1999 and 1999 (update); IMF, International Financial Statistics,1996, 1999; IMF, World Economic Outlook, December 1997.

TABLE A5.2.3a
AVERAGE ANNUAL GROWTH IN SOME ECONOMIC PARAMETERS FOR MALAYSIA

(%)

	1989	1990	1991	1992	1993	1994	1995	1996	1997	1998
GDP at constant prices	12.5	9.6	8.6	7.8	8.3	9.2	9.5	8.6	7.8	-7.5
Pvt consumption expenditure		13.5	11.1	3.7	7.2	6.6	11.1	5.8	5.4	
Govt consumption expenditure	9.9	6.6	10.4	-0.4	9.9	5.9	3.0	-0.1	4.6	
Gross domestic investment	20.1	20.4	29.5	1.7	16.7	17.0	17.6	3.9	8.9	-22.4
Fixed capital formation			22.0	6.6	15.3	14.3	17.4	6.6	8.3	
M2		10.6	16.9	29.2	26.6	12.7	20.0	20.9	18.5	4.7
Domestic credit		18.0	18.5	16.6	12.3	14.8	29.5	31.2	29.3	-2.7
Merchandise imports ($)		28.2	26.8	10.1	17.8	28.1	29.4	1.7	7.0	-26.8
Merchandise exports ($)		16.3	17.0	18.1	16.1	23.1	25.9	7.3	6.0	-7.8
GDP deflator	3.4	2.9	2.9	5.3	1.8	5.1	4.9	5.1	2.5	
Consumer prices	2.7	2.7	4.4	4.7	3.6	3.7	3.4	3.5	4.0	5.2

Source: ADB, *Asian Development Outlook*, 1997, 1999 and 1999 (update); IMF, *International Financial Statistics*, 1996, 1999; IMF, *World Economic Outlook*, December 1997.

Table A5.2.3b
KEY MACROECONOMIC RATIOS OF MALAYSIA

(% of GDP)

	1989	1990	1991	1992	1993	1994	1995	1996	1997	1998
Gross domestic investment		31.2	37.2	35.1	37.8	40.5	43.5	41.6	42.0	33.2
Gross national saving		29.1	28.4	31.3	33.0	32.7	33.5	42.6	43.8	48.0
Current account balance		-2.1	-8.8	-3.8	-4.8	-7.8	-10.0	-5.0	-5.3	-1.8
Fixed capital formation		32.4	36.4	36.0	38.3	40.1	43.0	41.6	42.5	
Foreign liabilities of banks		7.3	9.0	13.0	19.5	8.8	6.5	11.4	17.4	12.2
External debt service		6.9	5.9	5.6	6.1	5.2	6.6	5.4	5.9	
Exports + services	73.0	76.3	80.8	77.2	81.2	89.8	97.7	92.2	94.9	
Imports	59.3	68.3	77.8	68.6	72.0	84.1	91.0	79.1	80.7	80.5
Trade balance	13.7	8.0	3.0	8.6	9.2	5.7	6.6	3.9	4.0	
Net fiscal balance	-5.1	-4.8	-4.4	-4.2	-5.3	2.4	0.9	0.7	1.8	-3.4
Revenue surplus	-5.4	-5.8	-4.4	-4.4	-5.2	2.4				
Official reserves/imports (in months)	4.2	3.7	3.3	4.7	6.2	4.5	3.3	4.0	6.0	5.1

Source: ADB, *Asian Development Outlook*, 1997, 1999 and 1999 (update); IMF, *International Financial Statistics*, 1996, 1999; IMF, *World Economic Outlook*, December 1997.

Table A5.2.4a

AVERAGE ANNUAL GROWTH IN SOME ECONOMIC PARAMETERS FOR PHILIPPINES

(%)

	1989	1990	1991	1992	1993	1994	1995	1996	1997	1998
GDP at constant prices		3.0	-0.6	0.3	2.1	4.4	4.8	5.8	5.2	-0.5
Pvt consumption expenditure	6.6	4.5	2.6	3.0	3.1	1.9	4.5	3.7	4.2	2.5
Govt consumption expenditure	12.0	9.1	-2.2	-2.4	7.0	11.4	10.6	9.7	14.7	2.6
Gross domestic investment		15.1	-18.6	4.3	15.9	4.6	-3.0	16.2	14.3	-20.2
Fixed capital formation			-17.2	4.9	16.3	3.5	-1.4	10.5	16.0	-14.4
M2		22.5	17.3	13.6	27.1	24.4	24.4	15.8	20.5	7.1
Domestic credit		30.7	-2.6	17.6	131.2	19.0	31.3	40.3	30.2	
Merchandise imports ($)	28.0	17.0	-1.7	20.1	21.2	21.2	23.7	20.8	14.0	-18.4
Merchandise exports ($)	10.6	4.7	8.0	11.1	15.8	18.5	29.4	17.7	22.8	16.9
GDP deflator	9.0	13.0	16.5	7.9	6.8	10.0	7.3	7.7	6.1	10.4
Consumer prices	12.2	14.2	18.7	8.9	7.6	9.0	8.1	9.1	6.0	9.7

Table A5.2.4b
KEY MACROECONOMIC RATIOS OF PHILIPPINES

(% of GDP)

	1989	1990	1991	1992	1993	1994	1995	1996	1997	1998
Gross domestic investment	21.6	24.8	20.3	21.1	24.0	24.0	22.2	23.1	23.8	19.3
Gross national saving	18.2	18.7	18.0	19.5	18.4	19.4	17.8	18.5	20.3	20.0
Current account balance	-3.4	-6.1	-2.3	-1.6	-5.6	-4.6	-4.4	-4.7	-5.3	2.0
Fixed capital formation		24.0	20.0	20.9	23.8	23.6	22.2	24.0	24.8	20.2
Foreign liabilities of banks		14.9	11.5	12.9	10.9	12.3	13.9	20.9	31.1	26.6
External debt service		8.1	9.0	7.2	7.8	7.2	6.5	5.1	5.7	6.8
Exports + services	26.0	25.8	27.5	27.5	29.5	31.6	36.2	40.4	49.1	56.8
Imports	26.3	29.5	28.3	29.1	34.7	35.2	38.3	41.2	46.5	47.2
Trade balance	-0.3	-3.7	-0.8	-1.6	-5.2	-3.6	-2.2	-13.7	-13.5	0.0
Net fiscal balance	-2.1	-3.5	-2.1	-1.2	-1.5	1.1	0.5	0.3	0.1	-1.9
Revenue surplus	-1.7	-3.1	-1.8	-1.9	-0.9	1.5	0.9	0.3		
Official reserves/imports (in months)	1.5	0.9	2.8	3.1	2.7	2.8	2.3	3.5	2.2	3.6

Source: ADB, Asian Development Outlook, 1997, 1999 and 1999 (update); IMF, International Financial Statistics, 1996, 1999; IMF, World Economic Outlook, December 1997.

Table A5.2.5a

AVERAGE ANNUAL GROWTH IN SOME ECONOMIC PARAMETERS FOR SOUTH KOREA

(%)

	1989	1990	1991	1992	1993	1994	1995	1996	1997	1998
GDP at constant prices	6.4	9.5	9.1	5.1	5.8	8.6	8.9	7.1	5.5	-5.8
Pvt consumption expenditure	11.0	10.4	8.4	6.3	5.5	8.4	7.3	7.9	4.5	-8.7
Govt consumption expenditure	14.3	8.6	10.7	11.0	4.8	7.0	6.5	10.1	7.6	-2.9
Gross domestic investment			14.7	-1.1	1.5	10.8	12.9	10.3	-5.8	-17.7
Fixed capital formation			13.0	0.1	4.1	7.7	11.6	7.7	-1.9	-16.4
M2		17.2	21.9	14.9	16.6	18.7	15.6	15.8	14.1	27.9
Domestic credit		24.8	22.4	11.7	12.7	18.4	14.7	19.4	23.2	11.6
Merchandise imports ($)		14.6	17.6	1.0	2.3	22.4	32.1	12.3	-2.2	-36.1
Merchandise exports ($)		2.8	10.2	8.0	7.7	15.7	31.5	4.3	6.7	-4.9
GDP deflator	5.3	9.9	10.1	6.1	5.1	5.5	5.4	3.7	2.8	13.4
Consumer prices	5.7	8.6	9.3	6.2	4.8	6.2	4.5	5.0	4.5	7.5

Source: ADB, Asian Development Outlook, 1997, 1999 and 1999 (update); IMF, International Financial Statistics, 1996, 1999; IMF, World Economic Outlook, December 1997.

Table A5.2.5b
KEY MACROECONOMIC RATIOS OF SOUTH KOREA

(% of GDP)

	1989	1990	1991	1992	1993	1994	1995	1996	1997	1998
Gross domestic investment		37.0	38.9	36.6	35.1	35.8	37.1	38.4	35.0	29.0
Gross national saving		36.1	35.9	35.1	35.2	34.6	35.1	33.7	33.1	42.3
Current account balance		-0.9	-3.0	-1.5	0.1	-1.2	-2.0	-4.7	-1.8	12.5
Fixed capital formation		37.1	38.4	36.6	36.0	35.7	36.6	38.4	35.0	20.9
Foreign liabilities of banks		6.5	7.7	7.6	6.9	8.0	10.1	12.8	15.8	17.4
External debt service	32.3	29.3	27.8	28.6	29.0	29.8	32.8			
Exports + services	27.7	27.5	27.7	26.6	25.2	26.9	29.7	31.7	37.3	
Imports	27.7	27.5	27.7	26.6	25.2	26.9	29.6	31.0	32.7	29.1
Trade balance	1.5	0.2	-0.7	-1.6	-0.5	0.6	0.3	-3.1	-0.7	
Net fiscal balance	2.6	1.5	1.7	0.6	0.6	0.3	0.6	0.5	-1.4	-5.0
Revenue surplus	3.0	2.3	1.8	2.2	2.5	2.6	2.5	2.3		
Official reserves/imports (in months)	3.0	2.5	2.0	2.5	2.9	3.0	2.9	2.6	1.6	6.7

Source: ADB, *Asian Development Outlook, 1997, 1999* and *1999* (update); IMF, *International Financial Statistics,* 1996, 1999; IMF, *World Economic Outlook,* December 1997.

Table A5.2.6a

AVERAGE ANNUAL GROWTH IN SOME ECONOMIC PARAMETERS FOR JAPAN

(%)

	1989	1990	1991	1992	1993	1994	1995	1996	1997	1998
GDP at constant prices	4.7	5.1	3.8	1.0	0.3	0.6	1.5	5.0	1.4	-2.8
Pvt consumption expenditure	4.3	4.4	2.5	2.1	1.2	1.9	2.1	2.9	1.1	-0.4
Govt consumption expenditure	4.2	4.6	4.0	3.6	0.4	2.6	3.8	1.9	-0.6	1.3
Gross domestic investment	8.6	8.1	4.3	-3.3	-3.4	-3.1	1.3	9.0	-3.4	
Fixed capital formation	10.5	11.4	2.8	-1.9	-3.0	-2.5	1.1	8.3	-3.4	-1.4
M2		8.2	2.5	-0.1	2.2	2.8	3.3	2.9	4.0	4.0
Domestic credit		9.2	2.9	2.9	0.8	-0.4	1.8	1.4	1.3	0.7
Merchandise imports ($)	12.1	11.3	1.3	-1.5	3.5	13.8	22.2	4.2	-3.0	-17.2
Merchandise exports ($)	3.8	4.0	9.9	7.9	6.0	9.4	11.2	-6.6	2.4	-7.8
GDP deflator	1.9	2.2	2.7	1.7	0.6	0.2	-0.6	-0.5	0.6	0.4
Consumer prices	2.2	3.1	3.3	1.7	1.2	0.7	-0.1	0.1	1.7	0.4

Source: ADB, Asian Development Outlook, 1997, 1999 and 1999 (update); IMF, International Financial Statistics, 1996, 1999; IMF, World Economic Outlook, December 1997.

Table A5.2.6b
KEY MACROECONOMIC RATIOS OF JAPAN

(% of GDP)

	1989	1990	1991	1992	1993	1994	1995	1996	1997	1998
Gross domestic investment	31.8	32.0	32.2	30.8	29.7	28.6	28.5	29.9	28.5	27.9
Gross national saving	33.8	33.5	34.2	33.8	32.8	31.4	30.7	31.3	30.8	30.8
Current account balance	2.0	1.5	2.0	3.0	3.1	2.8	2.2	1.4	2.2	3.4
Fixed capital formation	31.0	31.7	31.4	30.5	29.5	28.6	28.5	29.7	28.4	
Foreign liabilities of banks		19.4	15.3	12.4	11.0	9.7	10.0	10.6		
Exports + services	10.8	11.0	10.5	10.4	9.7	9.7	9.6	10.2	11.4	11.5
Imports	7.3	8.0	7.1	6.4	5.8	6.0	6.5	7.6	8.1	7.4
Trade balance	3.5	3.1	3.5	4.1	3.9	3.7	2.6	1.8	2.4	3.2
Net fiscal balance	-2.9	2.9	2.9	1.5	-1.6	-2.3	-3.6	-4.2	-3.1	-5.7
Revenue surplus	-2.8	-1.3	1.5	-0.3	-2.7					
Official reserves/imports (in months)	4.8	3.2	2.9	2.9	3.8	4.3	5.2	5.8	7.4	8.7

Source: ADB, *Asian Development Outlook,* 1997, 1999 and 1999 (update); IMF, *International Financial Statistics,* 1996, 1999; IMF, *World Economic Outlook,* December 1997.

Table A5.2.7a

AVERAGE ANNUAL GROWTH IN SOME ECONOMIC PARAMETERS FOR CHINA

(%)

	1989	1990	1991	1992	1993	1994	1995	1996	1997	1998
GDP at constant prices	4.3	3.8	9.2	14.2	13.5	12.6	10.5	9.7	8.8	7.8
Gross domestic investment			9.5	18.8	35.8	7.1	9.4	12.8	-0.8	
Fixed capital formation			17.8	29.6	36.4	8.1	6.5	12.4	9.4	
M2		28.9	26.7	30.8	42.8	35.1	29.5	25.3	17.3	15.3
Domestic credit		23.6	20.0	22.3	42.1	23.8	22.8	25.5	19.7	20.0
Merchandise imports ($)	5.3	-13.3	18.5	28.3	34.1	10.4	15.5	19.5	3.8	-1.5
Merchandise exports ($)	5.3	19.2	14.4	18.1	8.8	35.6	24.9	17.9	21.0	0.5
GDP deflator	8.9	5.6	6.7	7.9	14.6	19.5	13.0	6.6	0.8	
Consumer prices	16.3	1.3	3.0	5.3	13.0	21.7	14.8	8.3	2.8	-0.8

Source: ADB, *Asian Development Outlook*, 1997, 1999 and 1999 (update); IMF, *International Financial Statistics*, 1996, 1999; IMF, *World Economic Outlook*, December 1997.

Table A5.2.7b
KEY MACROECONOMIC RATIOS OF CHINA

(% of GDP)

	1989	1990	1991	1992	1993	1994	1995	1996	1997	1998
Gross domestic investment		34.7	34.8	36.2	43.3	41.2	40.8	39.6	38.2	39.0
Gross national saving		38.1	38.3	37.7	40.6	42.6	41.0	40.5	41.5	41.5
Current account balance		3.4	3.5	1.5	-2.7	1.4	0.2	0.9	3.2	3.1
Fixed capital formation		25.5	27.5	31.2	37.5	36.0	34.7	38.7	37.5	
Foreign liabilities of banks		3.5	4.6	4.0	5.4	7.1	6.4	5.6	6.7	
External debt service		1.7	1.7	2.3	2.5	2.4	2.2	2.0	1.9	
Exports + services	12.7	17.5	19.4	19.5	17	25.4	24.1	20.6	22.6	
Imports	13.2	13.8	15.7	16.7	17.2	21.4	18.5	16.7	15.5	
Trade balance	-0.5	3.8	3.7	2.8	-0.2	4.0	5.6	2.3	5.0	
Net fiscal balance	-0.5	-0.8	-0.9	-0.9	-0.6	-1.2	-1.1	-0.8	-0.7	-1.2
Revenue surplus	-0.5	-0.8	-0.9	-0.9	-0.6	-1.2	-1.1			
Official reserves/imports (in months)	3.6	7.6	9.7	3.4	2.7	5.7	6.7	9.1	11.8	12.4

Source: ADB, *Asian Development Outlook*, 1997, 1999 and 1999 (update); IMF, *International Financial Statistics*, 1996, 1999; IMF, *World Economic Outlook*, December 1997.

6

Crisis and Recovery: 1997–9
East Asia Revisited

INTRODUCTION

There seems to be no end to the way East Asia can baffle economists and remain at the centre of their attention. Belying the highly influential and widely accepted thesis of 'financial repression'[1], countries in this region recorded phenomenal economic growth and uplifted themselves from rags to riches in less than a generation. Until 1997, economists were unanimous with regard to the superiority of the East Asian model of development[2], characterized by, among other things, rapid capital accumulation backed by exceptionally high domestic savings, state guided allocation of finance, and close co-operation between the government and the private sector. Little wonder then, that the travails of Thailand in 1997 were, for quite

This is a truncated and revised version of the paper published in *Money & Finance*, January–March 2000.

1 Advanced by McKinnon (1973) and Shaw (1973). The thesis highlights the deleterious impact on growth of the system of state directed credit at interest rates below market clearing levels. The effect is supposed to operate through (a) a fall in the domestic saving ratio (at artificially low interest rates offered to depositors); and (b) inefficient allocation of investible resources. In East Asia 'financial repression' went hand in hand with high saving and high return on capital. It should, however, be noted that though interest rates were set below market clearing levels in East Asian economies, real rates were higher than those in other LDCs where the directed credit system was in force.

2 The ultimate accolade came from the World Bank (1993).

a while, viewed as no more than a little local difficulty, and practically all commentators expected the financial turmoil to blow over fairly soon without doing any serious damage to Thailand and her neighbours.[3] However, with the deepening and widening of the crisis across the region, there was a sea change in the climate of opinion concerning the economic strength of these nations.[4] Characteristics hitherto regarded as sources of strength were now identified as factors responsible for the region's economic woes: the relation between the government and the private sector came to be viewed as crony capitalism; directed credit as the mainspring of inefficiency; and large savings as an important reason for exceptionally high debt–equity ratio[5] in the corporate sector.

The complete reversal of the climate of opinion regarding merits of the 'Asian model' of development and economic prospects of the region was reflected in: (a) significant structural reforms forming an integral part of the IMF rescue packages[6]; (b) sharp downward revision of the projected growth of the East Asian economies; and (c) downgrading of these economies by several notches by Moody's, Standard and Poor's and other international credit rating agencies.

3 See our quotations from the ADB, IMF and World Bank in Chapter 4. It is also interesting to note that all international agencies, like Moody's, maintained high ratings for East Asian sovereign debts, even up to October 1997. Only in the last quarter of 1997 was there a sharp downgrading of these debts.

4 To be sure, even before the Asian economies started experiencing financial turmoil, there were some contrarians like Young(1994, 1995) and Krugman (1994). In popular circles, the Asian crisis was widely viewed as a vindication of the Young–Krugman thesis that there was nothing miraculous about the 'Asian miracle' and that the growth rates of these economies, driven almost entirely by employment of labour and capital, were bound to come down significantly over time. This belief in the extraordinary prescience of Krugman was quite widespread, despite his disclaimer that his 1994 thesis related to the long term behaviour of these economies and had nothing to do with the emergence of the currency crisis in 1997.

5 Universally considered to be one of the most important sources of financial turbulence.

6 It was widely held that recovery of the crisis economies would be difficult, if not impossible, in the absence of restructuring of the financial, corporate and other sectors, along with establishment of arms-length relationship between the authorities and enterprises.

Even as late as December 1998, the IMF envisaged a dismal economic scenario of the Asian–5[7] during 1999, and expected a modest recovery in their GDP growth only from the new millennium. However, the turn of events over the last one year and a half has proved all the pundits and analysts completely wrong in their prognosis of the economic health of the region. Throughout 1999, both the IMF and non-official agencies were busy making upward revisions in their forecasts concerning economic performance of the Asian–5.

Indeed, by the third quarter of the year, few could doubt that East Asia had staged a most remarkable recovery within an unexpectedly short period and was likely to attain its earlier growth trajectory, from which it had slipped so badly in 1998.

The unforeseen fall and fairly rapid recovery of Asia has produced voluminous literature dealing with a whole host of diagnostic and policy-related issues. The most important of these issues may be grouped under three broad (but interrelated) posers:

• What produced the crisis and its rapid contagion in countries which had been characterized by high growth, relatively equitable distribution of income, exceptionally large domestic saving, low inflation, noteworthy fiscal prudence, and progressive increase in trade–GDP ratios—features which made them poles apart from their crisis prone Latin American counterparts?
• What accounts for the rapid recovery of Asia?
• What lessons can we learn from the East Asian experience?

We propose to deal with the last question in the final part of the study. In the earlier chapters we have already recorded our views on the roots of the Asian crisis and factors promoting its rapid contagion. On the present occasion, we focus on other issues, though recapitulation of some of our earlier results will be useful in providing a backdrop to our discussion of the process of recovery of the Asian–5 and policy problems, including the role of the IMF and cross-border capital flows. The second section of paper provides an overview of different phases of the East Asian financial upheaval over the reference period. The next section examines the incidence of the crisis and indicates the leads and lags in movements of real and financial variables. The fourth section of paper is devoted to an

7 Consisting of Korea, Thailand, Malaysia, Indonesia, and the Philippines.

economic analysis of the interaction between domestic and international factors behind the crisis and its major turning points. The final section summarizes our main findings.

PHASES OF THE ASIAN CRISIS

The first to sink in the Asian financial turmoil was Thailand, when she gave up defending the baht against speculative attack and let the currency float on 2 July 1997. Soon other East Asian economies were infected by the Thai virus, and at one stage it appeared that the contagion would spread to the financial systems, not only of emerging market economies elsewhere, but even of advanced industrialized nations. The trouble turned out to be quite transitory in other parts of the world; but East Asia was not so fortunate. By far the hardest hit were the Asian–5, who had to endure severe meltdown in their financial markets and suffer from a sharp decline in output, employment and standard of living. Hence our focus will be on the experience of these five economies, though we have to take into account their interaction with others for an adequate appreciation of the course of the currency crisis.

Tables A6.1.1–A6.1.5 in Annexe 6.1, along with Figures 6.1, 6.2 and 6.3 give the time paths of the major financial and real variables of the five most severely crisis-ridden Asian economies during 1997–9.[8] On the basis of the behaviour of financial markets in these economies, we may distinguish five phases of the East Asian currency crisis:

• Phase 1: currency turmoil in Thailand between mid-June and early August 1997;
• Phase 2: contagion and deepening of the crisis, from mid–August to the third week of December 1997;
• Phase 3: temporary turnaround, from January to late March 1998;
• Phase 4: renewal of pressure and slide-back during April–September 1998; and
• Phase 5: bottoming out and recovery, from late September 1998.

8 The charts for the financial variables and our analysis of their behaviour are based on weekly, not monthly data. Space limitations have prevented us from giving tables for weekly data.

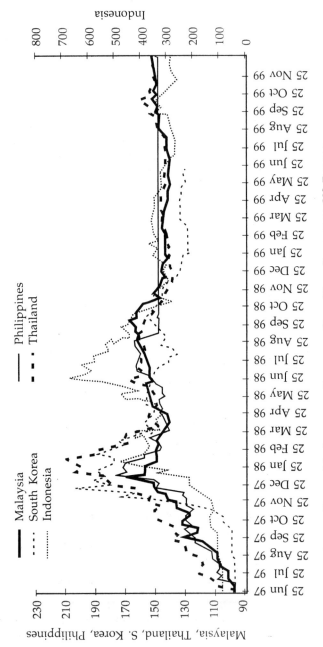

Figure 6.1: Indices of Exchange Rate With Respect to US Dollar (Base: 25 June 1997).

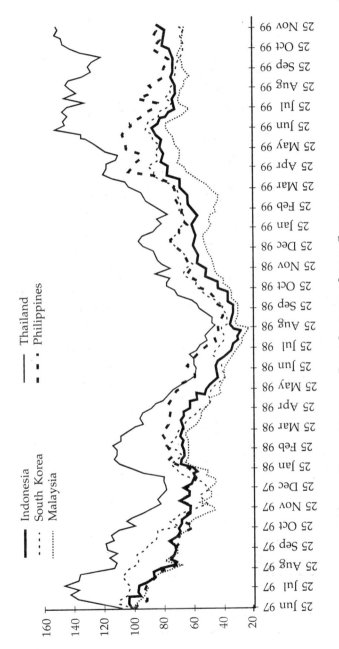

Figure 6.2: Stock Price Indices in Local Currency (Base: 25 June 1997).

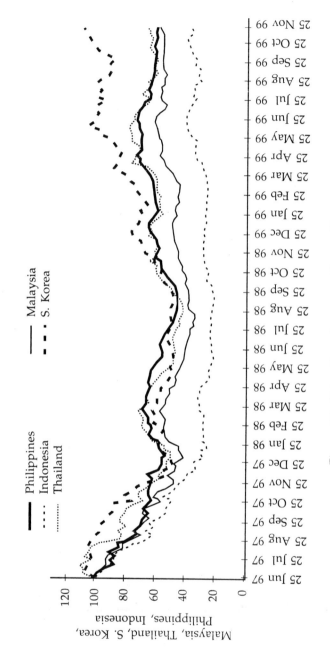

Figure 6.3: Stock Price Indices in Dollar Terms (Base: 25 June 1997).

PHASE 1: CRISIS IN THAILAND

As we have already discussed earlier, though troubles had been brewing in Thai financial markets from April 1997, it was the mid–June speculative attack on the baht and collapse of its defence on 2 July 1997, that marked the onset of the East Asian currency crisis. Until early August 1997, the crisis was confined primarily to Thailand, though financial markets in the Philippines did experience some pressure in this period. The most interesting feature of this phase[9] consisted not only in the absence of any pronounced contagion, but also in restoration of stability in financial markets in Thailand and elsewhere by the last week of July, inducing the observers to believe that the crisis had already been resolved.

PHASE 2: CONTAGION IN EAST ASIA

However, the stability lasted only for two to three weeks and proved no more than a lull before the resumption of the storm with renewed fury. The second phase of the crisis, starting from mid–August 1997, was characterized by rapid contagion and may be divided into two sub-periods.[10] Between August and the third week of October the contagion was largely confined within the ASEAN group of countries, while the last week of October witnessed clear symptoms of the Thai malady spreading to countries outside the ASEAN block.

Indeed, during the closing days of October, 1997 not only the whole of East Asia, but other emerging economies elsewhere also experienced substantial pressure in their financial markets. While

9 The other interesting and paradoxical feature in this period was the rise in Thai share prices, along with a depreciation of her currency. Indeed, between 25 June and 30 July 1997, a 25 per cent gain of US dollar against the baht was accompanied by a 37 per cent increase in the Bangkok SET—something which is quite contrary to what normally happens in a currency crisis. As we have discussed elsewhere, abandonment of the currency peg and the consequent depreciation would, in the absence of contagion, be expected to provide a boost to exports, and hence, to output and employment, given the fact that exports constituted more than 40 per cent of Thailand's gross domestic product. See Chapter 4 for a more detailed analysis of the first phase of the currency crisis.

10 In our earlier discussion of the contagion in Chapter 4, these sub-periods were treated as two distinct phases.

other parts of the world recovered fairly soon, until late December, 1997 and January 1998, the pressure remained practically unabated in all East Asian economies including Japan, Singapore, Hong Kong, and Taiwan[11] (see Tables A6.1.1–A6.1.9). By far the most seriously afflicted were the ASEAN-4[12] and Korea, where exchange rates and share prices recorded almost a free fall during this sub-phase (Fig. 6.1–6.3).

Interestingly enough, the spread of the crisis across the Asian economies and its accompanying financial meltdown occurred despite[13] a series of rescue operations mounted under the IMF sponsorship and pursuit of widely recommended policies on the part of the beleaguered nations. The Philippines was the first to obtain a modest support of US$1.2 billion from the IMF in the early phase of the crisis. Over the period 29 July 1997–3 December 1997, the IMF put successively in place, bailout packages amounting to US$17.2 billion for Thailand, US$42 billion for Indonesia, and US$58.2 billion for Korea—an exercise that did not, however, seem to cut much ice with domestic or foreign investors.[14]

For comparing the extent of financial market meltdown (or recovery) across countries and for demarcating the approximate dates of transition from one phase of the crisis to another, it appears useful to consider the troughs and peaks of indices of share prices valued in US dollars.[15] In terms of these indices, the first bottoming out of financial market indices among the Asian-5 occurred in Korea[16] in the last week of December 1998, followed by those in Thailand,

---

11 However, among these countries, recovery of Taiwan was the fastest, though it was the abandonment of central bank support to the new Taiwan dollar in mid-October 1997 that marked the spread of the Thai virus outside the ASEAN block of nations.

12 Consisting of Thailand, Malaysia, Indonesia, and the Philippines.

13 Or perhaps, because of.

14 See Chapter 4 for an account of how each bailout package was followed within a few days by a surge of financial turmoil.

15 The indices reflect a combination of movements in exchange rates and share prices (in terms of local currency) and indicate the extent of capital losses (gains) foreign investors in domestic shares suffered (enjoyed) in the course of the financial turmoil.

16 Indeed, in Korea both the share and currency markets showed signs of recovery simultaneously. Malaysian financial markets also showed similar signs, but at a later date.

Malaysia, and the Philippines a fortnight later (see Table 6.1). Only in the Indonesian financial sector did the pressure continue for a further fortnight.

PHASE 3: TEMPORARY TURNAROUND

The turnaround in Asian financial markets was led by Korea, where both the exchange rate and share prices started recovering from the last week of December 1997. The intensification of crisis during the later part of the second phase, it is interesting to note, was also a fall-out of the revelation in early December of the precarious state of Korea's foreign exchange reserves in relation to her short term external debts. The announcement on 3 December of the US$58 billion IMF bailout package was of little avail, if not positively counterproductive, in stemming the rising tide of financial turbulence. The first sign of Korean recovery was discernible only after most of the country's bank creditors had agreed, in late December, to roll over the short term loans. With a lag of a couple of weeks, followed recovery of financial markets in other afflicted economies of the region.[17]

The financial recovery in this phase did not prove enduring; but neither was it quite insignificant (Table 6.1). Though exchange rates showed signs of improvement during this phase, much more prominent was the recovery of share prices (valued in local currency). Stock markets were also the first to turn bearish later on, significantly ahead of development of renewed pressure in foreign currency markets.

PHASE 4: RENEWAL OF PRESSURE IN FINANCIAL MARKETS

The second wave of meltdown in Asian financial markets started from the first week of March 1998, when the Korean and Thai share markets became jittery, and by early April, stock prices in all the 5 crisis countries were on a steeply downward course (Figure 6.2). The foreign exchange markets, as we have just seen, were the laggards in this phase of the financial turmoil, but they were the first to recover from the downward thrust. By the third week of June 1998, exchange rates stabilized everywhere in the Asian–5, but

17 The onset of recovery in the Indonesian foreign exchange market was delayed by a further fortnight.

Table 6.1
TROUGHS AND PEAKS OF EXCHANGE RATE AND SHARE PRICE INDICES
(Base: 25 June 1997)

| | | End of Phase 2 (Dec 97–Jan 98) | | End of Phase 3 (Mar–Apr 98) | | End of Phase 4 (Aug–Oct 98) | | Minimum over the crisis period* | | (December 1999)** |
		Indices	Date	Indices	Date	Indices	Date	Indices	Date	Indices (average)
Indonesia	Exchange Rate	485.2	28 Jan 98	320.7	15 Apr 98	688.5	17 Jun 98	688.5	17 Jun 98	296.1
	Share Prices	51.8	17 Dec 97	73.8	7 Apr 98	36.8	23 Sep 98	36.8	23 Sep 98	89.1
	Share Prices in US$	14.0	21 Jan 98	22.5	15 Apr 98	8.1	23 Sep 98	8.1	23 Sep 98	30.1
Malaysia	Exchange Rate	178.6	7 Jan 98	142.5	25 Mar 98	167.1	19 Aug 98	178.6	7 Jan 98	150.8
	Share Prices	48.7	7 Jan 98	68.9	25 Mar 98	27.5	2 Sep 98	27.5	2 Sep 98	70.1
	Share Prices in US$	27.3	7 Jan 98	48.3	25 Mar 98	18.2	26 Aug 98	18.2	26 Aug 98	46.5
Philippines	Exchange Rate	171.6	7 Jan 98	140.5	25 Mar 98	169.7	23 Sep 98	171.6	7 Jan 98	154.4
	Share Prices in	59.6	14 Jan 98	81.7	25 Mar 98	40.9	9 Sep 98	40.9	9 Sep 98	69.3
	Share Prices US$	36.0	7 Jan 98	58.1	25 Mar 98	24.2	23 Sep 98	24.2	23 Sep 98	44.9
S. Korea	Exchange Rate	206.0	24 Dec 97	150.7	29 Apr 98	157.9	23 Sep 98	206.0	24 Dec 97	127.2
	Share Prices	53.4	24 Dec 97	81.3	4 Mar 98	41.4	23 Sep 98	41.4	23 Sep 98	141.9
	Share Prices in US$	25.9	24 Dec 97	46.3	25 Mar 98	26.2	23 Sep 98	25.9	24 Dec 97	111.6
Thailand	Exchange Rate	212.3	28 Jan 98	151.8	25 Mar 98	174.5	10 Jun 98	212.3	28 Jan 98	152.4
	Share Prices	73.4	24 Dec 97	106.5	4 Mar 98	41.9	2 Sep 98	41.9	2 Sep 98	85.8
	Share Prices in US$	36.1	7 Jan 98	63.8	25 Mar 98	26.0	2 Sep 98	26.0	2 Sep 98	56.3

*For the exchange rate the minimum corresponds to the maximum value of the US$ in terms of the local currency.
**Upto 14 December 1999.

bottoming out of share prices came two to three months later (Figures 6.1–6.2). The extent of currency depreciation was also much less than the fall in share prices. In fact, September 1998 saw all the five share price indices plunge to their all-time minima; but, except for the Indonesian rupiah, the new lows of other currencies were higher than those obtaining at the end of the second phase (Figure 6.1 and Table 6.1).

The behaviour of share prices in terms of US currency suggests that the renewed financial pressure lasted until August–September 1998, when the bearish tendencies gradually tapered off. Except for Korea, the share prices (valued in US$) in the other four Asian–5 economies hit their ten-year minima during this phase[18] (see Figure 6.3). Compared to its pre-crisis level, the index, at the time of bottoming out, showed a loss of 74 per cent in Thailand and Korea, 76 per cent in the Philippines, 82 per cent in Malaysia, and 92 per cent in Indonesia. While Indonesia's was a basket case for a variety of reasons, figures for other countries also indicate the enormous pounding the stock and currency markets in the Asian–5 had to endure before the financial turmoil finally started abating, more than a year after the outbreak of the Thai crisis.

Phase 5: Sustained Recovery

The beginning of the end of the Asian financial troubles may be traced from May–June 1998, when first the won and then other currencies showed signs of stability, followed by gains against the US currency. The recovery of foreign exchange markets was somewhat halting up to September 1998, but more or less sustained thereafter (see Figure 6.1). The month also marked the onset of recovery of share prices in all the five economies, and may be regarded as the lower turning point of the final phase of the Asian crisis.

We have already observed how the lower turning point in share markets lagged behind that in currency markets.[19] There was another difference between the behaviour of exchange rates and share prices

18 Because of the relatively minor depreciation of the won, the minimum in Korea (at 26.2 on 23 September 1998) was almost the same as the earlier minimum (at 25.9) reached on 24 December 1998 (see Table 6.1).

19 The Philippines seems to be a contrarian in this respect: share prices in the country started recovering from early September, but stability in the currency market was attained only in the later part of the month.

that is of some importance to note. The recovery in the Asian–5 currencies during the final phase constituted, by and large, a process of correction from their unduly depressed levels and adjustment towards their new equilibrium values. The adjustment process was more or less monotonic[20] and the new equilibrium appears to have been attained by November 1998 in the Philippines, and by January 1999 in Thailand and Korea. The behaviour of the Malaysian and Indonesian currency markets deserves special mention. The slide in the ringgit during the fourth phase was quite moderate, and it started bottoming out in early July 1998, two months before the currency peg was introduced[21] (at 3.81 ringgit per dollar). Only in Indonesia did stability in the currency market prove elusive until the last quarter of 1999.

The final phase saw the share prices in all the five crisis-ridden economies staging a substantial recovery, but the upward adjustment was cyclical, rather than monotonic. The recovery was almost uninterrupted between September 1998 and July 1999, when share prices (in terms of both domestic and US currency) stood at their highest levels since the outbreak of the currency crisis. Over the next three months or so, stock markets experienced some downward thrust, but displayed unmistakable signs of stabilization and recovery during the last quarter of 1999. The significant point to note in this connection is that in all the Asian–5 economies, the troughs of the two stock price indices[22] during the downturn in the third quarter of 1999 were at much higher levels than the corresponding minima during the earlier phases of the stock market meltdown. Indeed, a glance at Figures 6.2 and 6.3 strongly indicates September 1998 as constituting the dividing line between deepening of the East Asian crisis and the process of recovery of the battered region.

The enduring nature of the financial market turnaround since September 1998 was attested by other factors as well. First, recovery and stabilization in the currency markets took place along with substantial build-up in foreign exchange reserves.[23] Second and

20 i.e., devoid of significant ups and downs.

21 The ringgit, it is of some importance to note, was pegged from September 1998 and the step seemed to provide an immediate and perceptible upward thrust to the Malaysian share prices.

22 For prices in local and the US currency.

23 Implying that the exchange rates were not propped up through sustained market intervention on the part of the central bank. Between

more significant, exchange rates gained and moved within narrow bands even while the central banks were pushing interest rates downward[24], ultimately to below their pre-crisis levels by several percentage points.[25] Interest rate reductions of such order without a crash in the exchange rates would have been impossible, were there no dramatic turnaround in market perception regarding the financial health of the East Asian economies.

REAL AND FINANCIAL VARIABLES

Our focus has so far been on the behaviour of financial markets, since these are generally the first to show palpable signs of any economic distress and mirror changes in investors' expectations, whatever be their source. However, while violent swings in financial markets are often the product of undue panics or herd behaviour, investors' sentiments would, over time, be based on trends in output, employment, and related variables. Hence arises the need for examining the behaviour of the real sector and its interaction with financial markets over our reference period.

As one would expect, the real variables did not display as wide fluctuations or as many turning points in the course of the currency turmoil as did their counterparts in the financial sector[26] (compare

---

August 1998 and November 1999 the build-up was also quite steady, with the reserves going up from US$25.9 to US$31.7 billion in Thailand; from US$8.5 to US$12.7 billion in the Philippines; from US$19.6 to US$31.1 billion in Malaysia; from US$19 to US$26.2 billion in Indonesia; and from US$45 to US$65.4 billion in Korea. Korea had, in fact, to use up some foreign exchange in order to prevent undue increase in the value of the won.

24 A cheap money policy, *a la* textbook results, should lead to a (nominal) depreciation of the exchange rate. That it did not in this instance, reflected growing improvement in investors' confidence in the countries' currencies.

25 Between June 1998 and November 1999, (short term) interest rates came down from 22.8 per cent to 4.1 per cent in Thailand; from 14.4 per cent to 8.7 per cent in the Philippines; from 11.1 per cent to 3.2 per cent in Malaysia; and from 17.2 per cent to 6.9 per cent in Korea. Even Indonesia started reducing interest rates during the final phase, with the rates registering a fall from 56.3 per cent in September 98 to 13.3 per cent in November 1999.

26 Note however, that fluctuations of the two sets of variables do not indicate their relative economic significance: a 20 per cent fall in GDP

Figure 6.4 with Figures 6.1–6.3). On the basis of the behaviour of exchange rates and share prices, we have distinguished five distinct phases and two pronounced cycles[27] during 1997–9. Adjustment in the real sector over this period was, however, characterized by a single cycle, with the GDP (and industrial) growth rates passing through a declining phase, followed by a phase of bottoming out and recovery (see Table 6.2 and Figure 6.4).

In general, adjustment in the real sector lagged behind that in the financial sector. The only exception seems to be Thailand where the downturn in the two sectors occurred in unison, during the third quarter of 1997. Though the other four members of the Asian–5 had also become victims of the currency crisis by late October 1997, setback in their real sector became manifest only in January–March, 1998. Recovery of the real sector also lagged significantly behind that in the financial markets. The exchange rates in the region started stabilizing from June 1998 and by end September financial recovery in all the countries was in full swing. But the upturn in the real sector was delayed by three months or more. After a continuous decline throughout 1998, GDP registered modest (year-to-year) growth in Korea, Thailand, and the Philippines during the first quarter of 1999. In this quarter, the Malaysian GDP, though on its declining phase, showed signs of bottoming out; but the fall in Indonesia's GDP was still a precipitous 10.3 per cent. Only from the second quarter of 1999 did the entire region begin experiencing sustained recovery of the real sector.[28]

INCIDENCE OF THE CRISIS

The relatively quick resolution of the currency crisis in East Asia and the strength of recovery of the entire region since early 1999 were beyond the most optimistic forecasts of economists and international financial institutions. However, the toll extracted by the crisis was not insignificant; nor are all its effects likely to be ephemeral. The impact of the crisis was the most severe on the

---

implies a substantial decline in a country's standard of living; a share price fall of a similar order would be of little consequence, unless it adversely affects investment, employment or growth.

27 Ignoring minor turning points and the setback in share prices in the third quarter of 1999.

28 Though the Indonesian recovery has been painfully slow and hesitant.

Table 6.2
QUARTERLY GDP GROWTH RATE

Country	1997				1998				1999			
	Q1	Q2	Q3	Q4	Q1	Q2	Q3	Q4	Q1	Q2	Q3	Q4
Indonesia	8.5	6.8	2.5	1.4	-7.9	-16.5	-17.4	-13.9	-10.3	1.8	0.5	5.8
Malaysia	8.2	8.4	7.4	6.9	-1.8	-6.8	-8.6	-8.1	-1.3	4.1	8.1	10.6
Philippines	5.7	5.7	4.9	4.7	1.7	-1.2	-0.1	-1.9	1.2	3.6	3.1	4.6
S. Korea	5.4	6.3	6.3	3.9	-3.8	-6.6	-6.8	-5.3	4.6	9.8	12.3	13.0
Thailand	7	7.5	-4.2	-11.5	-16.8	-15.3	-13.6	-4.95	0.9	3.5	7.7	6.5

Source: IMF, *World Economic Outlook, The Economist.*

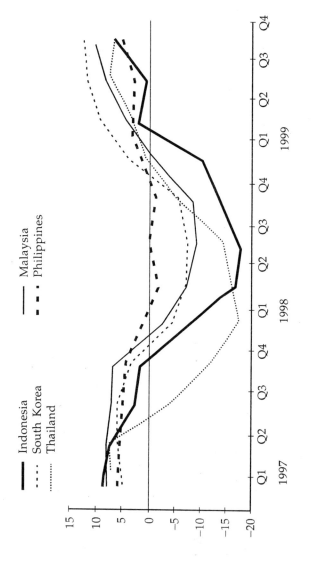

Figure 6.4: QUARTERLY GDP GROWTH RATE.

Asian–5[29], and among them, Indonesia and Thailand were the worst casualties, in terms of duration of the crisis, the extent of financial meltdown, as also the loss of output, employment, and other indices of the real sector. The time interval between the onset of the financial turmoil and beginning of more or less sustained recovery was about 15 months in Thailand (remembering that the speculative attack that culminated in the collapse of the baht was mounted in mid-June 1997). In Indonesia the crisis erupted in August, and the financial sector in general, and the exchange rate in particular, continued to experience significant volatility even up to March 1999, more than six months after markets elsewhere had started recovering. The duration of the crisis was the shortest in Korea: the currency and share markets were first rocked in October 1997, but fairly clear signs of stabilization were evident in less than nine months. The crisis lasted longer, for thirteen and fourteen months respectively, in Malaysia and the Philippines.

Figures 6.1–6.3 and Tables A6.1.1–A6.1.5 indicate the extent of battering financial markets in the Asian–5 had to undergo in the course of the currency turmoil. Before recovering, the fall in the exchange rate from its pre-crisis level was 85.5 per cent in Indonesia, 42.7 per cent in Thailand, 40.1 per cent in Malaysia, 41.1 per cent in the Philippines and 36.7 per cent in Korea. By mid-December 1999, the extent of depreciation was reduced to 21.4 per cent in Korea, and ranged between 34 to 35 per cent in Thailand, Malaysia, and the Philippines; but the rupiah's fall was still a staggering 66.2 per cent.

A more accurate index of financial stress is provided by the behaviour of share prices in dollar terms. In terms of this index, at the height of the pressure in the financial market, the meltdown[30] amounted to as much as 92 per cent in Indonesia, and was between 74 and 82 per cent in the other four crisis countries (see Table 6.3). By the second week of December 1999, Korean share prices (in dollar terms) staged a remarkable recovery and their index stood above the pre-crisis level by nearly 12 per cent. Others were not so fortunate. The loss, though less than at the end of Phase 4, was still 42 per cent in Thailand, 52 per cent in Malaysia, 54 per cent in the Philippines, and 70 per cent in Indonesia (see Table 6.3).

29 The loss suffered by Hong Kong, has also been substantial. See Table A6.1.8.
30 From the pre-crisis value of the index.

One of the most remarkable features of the Asian currency crisis was the mounting difficulties being faced by the banking system.[31] The troubles were particularly serious in Thailand, Indonesia, and Korea. Out of a total of 90 finance companies in Thailand, the economic condition of as many as 58 was regarded as extremely precarious and their operation suspended by the end of July 1997. Barring two, all of these companies were eventually shut down and their assets auctioned off. At the height of the crisis, the government of Thailand had also to nationalize 'temporarily' quite a few problem-ridden commercial banks in order not to seriously disrupt the financial system of the country. In Indonesia 16 banks were closed down in November 1997, and later, a large number of other banks were put under the control of bank restructuring agencies. Before the end of September 1998, 10 merchant banks in Korea had to be closed, and 6 commercial banks nationalized (for the time being) in view of the extremely precarious condition of their balance sheets. The ratio of capital–risk-adjusted assets of a large number of banks in all the three countries fell far short of the Basle norm. Indeed, the funds required for recapitalizing the potentially viable banks were estimated at 16 to 20 per cent of GDP for Korea, and were put at much higher levels for Thailand and Indonesia.

Financial sector distress is, no doubt, an important indicator of the seriousness of the crisis; but what matters ultimately is the countries' loss in terms of output, employment or economic and social well-being. In view of the paucity of data for other relevant variables, our analysis of the damage caused by the crisis will be based on the behaviour of GDP and consumer price inflation[32] over the period 1997–9. Thailand had to endure 6 consecutive quarters of negative GDP growth from July 1997 onward and posted a meagre 0.9 per cent growth in January–March 1999[33] (see Table 6.2).

31 Many an economist, in fact, regards the financial sector fragility as lying at the heart of the East Asian currency turmoil. See Chapter 5 in this connection.

32 The reason for tracking the time profile of the variable is that, other things remaining the same, higher consumer price inflation generally causes greater misery among the lower income households.

33 Given the 16.8 per cent fall in Thai GDP in the first quarter of 1998, the 0.9 per cent (year-to-year) growth during January–March 1999 did not constitute any significant turnaround of the economy. Hence, in Table 6.3 we put the duration of the crisis in the real sector at 7 quarters.

Table 6.3
INCIDENCE OF EAST ASIAN CRISIS

Country	Duration		Extent of financial meltdown* (%)		Output loss as % of 1996 GDP	Maximum inflation rate
	Financial sector (months)	Real sector (quarters)	Maximum during the crisis	In mid-December 1999		
Indonesia	20	8	-92	-70	65	82.4 (Sep 98)
Malaysia	13	5	-82	-52	44	6.2 (June 98)
Philippines	14	4	-76	-54	12	11.6 (Jan 99)
S. Korea	9	5	-74	12	44	9.5 (Feb 98)
Thailand	16	7	-74	-42	64	10.7 (June 98)

*Percentage change of share prices in dollar terms from the pre-crisis level

Negative growth in Indonesia lasted for 5 quarters, over January 1998 to March 1999; but the country's GDP growth had already nose-dived in the second half of 1997. What is more, considering the sharp fall in the absolute output level throughout 1998, growth since March 1999, though positive, cannot but be regarded as abysmally small. As far as the other countries are concerned, GDP remained depressed for 5 quarters in Malaysia and 4 quarters in Korea and the Philippines.[34] The duration of the crisis in the Philippines was relatively short, but except for Indonesia, her recovery has also been less robust.[35]

The single most satisfactory measure of the damage caused by the currency crisis is the output loss suffered by a country, and this loss consists in the difference between the country's potential and actual GDP over the relevant period. A back-of-the-envelope calculation[36] suggests that the output loss in the period 1997–9, as a proportion of the 1996 GDP level, was a moderate 12 per cent in the Philippines[37]; but the loss amounted to 44 per cent in

34 The Philippines recorded negative growth for 3 quarters. However, the growth rate fell sharply to 1.7 per cent in the first quarter of 1998. Hence, we have taken the entire year as the duration of the country's crisis in the real sector. Note that the 1.2 per cent (year-to-year) growth in Q1, 1999 was on top of the positive growth a year back, January–March 1998.

35 The recovery should, however, be judged against the relatively small decline in GDP during 1998.

36 Remembering that 1996 was a period of abnormally low export growth, the potential output over the period 1997–9 is estimated on the basis of the assumption that, in the absence of the crisis–GDP would have grown in this period at the (average) rate the country had attained during 1995–6. The purist, we may well admit, will feel uncomfortable with the procedure on at least two grounds. First, if the currency crisis was not a product purely of herd behaviour or expectations lacking any firm foundation, the growth rate during the crisis period would anyway have been lower than in earlier years. Second, the crisis itself may have some longer term impact. If the reforms the countries have been forced to undertake because of the crisis raise their long term growth potential, the net effect of the financial upheaval could be salubrious rather than adverse. It is also perfectly possible, however, that the economic fundamentals got seriously damaged because of the crisis, in which case, ours will be an underestimate.

37 Apart from the fact that the fall in the Philippine GDP was not as steep as in other members of the Asian–5, the country's long term growth rate was also significantly lower.

Malaysia and Korea, and nearly 65 per cent in Thailand and Indonesia.[38]

The impact of inflation was also the most severe in Indonesia. Apart from the fact that her peak rate of inflation at 82.4 per cent (in September 1998) was by far the highest among the Asian–5, the high-inflationary phase of the country was also unusually long (Tables A6.1.1–A6.1.5, Figure 6.5). Not only in comparison with the Indonesian experience, but in absolute terms also, the inflation rate was quite moderate in the other countries. The most impressive in this respect was the record of Malaysia, where the peak rate of inflation at 6.2 per cent was the lowest, and the volatility of price increases was also the least.

On the basis of the behaviour of the real sector, the cost of the crisis seems to be the largest in Indonesia and Thailand, and the least in the Philippines. However, as of December 1999, the turnaround in the Philippines and Indonesia has not been very strong, while prospects of resumption of a high-growth phase appear brightest in Korea, followed by Malaysia and Thailand.

MECHANICS OF THE EAST ASIAN CRISIS

The East Asian financial turmoil exposed serious limitations in the theories developed in the context of the Latin American currency crises. The limitations arose out of the fact that the South East and East Asian economies, with their high growth, unrivalled export competitiveness, exemplary fiscal prudence, and low inflation, were radically different from the crisis-prone Latin American countries. Hence arises the importance, from both theoretical and policy viewpoints, of understanding the economic mechanism behind the Asian currency crisis, its spread, and its resolution. We have already discussed in the earlier chapters the origins of the crisis and the process of contagion till early December 1997. In the present chapter, we propose to examine the rest of the issues, after a brief recapitulation of our previous results.

38 For Indonesia ours' is an underestimate, since GDP is most likely to fall far short of its potential level in 2000, if not much beyond that.

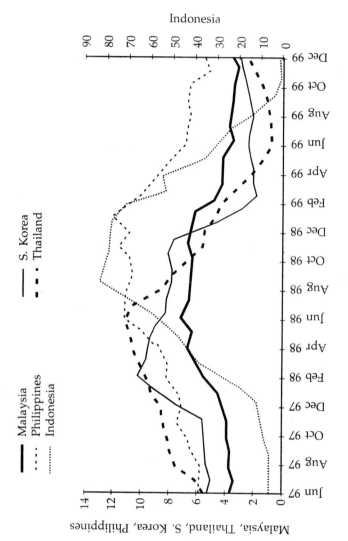

Figure 6.5: Consumer Price Inflation.

ORIGINS OF THE CRISIS

In explaining the roots of the crisis we focused first[39] on the disproportionately high concentration of investment in a few exportable goods by the East Asian economies and a precipitous drop in their export growth in 1996, due in part, to cyclical factors, but also because of sectoral over-capacity at the global level in major export items.[40] The increasingly high outward orientation, which had so far propelled growth in these countries, now turned into a veritable bane in more ways than one. For one thing, the exceptionally high export–GDP ratios the countries had attained by the mid-1990s implied that the negative impact of decelerating exports on GDP growth was also correspondingly large. What was more important was that with the Asian–5 enjoying a long spell of export growth at 10 per cent or more almost every quarter, investors' behaviour came to be based on expectations of continuance of such growth in the foreseeable future. The 1996 rupture in the export trend prevailing for more than a decade administered a rude shock to investors' confidence, produced a sharp decline in the rate of capital formation, and magnified thereby the adverse consequences of developments in the countries' external trade.

While the origins of the Asian troubles may thus be traced to factors operating in the real sector, the turbulence would, in all

39 The two widely proposed explanations, that we found wanting (see Rakshit 1998), ran in terms of (a) large current account deficits and pegged exchange rates, along with the 1994 Chinese devaluation; and (b) high risk investment by banks due to moral hazard problems (Krugman 1998). Since our writings on the subject, the World Bank (September 1998) has discounted the role of the Chinese devaluation as a factor responsible for downturn in the Asian–5 exports. Krugman, it also seems, no longer considers moral hazard problems in the banking sector as the major source of Asian troubles.

40 The role of cyclical factors is indicated by the 16 percentage point drop in world export growth between 1995 and 1996; and that of overcapacity by the 70 to 80 per cent decline in prices of electronic articles, in which the Asian–5 had undertaken massive investment in the first half of the 1990s. By 1995, electronic goods accounted for 50 per cent of total exports in Malaysia, 45 per cent in the Philippines, 40 per cent in Korea, and 33 per cent in Thailand. Given the narrow range of specialization and high export-dependence of these countries, the Asian crisis may be ascribed to structural factors or disproportionality, *a la* Marx (see Rakshit, 1998).

probability, have blown over without inflicting serious damage upon the economies, had not financial factors set a reinforcing mechanism in motion. From the mid 1980s the East Asian economies had started liberalizing their financial sectors and by the early 1990s, considerably relaxed controls on cross-border capital flows. A move towards capital account convertibility and high expectations of international investors regarding the economic prospects of the region produced an accelerated increase in private capital movements into the Asian–5, reflected in a surge of the net inflow from US$20.8 billion in 1990 to US$60.6 billion in 1995 (see IMF 1999). With the setback on the export front, the inflow increased only marginally, to US$62.9 billion in 1996, and as the domestic financial sector came under stress in 1997, international investors started having doubts regarding the sustainability of the currency peg and the economic health of borrowers, both banks and corporates. The result was a US$22.1 billion net outflow of capital in 1997, amounting to a reversal of US$85 billion from the earlier year's flow.[41] Thus, while happenings in the real sector triggered off the crisis, there can be little doubt that it was deepened and prolonged by the large swing in international capital movements. As we have noted in the earlier chapters, the sharp reversal and the accompanying financial meltdown were due in no small measure to (a) preponderance of short-term loans and FII investment in total inflows[42], and (b) absence of any hedging against depreciation for foreign currency loans taken by domestic banks and corporates.

There were other routes through which foreign capital inflow and liberalization of banking promoted structural imbalance and financial fragility, given the lax regulatory environment and woefully inadequate skill of banks in respect of risk management. The liberalized regime saw a surge of domestic credit, a substantial part of which went to support (a) investment in real estates and construction; and (b) spending spree of corporates in building up huge capacity in a few export industries like electronics and

41 Which equalled nearly 9 per cent of the countries' GDP. The net outflow in 1998 at US$29.6 billion was larger, but the incremental outflow amounted to only US$7.5 billion, the reason being that the volatile part of the foreign funds had already left the crisis-ridden countries, and financial markets showed signs of recovery from April–May 1998.

42 A point we discuss in the next chapter in connection with policy lessons of the Asian debacle.

automobiles.[43] The resulting asset price bubble, vulnerability of exports, highly unbalanced structure of the countries' external liabilities and the exceptionally high debt–equity ratios of big firms— all these factors made the situation ripe for a cumulative downward spiral in the event of some adverse shock.

COURSE OF THE CURRENCY CRISIS: AN ECONOMIC INTERPRETATION

The East Asian currency crisis, over the period 1997–9 was, as we have noted in the previous section, characterized by a single cyclical movement in gross domestic product, but by two major cycles in exchange rates and share prices. Before discussing the economics of these cycles and their turning points, it is useful to keep in view some features of the way real and financial sectors generally adjust over time in response to some perturbations, whatever be their source.

First, when an economy is buffeted by a major shock, it takes some time before the system fully adjusts to the shock and attains a new equilibrium.[44] However, the process of adjustment to the new equilibrium is generally cyclical, with overshooting of economic

43 Particularly instructive is the case of Korea. The Korean growth had, for long, been promoted by directed credit, under which not only was there a fair degree of co-ordination in respect of major investments, but small and medium enterprises also had access to bank loans. Under the liberalized regime, the large corporates cornered the lion's share of credit and financed their massive investments largely through loans with a corresponding increase in their debt–equity ratio. Quite clearly, there was a failure of both domestic financial institutions and foreign lenders in assessing the risk of their exposure. Thus, while the state gave up its role in co-ordinating investment decisions, the task proved too difficult for banks to perform.

44 When there is no persistent tendency for the variables to change, the presumption being that the economic system is (a) inherently stable; and (b) not subject to other major shocks in the meantime. Given these two conditions, the economy will regain its old equilibrium or attain a new one, depending on whether the shock was temporary or permanent. However, when the shock is a major one, it may so change the perception of economic agents and policy makers that the economy is shifted to a new trajectory altogether, even though the original source of the shock has disappeared. This, incidentally, is related to a perennial question to which no satisfactory answer is readily available: to what extent is the long term behaviour of an economy dependent on initial conditions, or, does history matter?

variables and subsequent corrections. The basic reason for such fluctuations lies in interdependence among different sectors of the economy and the time required by economic agents to execute revised plans under the evolving economic scenario.[45]

Second, driven as they are by expectations and herd behaviour, financial variables, even without any major shock, show considerable ups and downs, as market participants tend to over react to changing events, new information or unfounded rumours, and as there is a rapid feedback from one financial market to another.[46] Real variables, though influenced by expectations, are far less volatile, the reason being that unlike share prices and exchange rates[47], money wages and prices are slower to adjust, and it requires time for firms to effect changes in production and employment. Larger amplitudes of fluctuations and occurrence of turning points at shorter intervals are, thus, a normal feature of financial variables in an economy thrown off its long term trajectory.

Finally, the behaviour of an economy in the course of a crisis is governed by (a) endogenous mechanism, operating through interdependence among various markets; and (b) the chain of external shocks, including policy changes. A satisfactory explanation of the incidence and turning points of the Asian crisis has, thus, to be sought in the operation of both sets of factors.

EXOGENOUS SHOCKS AND REINFORCING MECHANISM

The rapid spread of the financial turmoil and the accompanying meltdown, as we noted in Chapter 4, were due in part to an unduly

45 (Readers not interested in technicalities may skip the footnote.) Recall the text-book trade cycle theories cast in terms of second (or higher) order differential (or difference) equations. The equations imply that (a) economic agents are guided by past and current happenings in forming their expectations and formulating plans; (b) all relevant items of information are not available instantaneously; and (c) due to technical and economic reasons, full adjustment to revised targets requires some time. Recall also that even if the adjustment function in each market is given by a first order differential equation—so that a single market, on its own, does not display cyclical adjustment— the dynamic process of an economy with n markets is governed by an nth order differential equation, so that the adjustment process is unlikely to be monotonic.

46 We shall presently note the reinforcing mechanism through interaction among financial markets.

47 Under a free float.

large reversal of investors' expectations and herd behaviour; but there were also tangible factors driving these expectations. Consider, for example, the series of shocks[48], which, along with the operation of endogenous forces, sent the Asian–5 tumbling between late July and end December 1997. The first consisted in the revelation in the later part of July regarding the precarious state of a large number of Thai finance companies and their suspension or closure by the authorities, both of which severely undermined the confidence of domestic and international investors and helped in transmitting the Thai virus to the rest of the region.

Second, matters were made worse by banking sector reforms, the fiscal squeeze, highly restrictive monetary measures, and other policies proposed to be undertaken under the IMF bailout package for Thailand, announced on 11 August 1997.[49]

Third, in response to a (relatively minor) slide of the rupiah in August 1997, the Indonesian authorities raised interest rates sharply and asked state enterprises and pension funds to shift their deposits from commercial banks to the central bank. The result was a banking crisis and a severe credit crunch.

Fourth, the IMF assistance sought by Indonesia on 8 October 1997 and closure of a number of banks along with adoption of highly

48 Some of the emerging events, e.g., policy changes, were no doubt responses to the currency crisis and may not thus be considered 'exogenous' in the strict sense of the term. Similarly, problems in Japan were aggravated by meltdown in other countries of the region. More generally, in a completely interdependent universe it is not strictly appropriate to talk of external shock as the first cause. However, such a position is not helpful in understanding an economic phenomenon. In the present context, since the IMF recommendations and policies pursued by the governments were not inevitable outcomes of the crisis, it makes good economic sense to treat them as exogenous, especially if we want to draw policy conclusions. Again, though Japan has close economic ties with the rest of East Asia, her problems in 1997–8, as we noted earlier (see Rakshit 1997c, 1999), were primarily of her own making. Given the large size of the Japanese economy and its relatively low trade–GDP ratio (at about 15 to 16 per cent), the feedback from Japan to the Asian crisis economies could not have been very large.

49 Thailand approached the IMF for financial help on 29 July 1997 and an assistance programme was put in place in less than a fortnight; but as we have seen, mid–August 1997 also marks the beginning of rapid contagion and financial meltdown in the ASEAN economies. The sequence of events, as we have already argued (see Rakshit, 1997c), was by no means accidental.

restrictive monetary and fiscal measures as part of the IMF programme (announced on 1 November 1997), set the stage for sucking the rest of the region into the vortex of the financial turmoil.

Fifth, the despondency was deepened in the last quarter of 1997 by a depreciating yen, along with a fall in GDP, industrial production, and retail sales in Japan.

Finally, the sharp downgrading of the East Asian economies by international credit rating agencies, information concerning the critical payments position of Korea[50] and the announcement of the IMF bailout programme for the country strengthened the financial turbulence during the closing months of 1997.[51]

Our account of the chain of 'exogenous' events indicates the significant role that new and unexpected information plays in influencing the economic process, especially when the system is in a state of flux. The reason is that when data relating to the balance sheet of banks including their non-performing assets, the magnitude of unhedged external exposure of financial firms and corporates, the amount and composition of a country's foreign debt, and foreign exchange reserves of the central bank net of commitments in the futures market to sell foreign against domestic currency[52]—are hard to come by or turn out to be quite unreliable, new information of a negative nature is not only considered to reveal nothing more than the tip of the iceberg, but also creates serious misgiving regarding the true balance sheet position of other financial intermediaries and neighbouring countries, for which no such information has come to light, and whose economic health may well be robust. Hence arose the link between the rapid spread of the Asian crisis and inadequate data or lack of transparency in the entire region, including its two OECD members, Japan and Korea.

50 At the end of October 1997 Korea's foreign exchange reserves were about US$30 billion, but her short term foreign debt amounted to nearly US$73 billion.

51 South Korea sought IMF help on 21 November 1997 and the bailout package was announced on 3 December. On the heels of the announcement, there was heightening of pressure in financial markets until private lenders agreed (in late December 1997) to roll over the Korean debt.

52 The usual data for foreign debt do not include these commitments, so that there can be a substantial difference, as happened in the Korean case, between the actual and useable foreign exchange reserves that can be deployed to defend the country's currency.

While lack of information and loss of credibility engendered by new revelations played some role[53] in the Asian debacle, of far greater importance was the reinforcing mechanism, providing as it did, a rational basis for revising expectations with the unfolding of events and causing rapid adjustments, especially in the financial sector. The mechanism consisted in close inter-linkages (a) among financial markets; (b) between the real and financial sectors; and (c) among neighbouring economies.

Note first that a sudden loss of confidence in a country's currency and its consequent depreciation are associated with a bearish share market, as also financial disruption, as (a) foreign (or domestic) investors scramble to take their funds away before the exchange rate hits rock bottom; (b) balance sheet positions of banks and corporates with large and unhedged external borrowing worsen dramatically and widespread bankruptcies loom large; and (c) bank credit shrinks, risk premia on loans rise sharply, and borrowers face a credit crunch. Development of pressure in stock and loan markets produces, in its turn, a negative feedback in the currency market, with investors seeking safer havens for their financial assets. The reinforcing mechanism, operating through interaction among currency, share, and loan markets, proved exceptionally strong in the Asian–5, as corporate investment was highly leveraged, bonds or other non-bank sources of loans were practically non-existent[54], and there was substantial exposure of banks to real estate (as in Thailand) or to a handful of big borrowers (as in Korea).

REAL SECTOR LINKAGES

In tracing the roots of the currency crisis in East Asia, we have already discussed how rapid and unbalanced investment, along

---

53 An unduly large swing in expectations, let us remember, may make the new ones self-fulfilling, and subject the countries to sufferings not warranted by their economic fundamentals.

54 The importance of the factor lies in producing greater dislocation in the financial market, since a crisis produces a sharp decline in bank loans, so that in the absence of alternative sources of funds, producers find it difficult to sustain their operations. The result is a worsening of financial position of firms which, in its turn, tends to make bank loans non-performing.

with its mode of financing, made the Asian–5 economies ripe for financial turbulence. However, the fundamentals of these countries were much stronger than most emerging market economies and the crisis would have been short-lived, had not mounting pressure in financial markets produced a downturn in real variables and transmitted thereby a negative feedback to the financial system.

The slide of the real sector may be traced to the operation of mainly demand side factors, though supply side failure also played a none-too-peripheral role. The most important factor producing the depressionary impact was the fall in investment demand. Note first that a financial meltdown, with uncertainty regarding future prospects of the economy, could not but prompt most investors to go slow, or abandon their investment plans. Even producers, who expected the currency turmoil to subside fairly soon, had to cut back their investment in view of the prevailing financial constraints: banking problems and share market meltdown ruled out availability of funds for investment on a significant scale.[55] The downward thrust on the real sector, imparted by the initial fall in investment, irrespective of its source, was magnified over time through operation of the multiplier–accelerator mechanism.[56]

THE PARADOX OF ASIAN CONSUMPTION AND SAVING

A highly interesting feature of the East Asian crisis was that, contrary to the text book proposition, *a la* Keynes, consumption demand failed to play a stabilizing role during the downward phase of the income movement.[57] In all the crisis countries barring Indonesia households reduced their consumption at a rate much faster than the fall in income, so that a negative GDP growth was associated

55 Consider also the sharp fall in profits due to high interest rates and credit crunch, even if producers were yet to experience a fall in demand.

56 The multiplier refers to the change in income due to a change in autonomous (here investment) expenditure (by one unit) after adjustment of consumption to variations in income. The accelerator operates when investment itself depends on changes in income, so that a fall in GDP induces firms to reduce their investment expenditure.

57 The fact that in general consumers reduce their demand to a much smaller extent than the decline in their income tends to reduce the value of the multiplier and moderate the fall in GDP due to an adverse shock.

with a rise in the household saving ratio.[58] Such changes in the private saving or consumption ratio go against one of the most robust empirical findings in economics, viz., the positive association between the saving ratio and GDP in the course of a trade cycle[59] (though not in the long run). Much more puzzling were the cases of Korea, Malaysia, and Thailand, where the absolute level of private saving rose even while incomes fell[60], so that the fall in GDP induced through a downturn in investment tended to become cumulative.

The paradox of the rise in saving ratio and the larger fall in consumption than income may, at first sight, be attributed to the operation of 'wealth effect' arising out of the share market meltdown, along with consumer price inflation. The presumption may not appear unreasonable in view of the large erosion of the real value of shares in 1998: the decline[61] was 43.2 per cent in Thailand, 48 per cent in Malaysia, 39.3 per cent in Korea, 34.7 per cent in the Philippines, and 56.5 per cent in Indonesia.

58 Thai GDP registered a marginal decline of 0.4 per cent in 1997, but private saving ratio went up to 33.8 per cent compared to its value at 31.3 per cent in the previous year. In 1998, all the crisis countries experienced a fall in their GDP, ranging from 0.5 per cent in the Philippines to 13.7 per cent in Indonesia. However, between 1997 and 1988, the private saving ratio increased substantially, from 33.8 to 38.4 per cent in Thailand, from 42.0 to 51.4 per cent in Malaysia, from 34.5 to 47.3 per cent in Korea, and from 20.2 to 21.9 per cent in the Philippines; only in Indonesia was there a fall in the household saving ratio, from 29.9 to 23.8 per cent.

59 The relationship appeared as casual empiricism in Keynes's *General Theory*, was confirmed through exhaustive studies by Kuznets (1946, 1946a) and constituted one of the most important regularities all consumer behaviour theories, formulated in the late 1940s and 1950s, tried to explain.

60 In other words, the fall in private consumption was larger than that in income. This violates perhaps the most fundamental proposition of all consumption function theories, viz., that the marginal propensity to consume is a positive fraction. Were it larger than unity, the macroeconomic system would tend to become unstable. Even when the system as a whole is stable, a larger-than-one marginal propensity to consume accentuates the downward (or upward) thrust of an adverse (or favourable) shock on the country's gross domestic product.

61 Estimated from the average prices of shares in 1997 and 1998, and average rate of consumer price inflation in 1998.

Note, however, that the consumption behaviour in the country with the sharpest decline in the purchasing power of shares was in conformity with orthodox economic theories: not only did the Indonesian personal saving ratio fall, but the decline in household consumption was also significantly less than the fall in income. Even in the case of other countries, it is doubtful whether the wealth effect *per se* was strong enough to produce the consumption paradox. The reason is that the major part of financial wealth of households in the crisis economies was held in the form of bank deposits or other fixed-return assets, not equities. Doubts regarding the viability of banks or other financial firms could, to be sure, have produced a (negative) wealth effect. But the quantitative impact of this does not appear significant either. Though some of the financial intermediaries were closed or suspended, and others faced serious troubles, central banks' intervention, together with government assurance, allayed depositors' fears and there was no major run on banks during 1998.[62]

The resolution of the consumption paradox in Thailand, Malaysia, and Korea has to be sought partly in Asian consumers' time preference, coupled with high degree of risk aversion, but mostly in the sea change in their perception regarding the future.[63] The

---

62 Note that except in Indonesia, the price increase was fairly minor in other countries, so that the fall in the real value of deposits on account of inflation was not very large. It is also worth noting that during the Great Depression, there was large scale failure of banks and sharp fall in share prices; but household consumption as a ratio of disposable income registered a rise.

63 Another factor behind the unusually sharp fall in consumption was, perhaps, the credit crunch faced by households. This factor was, to be sure, inoperative for households who had not lost their livelihood or whose intended consumption fell short of their income plus available liquid assets. Credit constraint could, however, still have played some role in reducing overall consumption, with people of small means and suffering from large income falls unable to implement their consumption plans, but the relatively better off households raising their saving in the bleak environment. Note however that the crucial factor here was the larger cut in consumption than their incomes on the part of the more affluent members of the society, since absence of such behaviour would preclude the consumption paradox at the aggregate level. Hence arises the need for examining the economic rationale of behaviour of households whose income, even after the decline, was not too low.

pre-crisis household saving ratios, ranging from 35 to 37 per cent in the three countries, attest to the exceptionally high telescopic faculty of their consumers; extreme aversion to risk is reflected in households' holding of the overwhelming part of their savings in the form of bank deposits or safe, fixed-return assets. A sharp break in the consumption–saving pattern of such consumers, when confronted with a major and wholly unexpected shock, should not thus, with the benefit of hindsight, appear highly perplexing.

In order to appreciate the Asian departure from the Keynes–Kuznet regularities[64], consider the difference between the pre-Second World War experience of western consumers and economic environment in the crisis countries between the early 1960s and mid-1990s. Regular cycles in income and employment, generally occurring over ten-year periods, were an important feature of western economies since the onset of the Industrial Revolution until 1939, even though per capita income in these countries showed a rising trend throughout. Consumers thus came to regard business cycles as quite normal, expected a sharp fall or rise in income to be reversed within a short while, and hence tended to raise their saving ratio during a boom and reduce it in times of depression.

The Asian experience, since the early 1960s, was radically different. Except the Philippines, not only did the crisis countries enjoy an average growth that was way above anything attained during the recorded history of mankind, but the growth was also uninterrupted and completely devoid of cycles.[65] By the late 1980s and early 1990s the labour market in Asian economies had become tight, job losses rare, and duration of even search unemployment exceptionally short. No wonder, households in the tiger economies (as also the outside world) had come to expect continuance of this happy state of affairs for years to come.

64 Concerning the marginal and average propensity to consume.
65 Between 1965 and 1997, the Thai GDP fell for the first time in 1997 (by 0.4 per cent); Indonesia did not experience any negative growth; Korea and Malaysia suffered from a GDP decline only once, the former in 1980 (at 2.2 per cent) and the latter in 1985 (at 1 per cent); only the Philippines had to endure two consecutive years of plummeting GDP at 7.3 per cent per annum in 1984 and 1985. Over the period 1985–95, GDP grew at an average rate of 8.4 per cent in Thailand, 7.7 per cent in Korea, 5.7 per cent in Malaysia and 6.0 per cent in Indonesia; the Philippines, with an annual average growth of only 1.5 per cent, was once again an outlier.

The sharp break from the past in 1997–8, the humiliation of having to beg for financial assistance from the IMF and industrialized countries, and the change in perception of the future by end 1997, induced in no small measure by pronouncements of the large majority of financial pundits and international organizations, to the effect that the East Asian economies were fundamentally flawed—all undermined the long held expectations of households regarding their economic prospects. Particularly unnerving, even for those who had yet to lose faith in the inherent strength of their economies, was the economic programmes initiated by the governments. These programmes, with their emphasis on severe monetary-cum-fiscal restraints[66] and unhindered operation of market forces, a rational household perhaps foresaw[67], would (a) doom the countries to growing unemployment and falling per capita income in the near, or even foreseeable, future; and (b) pave the way for cyclical fluctuations with frequent bouts of depression and unemployment.

Such a reversal in the beliefs and expectations on which household behaviour had, for so long been based, and the absence of social security arrangements[68] could not but induce consumers, renowned for their caution and propensity to value the future no less, if not more, than the present, to take urgent steps for augmenting their assets, even at the expense of a substantial cut in current consumption.[69]

66 Even Malaysia applied a fiscal squeeze and initiated economic reforms measures, even though she did not seek IMF assistance. It was only from the third quarter of 1998 that the country started following an expansionary policy and imposed some control on capital movement.

67 The presumption here is that the average household had a much better grasp of economic principles than the government or the IMF!

68 Only Korea had some social security system, but that covered only workers in relatively large enterprises.

69 It is instructive to consider the difference between the consumption behaviour in Thailand, Malaysia and Korea on the one hand, and that in Indonesia and the Philippines on the other. The consumption paradox surfaced in the first, but not in the second group of countries. In the Philippines private consumption went up between 1997 and 1998, but so did GNP and household disposable income (even though GDP registered a fall). Indonesia was the proper contrarian in that, unlike the first three countries, Indonesia saw a sharp fall in the private saving ratio, along with a decline in income in 1998. In order to appreciate the sources of difference between the savings behaviour in the two groups of countries, note first

SUPPLY-SIDE FAILURE

The downturn in the real sector was aggravated by supply-side factors as well. The most important of these was the credit crunch, which forced some producers to cut back on their scale of operation and reinforced thereby the depressionary pressure in the system.[70] The source of this supply side failure lay not so much in the overall shortage of production loans in relation to their demand, but more

---

that per capita GNP in Indonesia and the Philippines was a fraction of that in the other three countries. The implication is that unlike their counterparts in Indonesia and the Philippines, households in these three countries could afford to raise their saving without an unbearable cut in their standard of living. Second, the first group of countries had always been much more thrifty, with their saving ratios exceeding Indonesia's by 7 to 9 percentage points, and the Philippines' by 15 to 17 percentage points. Finally, for the vast majority of the Indonesians, the sharp rise in food prices left little scope for saving without serious deprivation and suffering.

70 See Blinder (1987) and Rakshit (1986). In the usual macroeconomic models, characterized by a single production sector, demand and supply side constraints cannot operate simultaneously. If producers are unable to sell their output anyway, the fact that banks have reduced their production loan is of no relevance. Were the latter the decisive factor, output would be constrained from the supply rather than the demand side. However, in a multi-sector economy, the two sets of constraints may operate simultaneously. Thus, some firms may have sufficient access to credit, but are forced to cut back on production because of demand deficiency; but there may be others who are unable to meet (potential) demand due to insufficient supply of credit. The basic reason for co-existence of the two constraints arises from the fact that buyers from the second group of producers do not shift their demand to the first group, or there is no significant lending and borrowing among firms. Again, such a shift in demand or arbitrage in the loan market, even if possible, generally requires time, so that in the intervening period fall in output and employment tends to get aggravated with the operation of the multiplier on the one hand, and greater reluctance on the part of banks to remain exposed to small and medium enterprises on the other. The supply-side failure can be quite important in export industries, where failure on the part of some producers to meet international demand generally leads to its diversion to producers elsewhere, rather than to other domestic firms. It is reported that during the currency crisis, tottering economic conditions of some Korean ship builders led to an increase in export demand for ships from Indian manufacturers.

in disruption of credit flows to particular sectors or producers[71], with the suspension/closure of banks, rise in risk perception on the part of financial intermediaries, and introduction or strict enforcement of capital adequacy norms.[72] The interesting point to appreciate in this regard is that though the credit crunch was sector-specific rather than economy-wide, by depressing output and employment in some sectors, it produced a negative impact on firms whose production was not credit constrained.

Similar was the effect of bankruptcy of firms and the dislocation associated therewith. Under an oligopolistic or monopolistic market structure, the demand hitherto met by bankrupt firms could not be wholly transferred to the surviving ones. The consequent slide in GDP was magnified by the fact that bankruptcy tended to have a much more shattering impact on consumers', lenders', and investors' confidence than a decline in economic activity of the same order, but distributed over a large number of firms and industries. In other words, even within the real sector, demand and supply side factors played a mutually reinforcing role in accentuating the incidence of the currency crisis.

Intra-Regional Linkages

The rapid spread of the Thai virus and its unusual virulence were due in no small measure to close ties among the East Asian economies and broad similarities in their institutional arrangements and financial systems.[73] These strong ties and the similarities led to the apprehension that countries in the region, which had not yet shown any symptoms

71 On the basis of the gap between the lending rates of banks and corporate bond rates, Ding, Domac, and Ferri (1998) estimate that credit crunch, especially for small-sized enterprises, was widespread in the Asian–5 in the first few months after the crisis.

72 See Rakshit (1998a) for the relationship between capital adequacy norms and loans to producers with low credit rating, in times of an economic downswing.

73 The major exception was China which did not adopt capital account convertibility. With its currency board system Hong Kong was also different from others, but the difference was minor in view of the fact that before 1997 all the crisis countries more or less pegged their currencies to the US dollar. It was only after the crisis that the difference became important, with Hong Kong still sticking to the currency board system, and others letting their exchange rates float.

of the malady, were going to suffer from it fairly soon—an apprehension that hastened the spread of the ailment to all parts of the region. The initial route of contagion was large scale withdrawal of foreign capital primarily by way of non-renewal of bank loans to the crisis countries. The aggregate net private capital flow to the Asian–5 plummeted from US$62.9 billion in 1996 to minus US$22.1 billion in 1997—a net reduction of US$85 billion[74] that exerted massive pressure on exchange rates and share prices in the region.

Of the real sector links leading to rapid spread of the Thai troubles across East Asia, the most important was the unusually large proportion of intra-regional trade. Out of total exports of 10 major East Asian countries[75] in 1996, 49 per cent was accounted for by trade among the countries themselves (World Bank, 1998). As far as the Asian–5 were concerned, sales to other countries in the region as a proportion of total export proceeds were 48 per cent for Thailand, 58 per cent for Indonesia, 53 per cent for Malaysia, 45 per cent for Korea, and 40 per cent for the Philippines. The most important export market of these 5 countries was Japan, followed by Singapore.[76] Particularly strong were the bilateral trading ties between Hong Kong and China[77], between Malaysia and Singapore, and between Korea and Japan.[78] It is also important to recognize that the Asian countries not only bought considerable quantities of each other's products, but they also very often competed in intra-or/and extra-regional markets. Korea, as also Taiwan, Singapore, and Malaysia had to face stiff competition from Japan in the extra-regional export market. In the intra-regional markets, the main

74 The reduction was accounted for almost entirely by the US$45.3 billion net withdrawal of foreign loans in 1997, compared with a US$32.2 billion net inflow in 1996.

75 The 10 countries were China, Hong Kong, Singapore, Japan, Taiwan, and the 5 crisis countries.

76 For Malaysia, however, the rank was reversed, with exports to Singapore and Japan amounting respectively to 20 per cent and 13 per cent of total exports.

77 China and Hong Kong accounted for 13 and 23 per cent of the Taiwanese exports respectively, but sold only 2 to 3 per cent of their exports to Taiwan.

78 China's share in Hong Kong's exports was 27 per cent and Hong Kong's in China's 24 per cent; the corresponding figures for the Malaysia–Singapore trade were 19 per cent and 20 per cent, and for the Japan–Korea trade 14 per cent and 7 per cent.

rivalries were between Korea and Japan, between Malaysia and Singapore, and between Korea and Taiwan.

The reinforcing mechanism under the exceptionally strong trading ties among the East Asian economies operated through (a) a fall in GDP or the exchange rate of some country causing substantial decline in imports from its neighbours; (b) a decline in exports of these countries producing a cutback in their output[79] and heightened pressure in currency markets; (c) the resulting fall in their imports[80], causing yet another round of downturn in the region's output and exchange rates; and so on. Again, substitutability of the countries' traded goods in intra- and extra-regional markets implied that simultaneous depreciation of their exchange rates would fail to provide any significant boost to the economies (through enlargement of their net exports) or to relieve pressure in currency markets.

While the overall implications of intra-regional trade for the currency crisis are fairly easy to discern, it appears necessary to take separate note of Japan, Singapore, China, and Hong Kong because of the special features of these countries. Given the importance of the Japanese market, changes in the country's GDP or the exchange rate tended to produce a strong impact on the rest of Asia. However, though the real sector downturn and currency depreciation elsewhere did hit exports from Japan, the large size of the country's economy and its relatively low trade–GDP ratio (at around 15.5 per cent) implied that the fall in Japan's income, due solely to lower exports to other Asian countries, could not have been large enough to produce a significant fall in her imports from these countries.[81] In explaining the course of the Asian crisis, the Japanese connection should, thus, be regarded as mostly a one-way channel of transmission, with income and exchange rate movements in Japan impacting on the crisis countries, but producing very little feedback from Japan to these economies due to the initial change in their imports.

Singapore stood on a different footing altogether. It was also a major importer from the Asian–5 and the second richest country in

79 Through operation of the foreign trade multiplier.
80 Which produced a negative feedback effect on the country initially subjected to the downward thrust.
81 In technical terms, the crisis countries did not experience any significant feedback effect from Japan.

the region. However, the trade–GDP ratio of Singapore was more than 400 per cent and East Asia excluding Japan constituted 45 per cent of its export market. The result was that Singapore's fate was inextricably linked with the crisis countries, and these links provided fast routes for transmission of cumulative, negative impulses as the currency turmoil hit the Asian shores.

In spite of the huge size of the Chinese economy, its trade with other countries did not form part of the reinforcing mechanism aggravating the crisis. The reasons were manifold. First, East Asia, excluding Japan and Hong Kong, contributed only 13 per cent of demand for Chinese exports. Second, China was not an important competitor of other countries except Hong Kong in either intra- or extra-regional trade.[82] Third and the most important, not only did China refrain from devaluation, but she also took corrective steps to prevent a slide in her GDP in the face of a sharp slowdown in her export growth, from 21 per cent in 1997 to only 0.5 per cent in 1998.[83]

Quite different was the behaviour of Hong Kong, which, in order to keep the exchange rate in terms of the US dollar unchanged, let the money supply plummet, suffered a substantial decline in the level of economic activity, and thus contributed to the contractionary process in the region.[84]

Apart from trade, intra-regional capital flows provided a direct and immediate means of transmission of troubles among East Asian economies. As in the sphere of trade, in this respect also the dominant player was Japan, followed by Singapore, constituting as they did the largest investors in crisis countries. The result was that the declining business conditions in these countries created difficulties for banks and corporations in Japan and Singapore. Much more important was the impact of changes in financial conditions in the two countries on capital flows to Thailand, Malaysia, and Indonesia.

82 In extra-regional trade, Chinese exports were only mildly competitive with those from Singapore and Indonesia, the export–share correlations in such trade between China and the two countries being .54 and .53 respectively (see World Bank, 1998).

83 Note that despite such a fall, the 1998 Chinese GDP growth at 7.8 per cent was the highest in the world.

84 Apart from the fact that Hong Kong formed a much larger market than China for other Asian economies, these economies also faced stiffer competition from Hong Kong in both intra- and extra-regional trade.

Indeed, an important reason for withdrawal of funds by Japanese banks from the crisis countries was that, apart from the deteriorating financial health of the region, the banks were encountering serious problems in the domestic sector itself (see Rakshit, 1999).

THE TURNING POINTS

Even without any operation of external factors, the currency crisis would have waned and passed off sooner or later, and in the process displayed cycles in major economic variables. The process could, however, be hastened or prolonged, and fluctuations enlarged or moderated, by the impact of exogenous elements, including policy initiatives.[85] We have indicated how a series of external shocks, together with the working of endogenous mechanism, sent the Asian economies reeling in the second half of 1997. Our explanation of other major phases of the currency crisis will also focus on the operation of these two types of factors.

The sharpest fall in exchange rates and stock prices, as noted earlier, occurred after investors had come to know, in early December 1997, of the extremely precarious liquidity position of the Bank of Korea.[86] It was the resolution of this problem in late December, through a rollover of Korea's short term external debt by foreign banks, that set the stage for financial market recovery in the region during January–March 1998. Second, strengthening of the yen from the second week of January to early March 1998, and of the Singapore dollar from mid-January to early April also contributed to recovery of share and currency prices in the crisis countries. Finally, even though the Thai turmoil had turned into an Asian one in the last quarter of 1997, the real sectors in countries other than the Asian–5 were yet to experience a serious decline.[87] The result was

85 See footnote 44 in this connection.

86 Recall that Korea was the second largest economy in the region.

87 During October–December 1997 and January–March 1998, GDP growth rates in Singapore were 7.4 and 5.6 per cent respectively. The corresponding rates were 7.2 and 6.8 per cent in China, 7.1 and 5.9 per cent in Taiwan, and 2.7 and –2.8 per cent in Hong Kong. In Japan, however, gross domestic product fell in both quarters, by 0.2 per cent in the first and by 3.7 per cent in the second; but in the short run strengthening of the yen may be expected to exert a greater influence on financial markets elsewhere, especially since there was as yet no perceptible rise in unemployment in the country.

that the positive developments noted above had a decisive impact in turning the tide of investors' expectations.

However, in the context of the lagged but significant effect of currency turmoil on the real sector in the region and the mounting problems faced by the Japanese economy, the reversal of financial recovery in April 1998, and resumption of pressure in the crisis countries over the next 3 to 4 months are not too difficult to rationalize. Note first that gross domestic product and industrial output in Japan registered a continuous fall throughout 1998, and so did employment, especially since March 1998. What was of more immediate relevance for crisis countries, between late March and end August 1998, the yen underwent a more or less continuous depreciation, falling from 125 per dollar in late March to 145 per dollar by late August 1998. In Singapore, industrial growth plummeted in April 1998 and became negative thereafter till November 1998; GDP growth came down sharply from 5.6 per cent in the first quarter to 1.6 per cent in the second, and was negative over the last two quarters of 1998; and downward trend was exhibited by the country's currency as well, as it fell from 1.59 to 1.78 per US dollar between 29 April and 26 August 1998. Given such slides of the two economies having the strongest trading-cum-financial links with the Asian–5, it is no wonder that the currency and stock markets in these countries suffered a renewed meltdown.

Problems were aggravated in the fourth phase[88] by the Japanese banks' large withdrawal of funds from the rest of the region, following deterioration in their balance sheet positions[89], and by palpable difficulties faced by Hong Kong and China. In the second and third quarter of 1998, gross domestic product of Hong Kong fell by 5.2 per cent and 7.1 per cent respectively. Even China experienced negative industrial growth from March to May 1998. This, along with the fall in Chinese export growth, fuelled the apprehension that devaluation of the yuan was round the corner. Thus, it was in this phase that the full force of the reinforcing mechanism, encompassing the entire region and covering the financial as well as the real sector, came into play, and the crisis countries suffered the steepest fall in their output and experienced the severest pressure in their financial markets.

88 Lasting over the period April–September 1998.
89 Especially since banks had to meet tightened capital adequacy requirements (see Rakshit, 1999).

RECOVERY AND GROWTH

As in the case of the downturn, the process of recovery and tangible improvements in the real sector lagged behind those in financial markets.[90] However, in order to appreciate what caused the general recovery and why it did not prove ephemeral, we need to pay close attention to factors promoting the reversal of the slide in output and employment the economies had been experiencing since late 1997.

Note that though the financial turmoil engulfing the East Asian countries was quite severe, their recovery was much faster and more robust than what most observers—including the IMF— could foresee. Indeed, while the Latin American countries had to suffer for nearly 7 to 8 years from the impact of the currency crisis erupting in the early 1980s, it took the Asian economies less than 18 months to recover and start recording sustained growth in their industrial output and gross domestic product.

With the benefit of hindsight, it is not very difficult to identify the major factors contributing to the turnaround of East Asian economies. Arguably, the most basic of these factors was the strong fundamentals which distinguished the Asian economies from their Latin American counterparts. The rapid and uninterrupted advancement of these economies between the early 1960s up to 1997 was driven by high domestic saving, export competitiveness, and remarkable fiscal prudence. Except for Thailand and Indonesia, external balances of these countries were also quite comfortable before the onset of the currency crisis. The result was that the countries were well placed to take corrective steps in order to counter the economic downturn. The Asian paradox, it thus seems, consists not so much in the rapidity of the region's revival, but more in why countries with such strong fundamentals had to endure such suffering for so long.[91]

---

90 The main reason was that, any development, e.g., expansionary fiscal or monetary policy proposals, that was expected to favourably impact the real sector in the future, would immediately affect current share prices and exchange rates.

91 In Chapters 3 and 4 we drew attention to the exceptionally strong economic fundamentals of these countries, suggested that Korea's was basically a liquidity problem, and indicated how IMF-sponsored measures in the crisis countries and the suicidal policies of Japan deepened and prolonged the Asian troubles.

SHIFT IN POLICY STANCE

Among the immediate sources of turnaround of the beleaguered economies, the most crucial was their change in policy stance in the face of falling domestic production and rising unemployment. Following the IMF prescription and conventional wisdom, all countries in the region, barring China, initially tried to stem the tide of currency turmoil through restrictive monetary and fiscal policies along with structural reforms in the financial and corporate sectors. The expectation was that these measures would restore investors' confidence and the export growth resulting from the lowering of real exchange rates would prevent a slide in the real sector. As the failure of the policy mix became more and more glaring over the course of the crisis, the International Monetary Fund showed signs of relenting, and the countries gradually shifted their policy stance. Instead of trying to generate fiscal surpluses, as planned earlier, the governments started planning to run, first moderate, and then substantial, budgetary deficits. Monetary policies were also being relaxed at the same time, with the central banks scaling down interest rates, in some cases to below their pre-crisis levels.

The chain of events clearly underlines the close connection between policy changes and the onset of the East Asian recovery. Korea, the second largest economy of the region, led the recovery posting, positive and sustained industrial growth from November 1998.[92] Soon other countries joined Korea, and by February 1999, output and employment were on the rise over the entire region.[93]

The sequence of policy changes is worth recounting in order to appreciate their role in (aggravating and) resolving the currency crisis. Under the Stand-By Arrangement with the IMF (approved on 4 December 1997), apart from undertaking rapid structural reforms, Korea was required to tighten monetary policy and aim for a fiscal surplus of about 2 per cent of GDP in 1998 (compared to the then

92 Before that, industrial growth in Korea had remained negative for 10 consecutive months.

93 Even Indonesian industrial production recorded a marginal growth at 0.1 per cent in February, though the country lagged far behind others in the process of recovery. The only exception was Hong Kong, whose currency board system proved a veritable albatross round its neck and prevented it from posting positive growth until recovery in other countries was sufficiently strong to provide the required stimulus.

estimated fiscal deficit of over 1 per cent during 1997). Under the IMF's first quarterly review, completed on 17 February 1998, the fiscal target was lowered to a deficit of 0.8 per cent of gross domestic product, but monetary measures were scheduled to remain restrictive until the currency market had stabilized. Further declines in output and employment made the IMF relent somewhat in the second quarterly review (ending on 29 May 1998), and the fiscal stance was permitted to be neutral, by way of letting the automatic stabilisers work.[94] However, monetary policy was still to focus solely on securing stability of the currency market. The major shift in the Korean policy stance came only after the IMF's third quarterly review (completed on 28 August 1998), when a supplementary budget, incorporating substantial increases in government expenditure and targeting a fiscal deficit of 4 per cent of GDP[95], was introduced in September 1998. Monetary policy was also loosened, with the central bank cutting interest rates from 16 per cent in June 1998 to 7 per cent by the end of September 1998. The steps on the fiscal and monetary front were supplemented by (a) a 64 trillion won (US$47 billion) injection into the financial system in September; (b) setting up of the Corporate Restructuring Fund in October 1998 with an initial capital of about US$1.2 billion in order to provide credit to smaller firms[96]; and (c) announcement in December 1998

94 In plain English, the government would keep the tax rates and expenditure programmes unchanged, i.e., not manipulate them in order to attain a pre-stipulated fiscal target. A fall in gross domestic product would then automatically reduce tax collections and moderate the extent of GDP decline. But such a policy is not only incapable of producing an expansionary impact, it cannot even prevent an economic downturn, whatever be its source.

95 The actual deficit turned out to be 5 per cent of GDP in 1998.

96 We have already noted how the crisis was aggravated by credit crunch felt by the smaller firms, even though there was no overall shortage of funds. In order to meet the credit requirement of smaller firms, a new rule was imposed from 28 October 1998, under which bonds issued by the 5 biggest chaebol could be held by investment trust companies only upto a maximum of 15 per cent of their total corporate debt holding. Consequently, there was a sharp drop in the chaebol bond issue, a fall in corporate bond yield, and a significant increase in credit flows to smaller firms. The interest on corporate bonds came down from 10 per cent at the end of October to 9.25 per cent by 1 December 1998. Bond issues by smaller firms doubled in November and their share in total credit flow rose

by state controlled banks to help restructure the conglomerates through conversion of major part of their debts into equities.[97] In the light of these policy initiatives, it is not very difficult to appreciate why there was a robust financial recovery in Korea from the last week of September 1998, and an expansionary process in the real sector was clearly discernible with a lag of about a month.

Similar chains of events could be observed in other crisis-ridden countries as well. Highly contractionary fiscal and monetary policies pursued in Thailand since early August 1997[98] were slightly modified after the IMF's second quarterly review (completed on 4 March 1998), when the fiscal stance was made somewhat accommodating[99]

---

significantly. Indeed, the Korean recovery in the early stages, it is interesting to note, was characterized by enlarged activity of medium and small scale enterprises, and rapid increase in the number of such firms through new entry, even while financial troubles were taking a heavy toll of pre-existing firms.

97 The conversion of debt into equity went a long way in promoting the turnaround of the chaebol and was expected to enable them to bring down their debt–equity ratios from 400–500 per cent in 1998 to a maximum of 200 per cent by end 1999, as required under the new rule. The conglomerates were thus freed to design their activity on the basis of expectations regarding the future, unburdened by their past mistakes.

98 Thailand approached the International Monetary Fund for financial assistance on 29 July 1997; outlines of the IMF assistance proposals were announced on 11 August 1997; and the Stand-By Arrangement was approved by the IMF's Board of Directors on 20 October 1997.

99 Under the initial Stand-By Arrangement, approved on 20 October 1997, the planned fiscal adjustment was to be 3 per cent of gross domestic product (required to turn the fiscal balance into a surplus during the financial year October 1997–September 1998, from the deficit recorded in the previous financial year); domestic credit to be severally controlled, with indicative ranges of interest rates; and the financial reforms programme requiring (among other things) closure of insolvent institutions to be speedily implemented. Even though the economy was clearly in the downswing, the first quarterly review (8 December 1997) laid down additional restrictive measures in order to attain the original targets: attainment of 3 per cent fiscal surplus in the context of lowering of projected GDP required a tighter budget than originally envisaged. The mounting pressure in the currency market was proposed to be countered through (a) an increase in the indicative range of interest rates, (b) scaling down the initial targets for reserve money and domestic assets of the Bank of Thailand, and (c) announcement and implementations of a specific time

and a 2 per cent deficit was allowed in view of the expected fall in GDP. Under the third quarterly review, completed on 10 June 1998, the fiscal deficit target for 1997–8 was raised further, to 3 per cent of GDP, with no sign as yet of bottoming out of output and employment; but the budgetary measures were still far from expansionary, and monetary policies directed solely towards attaining exchange rate stability. Only after the fourth quarterly review (11 September 1998) was the policy framework changed in order to promote recovery through budgetary expansion and lowering of interest rates.

Even though Malaysia did not seek IMF assistance, her overall policy response after the onset of the currency crisis was basically the same as that of the other crisis countries. However, unlike these countries, Malaysia had already had restrictions on short term borrowing in foreign currencies before the crisis, and supplemented these measures on 1 September 1998 by (a) further controls on capital account, of which the most important was banning of repatriation of funds from the stock market for one year, and (b) pegging the ringgit to the US dollar at a rate substantially higher than the previous month's close.[100] The tighter control of capital movement was immediately followed by a host of expansionary measures: the government announced a planned budget deficit of 6.1 per cent of GNP; interest rates were cut; and banks were offered funds for recapitalization and urged to expand credit.

Among responses to the crisis, perhaps the most bizarre was the way Indonesia tried to tackle the problem at its inception. Before the currency turmoil hit the Asian shores, Indonesia had generally had a fiscal surplus and a moderate current account deficit. Even so, the Stand-By Arrangement with the IMF, approved on 5 November 1997, imposed measures for strengthening the fiscal position, apart from recommending raising of interest rates, tightening of credit, and financial restructuring (including closure of problem-ridden

---

table for financial sector restructuring. Under the second quarterly review, budgetary policies were permitted to be accommodating, but high interest rates were required to be maintained till the foreign exchange market gained stability, and the scope for structural reforms was broadened considerably.

100 The exchange rate introduced on 1 September 1998 was 150.79 ringgits per dollar compared to the previous week's rate at 167.06 ringgits per dollar.

banks). A strengthened programme was announced on 15 January 1998 in order to arrest sharp decline in the rupiah, but large scale financial distress forced the Bank of Indonesia to provide liquidity support to banks. In the context of the unabated currency depreciation and raging inflation[101], the IMF's first quarterly review (finalized on 4 May 1998) programmed for (a) further tightening of monetary policy by way of sharp rise in interest rates and strict control over central bank's credit to the domestic sector; (b) some modification of fiscal targets in order to allow for the cost of bank restructuring and anti-poverty measures required under the sharply deteriorating economic conditions; and (c) rapid reforms, with emphasis on restructuring of banks, privatization and removal of price controls. The new programme was, however, derailed by severe civil unrest, fuelled by soaring food prices, that culminated in the President's resignation on 21 May 1998. Under the IMF's second review (15 July 1998) Indonesia's access to funds under the Stand-By Arrangement was raised by US$1 billion, fiscal policy was eased, but inflation and the exchange rate were to remain the prime concern of monetary measures. Sharp shrinkage of output and employment led to further fiscal easing in October 1998 and lowering of interest rates from December 1998, but it took a considerable while before the domestic policy reversal and improvement in the rest of Asia could extricate the Indonesian economy from the depths to which it had sunk.

Among the East Asian countries, China was the only one which consistently tried to counter recessionary tendencies by stimulating domestic demand, without taking recourse to devaluation—a policy initiative the country could take with relative impunity, in view of restrictions on capital movements already in force. From mid–1998, backed by further tightening of capital controls, China stepped up public investment on a massive scale, reduced deposit rates by 1.25 percentage points during the year, and continued to lower interest rates in 1999 as well.[102] The result was that the GDP growth in China jumped from 7.6 per cent in the third quarter of 1998 to 9.6 per cent in the next quarter, and amounted to a healthy 8.3 per cent during January–March 1999.

101 Along with falling output and employment.

102 By mid-1999, the bench-mark one-year interest rate in China fell below the corresponding US dollar rate by 350 basis points—a whopping differential, made possible only due to stringent capital controls.

Much more important for the crisis countries was the mending of ways by Japan and Singapore, the two countries having the strongest economic ties with the rest of the region. From August 1998, there was a significant shift in policies pursued by Singapore: interest rates were brought down sharply and fiscal tightening gave way to substantial budgetary expansion. The first sign of Japanese policy reversal came in April 1998 when, in the context of the continuing fall in output and employment, the government announced a supplementary fiscal package[103] of 20.7 trillion yen (US$158 billion). However, the amount was too small to arrest, let alone turn, the tide of economic contraction and restore investors' and consumers' confidence. The decisive shift in Japan's policy stance occurred in November 1998, when the government finally announced a wide ranging fiscal stimulus plan, involving an additional sum of 42 trillion yen (US$372.2 billion). The expansionary programme of the Ministry of Finance was supported by easy money policy, with the Bank of Japan pushing down short term interest rates to the near-zero level. Though there was a lag before production and employment recorded positive growth, the policies went a long way in reversing the slide of the yen from September 1998, and produced a positive impact on the rest of the region.

We have already examined how strong trading and financial links among East Asian countries caused a vicious circle in the process of their economic downturn. When countries in the region started to provide stimulus to their domestic demand more or less simultaneously, the circle turned virtuous, with expansion in one country helping recovery in others. The important point to note here is that, had one country tried on its own to follow expansionary monetary and fiscal policies, it would have benefitted others, but in the process the country itself would have incurred trade deficits, and perhaps, been subjected to stronger pressure in the currency market.[104] The East Asian expansionary process could become mutually self-supporting primarily since the major players in the region unfolded their stimulus packages almost in unison.

103 Over what had earlier been proposed in the year's budget.
104 Because of a rising trade deficit and its lower interest rates compared to those in other countries. China could carry through an expansionary programme on its own primarily since the yuan was not convertible on capital account and the country started with a large trade surplus, apart from more than US$120 billion worth of foreign exchange reserves.

EXTERNAL STIMULI

An important reason why domestic policies of East Asian economies could contribute to their financial stability and engineer real sector recovery from the last quarter of 1998 was the relatively favourable environment prevailing in the rest of the world. The Asian crisis, for one thing, did not produce any seriously debilitating impact on financial sectors in North America and Europe. Having burnt their fingers in the Latin American debt crisis during the early 1980s, major banks in the USA and other advanced countries (barring Japan) had already completed their risk management exercise well before the currency turmoil broke out in Thailand. These banks, with relatively small and well-provisioned on-balance-sheet exposures to the Asian–5, did not, as a result, create any systemic difficulties, and were able to resume their advances in the region once the crisis showed signs of waning.

Second, pursuit of expansionary monetary policies by East Asian economies was greatly facilitated by interest rate cuts in western countries.[105] Of particular importance was the series of reductions effected by the Federal Reserve Board of the United States: the federal fund rate, prevailing at 5.5 per cent since 25 March 1997, was brought down to 5.25 per cent on 29 September 1998, to 5.0 per cent on 15 October 1998, and finally to 4.75 per cent on 17 November 1998. Great Britain and quite a few other European countries outside the Euro zone also reduced their interest rates over 1999. By the time the federal fund rate was brought back to the 5.5 per cent level in three steps between 1 July 1999 and 17 November 1999, the financial as also real sectors of the crisis countries, had staged a robust recovery.

Finally, given the high degree of openness of the East Asian countries, the importance of export growth (which turned negative in 1998) for sustaining recovery can hardly be overemphasized. We have already dwelt on the role that intra-regional trading links played in aggravating the crisis, as also in acting as a reinforcing device in the course of the upswing.

However, around 50 per cent of East Asian exports were to the rest of the world, so that in the absence of a substantial rise in demand from this source, recovery in the real sector would have

---

105 In the absence of these cuts, easy money policy in East Asia would have discouraged capital flows into the region and produced pressure in foreign currency markets.

required either (a) a further fall in real exchange rates; or (b) massive inflow of foreign capital.[106] Fortunately for the region, demand for East Asian exports rose substantially during 1999. Unlike the early 1980s, when depressed economic conditions in the USA and Europe put obstacles to speedy resolution of the Latin American crisis, the United States in 1999 bettered her already impressive record of high GDP growth during the decade, and growth in Western Europe also started picking up in the same year. This expansionary process in advanced countries, together with substantial improvement in world demand for electronic goods including memory chips, provided a considerable boost to East Asian exports (see Table 6.4), promoted investors' confidence and permitted expansion in domestic demand, unconstrained by adverse developments in the sphere of external trade or international finance.[107]

SUMMARY AND CONCLUSIONS

On the basis of the behaviour of exchange rates, share prices and interest rates, one may distinguish between five phases of the Asian currency crisis. The crisis first erupted in Thailand, with speculative attacks on the baht from the second week of June 1997 and the collapse of its defence on 2 July; however, until the second week of August 1997 financial markets elsewhere in the region were yet to feel any significant impact of the Thai troubles. From mid-August to the third week of December 1997, the crisis engulfed other East and South East Asian countries, of which, apart from Thailand, the most seriously affected were the Philippines, Malaysia, Indonesia, and Korea. The third phase, lasting over January–March 1998, was marked by some recovery of both exchange rates and share prices in all the crisis countries. But the recovery did not prove enduring

---

106 It is, however, doubtful whether either of these two alternatives would have worked. Further depreciation would, in all probability, have triggered off outflow, rather than inflow, of capital. While expectations-driven capital inflow could be large, such inflows were unlikely to materialize in the absence of export growth, since sluggish exports would have acted as a damper on investors' expectations.

107 The negative export growth of China and Hong Kong during 1999 was due to their fixed exchange rates and the consequent appreciation of the yuan and the HK dollar against other currencies in the region.

Table 6.4
GROWTH RATE OF MERCHANDISE EXPORTS

(% per annum, in US$ terms)

Economy	1997	1998	1999
Hong Kong	4.0	−7.5	−5.5
Korea	6.7	−4.9	2.2
Singapore	−3.1	−5.6	6.5
Taiwan	5.4	−9.4	9.5
China	20.9	0.5	−2.0
Indonesia	7.9	−14.0	7.5
Malaysia	6.0	−7.8	6.0
Philippines	22.8	16.9	15.0
Thailand	3.8	−6.8	3.0
Japan	2.2	−8.8	7.3

Note: This table is based on data available upto 25 August 1999.

Source: Asian Development Outlook, update 1999, ADB website.

and the period August–September 1998 saw a severe meltdown in the region's currency and foreign exchange markets. It was only from late September 1998 that the markets bottomed out and started experiencing more or less sustained recovery.

While the financial variables went through two major cycles in the course of the crisis, behaviour of the real sector was characterized by a single cycle, with the GDP declining everywhere from September 1997 and showing an upward trend only after a year or so.

The proximate source of the Asian turmoil lay in large scale external borrowing by banks or corporates in order to finance long term investment and in inadequate foreign exchange reserves in relation to short term external liabilities. At the structural level, the origins of the currency crisis and its rapid contagion and deepening may be traced to the countries' exceptionally high trade–GDP ratios; large and unbalanced capital accumulation by highly leveraged firms in a handful of export industries and real estate; fragility of banks under a lax regularity environment; and unusually strong trading and financial links among countries of the region.

Matters were made worse by the restrictive fiscal and monetary policies the countries adopted under the IMF bailout programmes. In the context of large scale intra-regional trade and flow of finance, the restrictive measures, even when appropriate for an individual economy in isolation, could not but be deleterious for all the countries taken together. Of particular importance in worsening the crisis was the failure of Japan to arrest the slide in its GDP and the exchange rate and to resolve its growing banking sector problems—factors which produced negative impact on the crisis countries' export demand and inflow of external funds.

Apart from the strong long term fundamentals of the miracle economies, other factors promoting the recovery of the region from the last quarter of 1998 were (a) reversal of fiscal and monetary policies in the crisis countries as well as in Japan and Singapore; (b) continuing boom in the USA, along with resumption of growth in Europe; (c) reduction in interest rates by the central banks of the United States, Great Britain and some other European countries; and (d) resurrection of international demand for electronic chips, in which East Asia had built up huge capacity.

ANNEXE 6.1   ECONOMIC INDICATORS OF ASIAN COUNTRIES: 1997–9

Table A6.1.1
THAILAND

Month	Exchange rate (per US$)	Stk pr	Interest rate (short term % p.a.)	Forex reserve (US$ billion)	Consumer price inflation	% change on earlier year GDP	Industrial production
Jan 97	25.9	814.4	12.25	38.2	4.3	7 (Q1)	6.8
Feb 97	25.9	739.8	13.50	37.2	4.5		2.4
Mar 97	26.0	710.7	12.50	37.1	4.3		
Apr 97	26.1	661.3	10.75	36.3	4.3	7.5 (Q2)	6.1
May 97	25.8	562.8	12.00	32.3	4.4		
Jun 97	25.3	496.0	17.25	31.4	4.9		
Jul 97	31.7	679.5	18.00	29.4	6.6	-4.2 (Q3)	
Aug 97	33.9	523.7	18.00	25	7		
Sep 97	35.1	547.0	25.00	28.6	7.2		
Oct 97	39.1	457.2	16.00	30.3	7.6	-11.5(Q4)	-15.2
Nov 97	39.7	401.8	19.50	25.3	7.7		-10.7
Dec 97	47.0	365.8	26.00	26.2	8.6		-16.5
Jan 98	53.7	434.2	25.50	25.9	8.9	-16.8(Q1)	-13.7
Feb 98	43.3	513.0	24.50	25.4	9.5		-21.1
Mar 98	38.4	480.1	24.50	26.9	10.1		-16.2
Apr 98	38.6	412.3	22.50	28.7	10.2	-15.3(Q2)	-17.5
May 98	39.6	340.1	21.00	26.7	10.7		-11.9
Jun 98	41.1	267.7	23.50				

(Contd.)

Table A6.1.1 Contd.

Month	Exchange rate (per US$)	Stk pr	Interest rate (short term % p.a.)	Forex reserve (US$ billion)	Consumer price inflation	% change on earlier year GDP	% change on earlier year Industrial production
Jul 98	40.8	263.5	16.50	26	10		-13.9
Aug 98	41.8	227.5	13.50	25.9	7.6	-13.6(Q3)	
Sep 98	39.5	253.8	10.00	26.6	7		-6.1
Oct 98	36.9	330.5	9.00	27.8	5.8		
Nov 98	36.1	391.0	8.00	28.2	4.3	-4.95(Q4)	-3.2
Dec 98	36.7	355.8	7.25	28.8	4.3		
Jan 99	36.8	373.3	7.25	28.3	3.5		-1
Feb 99	37.6	336.2	5.75	28	2.9	0.9(Q1)	3
Mar 99	37.6	359.8	6.00	29.2	1.6		5.8
Apr 99	37.4	423.2	5.25	29.5	0.4		8.3
May 99	37.2	458.2	5.25	29.9	-0.5	3.5(Q2)	7.2
Jun 99	36.9	521.7	4.50	30.7	-1.2		8.8
Jul 99	37.0	461.9	4.00	31.2	-1.1		
Aug 99	38.3	468.7	4.00	31.5	-1.1	7.7(Q3)	17.7
Sep 99	41.3	391.1	3.73	31.7	-0.8		15.4
Oct 99	38.8	379.6	4.19	31.7	-0.5		14.4
Nov 99	38.8	399.2	4	32.1	nil	6.5(Q4)	23.4
Dec 99	38.6	438.2	5.41	34.1	0.7		15.3

Source: The Economist.

Table A6.1.2
MALAYSIA

Month	Exchange rate (per US$)	Stk pr	Interest rate (short term % p.a.)	Forex reserve (US$ billion)	Consumer price inflation	% change on earlier year GDP	Industrial production
Jan 97	2.50	1212.6	7.38	26.1	3.1	8.2(Q1)	11.9
Feb 97	2.49	1265.4	7.33		3.2		9.1
Mar 97	2.48	1217.3	7.32		2.6		9
Apr 97	2.51	1080.2	7.35		2.5	8.4(Q2)	11.4
May 97	2.51	1096.3	8.00	26.6	2.2		11.4
Jun 97	2.52	1070.0	7.70		2.1		12.2
Jul 97	2.63	1024.70	8.12		2.4		7.2
Aug 97	2.83	847.9	7.60		2.3	7.4(Q3)	13.2
Sep 97	3.06	779.4	7.83		2.6		7.5
Oct 97	3.40	662.5	8.67		2.6		9.8
Nov 97	3.51	526.1	9.33	21.7	2.6	6.9(Q4)	11.4
Dec 97	3.89	589.4	9.13		2.9		9.4
Jan 98	4.36	569.5	10.09		3.4	-1.8(Q1)	2.8
Feb 98	3.75	712.8	11.04		4.4		-2.2
Mar 98	3.59	736.8	11.00	21.3	5.1		-1.1
Apr 98	3.74	622.8	11.04	19.7	5.6	-6.8(Q2)	-3.4
May 98	3.85	552.3	11.03		5.4		-8.6
Jun 98	3.95	455.4	11.08		6.2		-6

(Contd.)

Table A6.1.2 Contd.

Month	Exchange rate (per US$)	Stk pr	Interest rate (short term % p.a.)	Forex reserve (US$ billion)	Consumer price inflation	% change on earlier year GDP	Industrial production
Jul 98	4.12	386.0	11.00	19.5	5.8		-8.0
Aug 98	4.21	324.5	10.0	19.60	5.6	-8.6(Q3)	-10.9
Sep 98	3.81	373.5	7.52	20.7	5.5		-10.5
Oct 98	3.80	410.5	7.24		5.2		-10.4
Nov 98	3.80	502.2	6.70	23.0	5.6	-8.1(Q4)	-11.5
Dec 98	3.80	574.6	6.53	25.6	5.3		-9.4
Jan 99	3.80	605.2	6.48	27.2	5.2		-11.2
Feb 99	3.80	553.1	6.40		3.8		3.9
Mar 99	3.80	498.6	6.35		3.0	-1.3(Q1)	-0.4
Apr 99	3.80	661.6	3.99		2.9		2.6
May 99	3.80	753.8	3.42		2.9		5.3
Jun 99	3.80	811.1	3.36	30.6	2.1	4.1(Q2)	8.3
Jul 99	3.80	782.4	3.33	31.6	2.5		7.6
Aug 99	3.80	768.4	3.21	32.5	2.3		12.9
Sep 99	3.80	683.5	3.17	31.1	2.1	8.1(Q3)	19.3
Oct 99	3.80	738.3	3.10	30.0	2.1		13.9
Nov 99	3.80	740.8	3.18	29.8	1.6	10.6(Q4)	23.1
Dec 99	3.80	769.9	3.19	30.6	2.5		16.2

Source: The Economist.

Table A6.1.3
INDONESIA

Month	Exchange rate (per US$)	Stk pr	Interest rate (short term % p.a.)	Forex reserve (US$ billion)	Consumer price inflation	% change on earlier year GDP	% change on earlier year Industrial production
Jan 97	2372	691.3	13.75	19.0	4.8	8.5(Q1)	15.6
Feb 97	2390	712.6	12.63	19.0	5.2		
Mar 97	2398	657.3	12.63	19.0	5.1		
Apr 97	2431	652	12.63	19.5	5.1	6.8(Q2)	9.0
May 97	2443	672.5	12.63		5		
Jun 97	2432	712.5	12.63	20.3	5.1		
Jul 97	2575	722	12.63	20.2	5.6	2.5(Q3)	10.7
Aug 97	2880	555.5	12.63	19.3	6.9		
Sep 97	3000	553.6	30.5	20.3	8.8		
Oct 97	3610	472.1	30.5	18.9	10	1.4(Q4)	
Nov 97	3660	398.5	30.5		11.6		
Dec 97	5570	401.7	30.5	18.1	18.1		
Jan 98	11800	485.9	30.5	15.5	31.7	−7.9(Q1)	−3.0
Feb 98	9450	483.4	34.91	16.3	39.1		
Mar 98	8375	504.1	34.73	16.9	45		
Apr 98	8150	465.2	35.45		52	−16.5(Q2)	
May 98	10500	417	45.76		59.5		
Jun 98	14750	431	47.32	18.0			

(Contd.)

Table A6.1.3 Contd.

Month	Exchange rate (per US$)	Stk pr	Interest rate (short term % p.a.)	Forex reserve (US$ billion)	Consumer price inflation	GDP	Industrial production
						\% change on earlier year	
Jul 98	13300	485.1	54.4		72		
Aug 98	11200	360.9	56.82	19	81.2	-17.4(Q3)	
Sep 98	10700	276.2	56.65	19.7	82.4		
Oct 98	7650	312.3	55.85	20.8	79.3		
Nov 98	7500	387.4	52.1		78.1	-13.9(Q4)	-14.2
Dec 98	8050	398	31.18	22.7	77.6		
Jan 99	9125	410.3	40.79	23.8	70.7		
Feb 99	8813	402	39.9		53.4	-10.3(Q1)	0.1
Mar 99	8725	393.6	39.68	23.2	53.4		
Apr 99	8515	481.3	35.82	24.9	38		
May 99	8100	605.8	28.42	25.4	30.7	1.8(Q2)	20.2
Jun 99	6573	662	19.95	26.3	24.5		
Jul 99	6840	599.3	14.57	26	13.5		
Aug 99	7520	585.3	13.72	26.2	5	0.5(Q3)	34.8
Sep 99	8360	526.5	13.41		1.3		
Oct 99	6825	576.5	13.58	26.3	1.6		
Nov 99	7135	599.7	12.5		1.6	5.8(Q4)	
Dec 99	7205	648.4	13.5	26.5	2		

Source: The Economist.

Table A6.1.4
SOUTH KOREA

Month	Exchange rate (per US$)	Stk pr	Interest rate (short term % p.a.)	Forex reserve (US$ billion)	Consumer price inflation	% change on earlier year	
						GDP	Industrial production
Jan 97	860.0	663.6	13.70	31.7	4.7		2.9
Feb 97	862.0	679.7	13.70	30.5	4.5	5.4(Q1)	9.1
Mar 97	889.0	638.9	13.75	29.9	4.3		10.7
Apr 97	892.0	703.2	13.05	30.6	3.8		6.1
May 97	893.0	738.1	12.65	32.7	4.0	6.3(Q2)	12.4
Jun 97	888.0	705.0	11.88	34.1	3.7		7.9
Jul 97	892.0	726.9	12.05				8.6
Aug 97	903.0	730.3	12.90	34.4	4.0	6.3(Q3)	10.1
Sep 97	914.0	655.8	13.30	31.2	4.2		12.2
Oct 97	967.0	506.6	13.85	31.3	4.2		6.2
Nov 97	1110.0	438.7	14.95	20.4	4.3	3.9(Q4)	2.4
Dec 97	1635.0	376.3	25.00	21.1	6.6		-10.3
Jan 98	1680.0	518.6	23.00	24.2	8.3	-3.8(Q1)	-1.9
Feb 98	1643.0	516.4	23.50	26.7	9.5		-10.1
Mar 98	1388.0	510.4	22.70	29.8	9.0		-10.8
Apr 98	1338.0	417.1	19.85	35.5	8.8	-6.6(Q2)	-10.8
May 98	1413.0	313.5	18.00	38.8	8.2		-10.8
Jun 98	1381.0	301.7	16.48	40.8	7.5		-13.3

(Contd.)

Table A6.1.4 Contd.

Month	Exchange rate (per US$)	Stk pr	Interest rate (short term % p.a.)	Forex reserve (US$ billion)	Consumer price inflation	% change on earlier year GDP	Industrial production
Jul 98	1244.0	344.4	13.00		7.3		-12.9
Aug 98	1310.0	317.6	11.40	45	6.9	-6.8(Q3)	-11.8
Sep 98	1391.0	310.3	10.30	47	6.9		0.3
Oct 98	1315.0	363.9	7.50	48.8	7.2		-8
Nov 98	1250.0	464.0	7.70	50	6.8	-5.3(Q4)	1.4
Dec 98	1201.0	562.5	7.70	52	4		4.7
Jan 99	1175.0	565.2	6.80	53.5	1.5		14.7
Feb 99	1218.0	498.4	6.70	55.4	0.2	4.6(Q1)	4
Mar 99	1223.0	618.1	6.55		0.5		18.4
Apr 99	1179.0	790.0	5.80	59.3	0.4		17.1
May 99	1191.0	720.1	6.28	61.3	0.8	9.8(Q2)	21.8
Jun 99	1158.0	883.0	6.40		0.6		29.5
Jul 99	1198.0	944.5	7.23	64.9	0.3		
Aug 99	1192.0	963.0	7.23	64.7		12.3(Q3)	29.9
Sep 99	1218	868.9	7.2	65.4	0.8		18.1
Oct 99	1200.0	793.4	7.00		1.2		30.6
Nov 99	1162	969.3	6.85	69.6	1.4	13.0(Q4)	26.8
Dec 99	1134	1002.6	7.2	74	1.4		24.1

Source: The Economist.

Table A6.1.5
PHILIPPINES

Month	Exchange rate (per US$)	Stk pr	Interest rate (short term % p.a.)	Forex reserve (US$ billion)	Consumer price inflation	% change on earlier year	
						GDP	Industrial production
Jan 97	26.3	3373.6	10.25	9.7	4.4	5.7(Q1)	-6.3
Feb 97	26.3	3349.8	10.19	10.3	4.8		-3.6
Mar 97	26.4	3204.1	10.19	10.4	4.8		9.3
Apr 97	26.4	2648.2	8.19	10.2	4.6		-0.5
May 97	26.4	2722.7	9.69	10	4.2	5.7(Q2)	-5.4
Jun 97	26.4	2829.3	10.13		4.8		5.8
Jul 97	29.8	2595.4	12.00	8.3	4.8		5.7
Aug 97	30.5	2284.0	10.63		4.5	4.9(Q3)	1
Sep 97	33.5	2077.0	12.00	9.4	5.3		4.3
Oct 97	35.1	1814.2	11.38		5.7		19.4
Nov 97	34.8	1799.4	13.37		6.5	4.7(Q4)	
Dec 97	40.5	1869.2	13.13		6.1		
Jan 98	42.2	1782.1	13.93	8.8	6.4	1.7(Q1)	-7.7
Feb 98	40.3	2153.7	14.87		7.4		
Mar 98	37.1	2311.4	14.37	7.8	7.3		-11.8
Apr 98	40.1	2134.0	14.43	9.3	7.9	-1.2(Q2)	
May 98	39.1	2060.1	14.43		9.2		
Jun 98	41.5	1712.9	14.43	9	10.7		-10.5

(Contd.)

Table A6.1.5 Contd.

Month	Exchange rate (per US$)	Stk pr	Interest rate (short term % p.a.)	Forex reserve (US$ billion)	Consumer price inflation	% change on earlier year GDP	Industrial production
Jul 98	42.1	1605.3	12.63		10.6		-12.1
Aug 98	43.6	1287.0	12.75	8.5	10.5	-0.1(Q3)	-17
Sep 98	43.8	1259.6	11.37	9.0	10.0		-16.4
Oct 98	40.9	1602.2	12.18		10.2		-16
Nov 98	39.4	1958.5	13.38		11.2	-1.9(Q4)	
Dec 98	39.2	1968.8	13.13	9.2	10.4		-10.6
Jan 99	38.7	1994.0	11.18		11.6		-3.7
Feb 99	39.1	1934.1	11.18	10.7	9.9	1.2(Q1)	-8.3
Mar 99	38.8	2012.0	10.56		8.7		-3.6
Apr 99	38.0	2460.0	10.81	12.2	8.0		1.8
May 99	38.1	2390.4	10.13	12.2	6.7	3.6(Q2)	
Jun 99	38.0	2487.0	8.06	12.3	5.8		-4.6
Jul 99	38.3	2353.0	8.06	12.4	5.7		-4.6
Aug 99	39.8	2260.1	7.75	12.7	5.5	3.1(Q3)	14.3
Sep 99	41.0	2081.4	8.00	12.7	5.7		4.2
Oct 99	40.1	1962.3	8.87		5.4		8.7
Nov 99	40.8	1964.2	8.68	12.9	3.9	4.6(Q4)	-11.7
Dec 99	40.7	2011.3	8.81		4.3		

Source: The Economist.

Table A6.1.6
SINGAPORE

Month	Exchange rate (per US$)	Stk pr	Interest rate (short term % p.a.)	Forex reserve (US$ billion)	Consumer price inflation	% change on earlier year	
						GDP	Industrial production
Jan 97	1.41	2220.1	3.00	77.3	1.90	3.8(Q1)	-7.2
Feb 97	1.43	2216.1	2.88	77.2	1.60		-5.5
Mar 97	1.44	2100.0	3.38	78.7	1.60		-8.5
Apr 97	1.45	2004.3	3.50		1.90		1.1
May 97	1.43	2046.4	3.88	80.4	1.60	7.8(Q2)	-1.6
Jun 97	1.43	2023.9	3.70	80.7	1.70		9.3
Jul 97	1.47	1966.4	4.34		2.10		7.7
Aug 97	1.51	1916.0	3.95	76.8	2.30	10.1(Q3)	6.5
Sep 97	1.51	1900.5	4.19	77.3	2.50		13.4
Oct 97	1.58	1541.4	7.25	74.5	2.50		6.4
Nov 97	1.60	1653.6	5.75	74.4	2.30	7.4(Q4)	10.3
Dec 97	1.68	1514.8	6.87		2.00		8.0
Jan 98	1.72	1259.9	8.13		1.20		-3.9
Feb 98	1.63	1583.2	6.09		0.90	5.6(Q1)	16.2
Mar 98	1.60	1667.2	5.03		1.00		8.5
Apr 98	1.59	1502.1	5.23	76.1	0.60		1.3
May 98	1.67	1295.5	5.89	71.9	0.50	1.6(Q2)	-4.5
Jun 98	1.66	1074.9	6.75	70.9	-0.20		-0.9

(Contd.)

Table A6.1.6 Contd.

Month	Exchange rate (per US$)	Stk pr	Interest rate (short term % p.a.)	Forex reserve (US$ billion)	Consumer price inflation	% change on earlier year GDP	Industrial production
Jul 98	1.72	1054.0	5.59	69.2	-0.40	-0.7(Q3)	-6.2
Aug 98	1.78	925.9	4.87	68.0	-0.80		-6.6
Sep 98	1.68	939.7	4.25	72.3	-1.40		-1.7
Oct 98	1.62	1180.2	3.12	75.9	-1.70		-7.9
Nov 98	1.64	1390.5	2.25	74.9	-1.50	-0.8(Q4)	-3.3
Dec 98	1.66	1394.7	1.75		-1.50		2.7
Jan 99	1.69	1457.4	1.96	74.0	-0.50		10.0
Feb 99	1.73	1411.0	1.87	72.1	-0.60	1.2(Q1)	2.8
Mar 99	1.73	1518.1	1.96	71.6	-0.60		6.2
Apr 99	1.70	1837.2	1.26		-0.30		4.8
May 99	1.73	1893.7	1.70	73.2	0.10	6.7(Q2)	16.4
Jun 99	1.70	2167.7	1.64	73.8	0.50		18.4
Jul 99	1.68	2077.7	2.23	75.1	0.60		17.4
Aug 99	1.69	2136.4	2.29	75.8	0.90	6.7(Q3)	18.4
Sep 99	1.71	2017.6	2.28	75.9	1.20		14.2
Oct 99	1.67	1989.0	2.53	75.1	1.50		22.6
Nov 99	1.67	2190.7	2.71	74.3	1.3	7.1(Q4)	18.0
Dec 99	1.68	2369.3	2.82	76.8	1.4		7.0

Source: The Economist.

Table A6.1.7
CHINA

Month	Exchange rate (per US$)	Stk pr	Interest rate (short term % p.a.)	Forex reserve (US$ billion)	Consumer price inflation	% change on earlier year GDP	% change on earlier year Industrial production
Jan 97	8.30	957.0	11.72	110.6	5.6	9.4(Q1)	10.4
Feb 97	8.29	1005.0	11.97		4.0		13.5
Mar 97	8.30	1216.3	11.61	114.0	3.2		11.9
Apr 97	8.30	1391.9	11.33	116.3	2.8		11.9
May 97	8.29	1442.5	11.21		2.8	9.6(Q2)	12.1
Jun 97	8.29	1287.2	12.03	122.8	2.7		8.4
Jul 97	8.29	1244.9	13.80	127.8	1.9		8.4
Aug 97	8.29	1194.4	10.58	132.3	1.8	8.1(Q3)	11.0
Sep 97	8.29	1217.1	10.80	136.0	1.8		11.8
Oct 97	8.28	1233.5	10.80	139.9	1.5		11.6
Nov 97	8.28	1241.4	9.00	141.3	1.1	8.1(Q4)	11.6
Dec 97	8.28	1207.7	9.03	142.8	0.4		9.2
Jan 98	8.28	1272.2	8.68	143.7	0.3		
Feb 98	8.28	1298.2	9.09		-0.1	7.2(Q1)	6.6
Mar 98	8.28	1258.3	9.18	140.6	0.7		-2.6
Apr 98	8.28	1400.0	9.00		-0.3		-4.4
May 98	8.28	1437.7	6.51	140.9	-1.0	6.8(Q2)	-5.6
Jun 98	8.28	1431.9	9.43	140.6	-1.3		7.9

(Contd.)

Table A6.1.7 Contd.

Month	Exchange rate (per US$)	Stk pr	Interest rate (short term % p.a.)	Forex reserve (US$ billion)	Consumer price inflation	% change on earlier year	
						GDP	Industrial production
Jul 98	8.28	1419.3	8.10		-1.4	7.6(Q3)	7.9
Aug 98	8.28	1197.0	8.10		-1.4		10.2
Sep 98	8.28	1331.8	6.96	141.1	-1.5		10.6
Oct 98	8.28	1282.2	7.92	143.7	-1.1		11.0
Nov 98	8.28	1366.6	7.48		-1.2	9.6(Q4)	
Dec 98	8.28	1258.8	6.60	149.2	-1.0		8.0
Jan 99	8.28	1225.8	7.92	149.2	-1.2		10.6
Feb 99	8.28	1160.6	9.00	150.4	-1.3	8.3(Q1)	9.0
Mar 99	8.28	1235.5	12.00	150.5	-1.8		9.0
Apr 99	8.28	1257.6	9.00	150.7	-2.2		9.0
May 99	8.28	1178.9	8.82	150.4	-2.2	7.1(Q2)	8.9
Jun 99	8.28	1548.3	7.70	150.6	-2.1		9.4
Jul 99	8.28	1710.7	7.60	152.3	-1.4		9.3
Aug 99	8.28	1680.7	6.60	154.0	-1.3	7(Q3)	9.5
Sep 99	8.28	1766.9	6.10	154.7	-0.8		8.1
Oct 99	8.28	1602.7	1.98	156.0	-0.6		7.0
Nov 99	8.28	1553.8	1.98	156.8	-0.9	6.8(Q4)	7.6
Dec 99	8.28	1512.2	1.98		-1.0		8.8

Source: The Economist.
Note: From 6 October 1999 interest rate of China: Proxy, due to lack of inter–bank market.

Table A6.1.8
HONG KONG

Month	Exchange rate (per US$)	Stk pr	Interest rate (short term % p.a.)	Forex reserve (US$ billion)	Consumer price inflation	% change on earlier year GDP	% change on earlier year Industrial production
Jan 97	7.74	13692.8	5.44		6.5	6.1(Q1)	-3.1
Feb 97	7.75	13106.3	5.65		5.7		
Mar 97	7.75	12651.4	5.71		5.2		
Apr 97	7.75	12581.3	5.94		5.8	6.4(Q2)	-0.8
May 97	7.74	14153.6	6.03		5.4		
Jun 97	7.75	14203.9	6.63	67.6	6.5		
Jul 97	7.75	15446.0	6.31	81.7	6.6	5.7(Q3)	0.5
Aug 97	7.74	15855.7	9.98	85.3	5.3		
Sep 97	7.74	14411.2	7.45		5.5		
Oct 97	7.74	13384.2	7.02	91.8	5.1	2.7(Q4)	-0.2
Nov 97	7.73	10154.4	11.32	96.5	4.8		
Dec 97	7.75	10692.7	9.63	75.3	5.1		
Jan 98	7.74	9246.8	13.26	80.3	4.7	-2.8(Q1)	-4.0
Feb 98	7.74	10671.0	9.24	78.6	4.8		
Mar 98	7.75	11121.7	6.57		4.7		
Apr 98	7.75	10977.5	6.09	96.2	4.5	-5.2(Q2)	-4.5
May 98	7.75	9549.2	7.81	96.4	4.0		
Jun 98	7.74	8004.4	13.54				

(Contd.)

Table A6.1..8 Contd.

Month	Exchange rate (per US$)	Stk pr	Interest rate (short term % p.a.)	Forex reserve (US$ billion)	Consumer price inflation	% change on earlier year GDP	% change on earlier year Industrial production
Jul 98	7.75	7.75	8420.70	8.41	96.5	3.2	
Aug 98	7.75	7622.6	12.05	92.1	2.7	-7.1(Q3)	-10.2
Sep 98	7.75	7504.4	9.42	88.4	2.5		
Oct 98	7.75	9662.1	5.91	88.7	0.1		
Nov 98	7.74	10213.4	6.33	88.6	-0.7	-5.7(Q4)	-13.8
Dec 98	7.75	9939.4	5.66	89.6	-1.6		
Jan 99	7.75	10314.9	6.09	90.1	-1.1		
Feb 99	7.75	9402.4	6.11	89.8	-1.7	-3.4(Q1)	-9.8
Mar 99	7.75	10940.1	5.48		-2.6		
Apr 99	7.75	12543.8	5.26	89.5	-3.8		
May 99	7.75	12403.1	5.18	88.9	-4.0	0.7(Q2)	-6.6
Jun 99	7.76	13155.1	5.63	88.6	-4.1		
Jul 99	7.76	13419.7	6.13	89.1	-5.5		
Aug 99	7.76	12993.1	6.45	89.2	-6.1	4.5(Q3)	-6.3
Sep 99	7.77	13187.6	5.87	90.4	-6.0		
Oct 99	7.77	12498.6	6.59		-4.2		
Nov 99	7.77	14704.5	6.17	92.1	-4.1	8.7(Q4)	-2.7
Dec 99	7.77	16282.7	5.97	96.3	-4.0		

Source: The Economist.

Table A6.1.9
TAIWAN

Month	Exchange rate (per US$)	Stk pr	Interest rate (short term % p.a.)	Forex reserve (US$ billion)	Consumer price inflation	% change on earlier year	
						GDP	Industrial production
Jan 97	27.5	7290.8	5.65		2.0	6.8(Q1)	0.6
Feb 97	27.6	7656.9	5.50		1.1		10.0
Mar 97	27.5	8441.5	6.25	88.8	0.5		6.1
Apr 97	27.6	8614.8	6.50		0.8	6.3(Q2)	7.3
May 97	27.8	8022.9	5.40		1.8		5.3
Jun 97	27.9	8713.5	5.75	90.0	3.3		7.2
Jul 97	27.9	9544.6	6.80	88.8	-0.6	6.9(Q3)	7.4
Aug 97	28.7	9855.2	7.75	87.8	0.6		9.0
Sep 97	28.6	9087.6	8.15		-0.3		10.8
Oct 97	30.4	7692.5	7.95	82.9	-0.5	7.1(Q4)	6.0
Nov 97	33.0	7705.4	8.25	83.1	0.2		8.1
Dec 97	32.5	8347.2	8.65		1.8		-6.8
Jan 98	33.5	8098.7	8.50			5.9(Q1)	19.9
Feb 98	32.9	8837.3	8.15	84.0	2.6		3.9
Mar 98	32.9	8952.7	7.70		2.1		6.3
Apr 98	33.0	8636.5	7.25	84.0	1.7	5.2(Q2)	0.7
May 98	33.7	8267.5	7.35	84.4	1.4		5.4
Jun 98	34.7	7466.4	7.75	83.3			

Table A6.1.9 Contd.

Month	Exchange rate (per US$)	Stk pr	Interest rate (short term % p.a.)	Forex reserve (US$ billion)	Consumer price inflation	% change on earlier year GDP	% change on earlier year Industrial production
Jul 98	34.4	7881.1	7.00	83.6	0.9		2.4
Aug 98	34.7	7293.4	7.10	83.7	0.4	4.7(Q3)	4.6
Sep 98	34.6	6972.5	6.65		0.4		6.7
Oct 98	32.9	7021.4	6.05		2.6		1.6
Nov 98	32.3	7100.1	6.25		3.9	3.7(Q4)	
Dec 98	32.3	6769.5	7.00		2.1		−0.8
Jan 99	32.3	6310.7	5.55	91.9	0.4		15.0
Feb 99	32.4	5798.0	5.45	92.6	2.1	4.3(Q1)	−6.3
Mar 99	33.2	6757.1	5.05		−0.5		7.9
Apr 99	32.9	7474.2	5.05	95.1	−0.1		6.4
May 99	32.8	7614.6	5.20		0.5	6.5(Q2)	10.8
Jun 99	32.4	8059.0	5.20		−0.8		10.0
Jul 99	32.3	7786.7	5.40	98.6	−0.8		7.1
Aug 99	31.9	7993.7	5.20	102.3	1.1	5.1(Q3)	9.0
Sep 99	31.8	7972.1	5.15		0.6		NIL
Oct 99	31.7	7666.6	5.40		0.4		7.5
Nov 99	31.7	7645.8	5.15	103.5	−0.9	6.8(Q4)	11.4
Dec 99	31.6	7850.1	5.53		0.1		10.9

Source: The Economist.

7

Lessons from the Asian Experience

Every economic crisis leads to a reappraisal of conventional wisdom, and the Asian one is no exception. The problem is that it takes a while, often a considerable while, before economists are able to put the events in their proper perspective, differentiate the core from the peripheral elements, and draw 'correct' analytical and policy conclusions. Anyone trying to follow the debate on the currency turmoil in East Asia cannot but be dazed by the voluminous literature on the subject and the diverse views expressed therein. However, there are some basic features of the turmoil on which the debate has produced some broad consensus, though there is considerable scope for serious differences of opinion in respect of others. Instead of going into the major areas of agreement and differences among the commentators, we propose in the final part of the present study to bring together the major theoretical and policy implications that are more or less immediate from our analysis of the East Asian upheaval during the period 1997–9.

It is useful to examine first whether our interpretations of the East Asian events suggest some advancement over the first and second generation theories of currency crises, summarized in Chapter 2. However, despite the analytical advancement, if any, it is highly unlikely that economists or policy makers can predict currency crises accurately or eliminate them altogether. But even so, the Asian troubles bring out the need for some policy measures, at the domestic and international level, that should go a long way in making countries less vulnerable to currency crises and mitigate their adverse consequences.

THEORIES OF CURRENCY CRISES IN LIGHT OF THE ASIAN EXPERIENCE

The first generation theories of currency crises, formulated in the context of the Latin American troubles, focus on the economic fundamentals and suggest how inconsistencies between domestic economic policies and a fixed exchange rate system[1] lead, sooner or later, to a speculative attack on the currency, followed by devaluation or abandonment of the peg. The second generation models were developed to explain currency turmoils faced by countries under the European Exchange Rate Mechanism (ERM). In these models, even though the basic economic forces at work permit the pegged exchange rate, when left on its own, to survive indefinitely, a speculative attack can very well cause a collapse of the currency. In both sets of theories, private economic agents are rational and guided by considerations of relative gains and losses of their alternative courses of action.[2] However, while the authorities in the earlier models give up the peg only when they run short of foreign exchange reserves, in the second generation models the government decision is based on evaluation of the net benefit to the economy of sticking to or abandoning the fixed exchange rate system. It is for this reason that the 'fundamentals' in the newer theories are much broader than in the older ones, the attack-contingent equilibrium can differ from the no-attack equilibrium, and currency traders' expectations may be self-fulfilling.

There is one important respect in which the East Asian experience resembled the Latin American rather than the ERM crisis. The proximate reason for abandoning the currency peg by Thailand and other Asian–5 countries[3] over July–October 1997 was paucity of their foreign exchange reserves, rather than problems of recession and unemployment, along with a growing trade deficit.[4] Indeed, compared to 1996, the first two quarters of 1997 saw the Asian economies enjoying substantial upturn in both their GDP and export

1 Leading to overvaluation of the country's currency and continuous loss of foreign exchange reserves. See Chapter 2 and Annex 2.1.

2 i.e., whether or not to attack the currency.

3 Consisting of Thailand, the Philippines, Malaysia, Indonesia, and Korea.

4 Devaluation or abandonment of the peg enables countries to tackle these problems effectively.

growth. As we have seen in Chapter 6, it was restrictive monetary and fiscal policies, following abandonment of the peg, that subjected the countries to a prolonged spell of declining output, employment, and standard of living.[5] There was thus a gulf of difference between the fall of Asian exchange rates and the European currency turmoils which the second generation models sought to explain.

However, the fact that drying up of external credit lines and inadequate foreign exchange reserves in relation to short term external liabilities forced the Asian-5 to let their currencies float does not make theirs parallel to the Latin American experience. We have emphasized in earlier chapters how the Latin American disabilities—e.g., fiscal profligacy, high inflation, low growth, and lack of export competitiveness—were conspicuous by their absence in the Asian tiger economies. The only serious flaw in the real sector of the East Asian economies, we have seen, lay in the huge capacity built up in some specific areas which, along with their high trade–GDP ratios—factors that made them vulnerable to external shocks. But in the context of their uninterrupted and consistently high GDP and export growth, neither the 1996 dip nor the pattern of their foreign liabilities should be viewed as constituting weak long term fundamentals.

Our analysis of the Asian episode brings out the crucial role of liquidity, informational problems, and fragility of short term expectations in triggering off and accentuating a currency crisis. To be more specific, a combination of factors like a downturn in export demand, disproportionately large external liabilities in relation to foreign exchange reserves, and weakening of banks' balance sheets may force a country to renege on its foreign dues and suffer a currency crisis. The case is not dissimilar to that of a firm which, following the Modigliani–Miller principle[6], does not bother about

5 Entirely different was the experience of Great Britain following her severance of ties with the European Exchange Rate Mechanism in 1992. This enabled the country to pursue expansionary policies and enjoy higher levels of output and employment, promoting many commentators to suggest that the British should look up to George Soros, the currency trader generally held responsible for the crisis, as their benefactor, rather than regard him as a malevolent speculator.

6 The principle suggests that for valuation it does not matter whether a firm finances its operations through debts or equities (see Modigliani and Miller, 1958). This would indeed be true, were financial markets perfectly

the composition of its liability or variability of its earnings, and relies primarily on short term loans to finance its fixed investment and current expenditure. It is well known that even though such a firm's long run prospects may be good, it can face serious troubles, if not go bankrupt, when an unexpected and large shock produces a liquidity problem and the heightened uncertainty raises the perceived risk of lending to the firm.

While distinguishing between the European and the Asian crises we have already emphasized how central banks in the Asian–5 were in no position to defend their currencies in the event of an attack. When private traders recognize this situation, the outcome, it may be argued, should be a (self-fulfilling) speculative attack. However, in order to rationalise the attack, it is necessary to show that not only will the central bank let the currency float when confronted with an onslaught, but the free market exchange rate is also expected to be lower than the pegged one.[7]

The most important reason behind the expected depreciation of the exchange rate following the float is likely to be the same as that limiting the central bank's ability to ward off the attack, viz., difficulty of arranging for external loans or drying up of external sources of finance. Had the international lenders not taken a dim view of the country's future, the central bank could have easily defended the exchange rate peg, nor would its abandonment have been followed by depreciation.

Such a reading of the East Asian chain of events does not attach any special role to speculative attacks or self-fulfilling expectations, *a la* the second generation models, but focuses more on economic 'fundamentals', albeit of a different nature than those emphasized under the first (and second) generation theories. The basic problem in this case lies in drastic revisions in investors' expectations as the economy is buffeted by an adverse shock, new pieces of information relating to shortfall of usable forex reserves or magnitude of banks' non- performing assets become available and uncertainty regarding the true state of economic health of the country looms large. Under these conditions, external credit becomes scarce, and when the central bank gives up intervening in the foreign exchange market,

---

competitive and economic agents risk neutral (i.e., are guided solely by expected returns and costs).

7 Since otherwise there will be no speculative attack on the currency.

attempts on the part of domestic banks or corporates to meet their external debt obligations cannot but drive the value of the currency down. It is thus clear that any factor that can create serious liquidity problems has the potential of pushing a country into a currency crisis, irrespective of its long term fundamentals.

The severity of external credit crunch a country faces following some large negative shock depends also on the country's standing in the international financial market. When faced with pressing balance of payments problems, along with depressed economic conditions at home, Great Britain or France could, in the early 90s, have kept their currencies within the ERM band by inducing capital inflows through jacking up interest rates, provided they were prepared to endure a prolonged spell of unemployment and output loss. However, even though the long term fundamentals of South Korea, Malaysia, and Thailand were stronger, at least not worse than the European economies in distress, the former failed to attract foreign capital even when their interest rates went through the roofs.

The difficulties faced by the Asian economies in this connection were due in no small measure to thinness of their external capital markets, compounded by imperfect information and lack of transparency. When the market for financial assets issued by an economic agent is narrow or lacks depth, as it generally is in the case of bonds of relatively minor players in the capital market, a small set-back in investors' expectations can not only cause a disproportionate increase in interest rates, reflecting the enlarged risk premium, but the agent very often fails to secure loans even if he is willing to pay a very high interest rate. The Asian–5 appear to have suffered from similar problems in the wake of revised expectations regarding their economic prospects. Capital flows to East Asian countries grew, to be sure, by leaps and bounds during the period 1989–96. But these countries still accounted for a tiny fraction of the global capital market, and international investors, including banks and fund managers, did not have sufficient knowledge regarding the strength and weaknesses of these economies. It is no wonder then that the unexpected negative shock created a serious pressure in the countries' financial markets, made the central banks incapable of defending the currencies and triggered off a meltdown in exchange rates.

SELF-FULFILLING EXPECTATIONS

Recall that while in the first generation models crises cannot be attributed to speculation[8], in the second generation models speculators play a pivotal role, since in the absence of their attack the currency peg can survive indefinitely. Our account of the factors driving the course of Asian events suggests that narrowness of the external capital market, liquidity or payments problems, and the consequent change in investors' expectations can well produce a currency turmoil, even without a speculative attack. In this respect the situation corresponds to that in the canonical crisis model, even though there is nothing basically wrong with the economies' long term fundamentals. However, under the scenario considered above, a speculative attack, as in the second generation theories, can turn out to be decisive in causing the currency turmoil.

Note first that given the thinness of the capital market and extremely shaky informational base for forming expectations, noticeable pressure in the foreign exchange market may itself be regarded by many an investor as a sign of inherent weakness of the currency, especially when the weakness is accompanied by some negative information. When speculators are aware of such a fragile state of expectations, surfacing of some balance of payments or liquidity problems may induce them to expect abandonment of the peg followed by currency depreciation, in the event of a speculative attack. Hence arises the possibility of self-fulfilling expectations.

From an analytical viewpoint, it is useful to distinguish between the attack contingent crisis just considered and the role of speculation in the second generation models. In these models, speculators consider how the government's policy stance is expected to change following the attack and what the corresponding shadow exchange rate[9] will be. Under the scenario considered in the context of the Asian crisis, the problem did not lie primarily with (a) whether abandonment of the peg following the speculative attack was expected to be optimal for promoting the government's objectives, or (b) if the post-float policies would be expansionary enough to bring about a fall in the exchange rate. Given the large (short term)

---

8 Speculation, as we have seen in Chapter 2, only advances the date of the crisis in these models; but even without any speculative attack, crisis is inevitable sooner or later.

9 Which is nothing but the free market rate under the pure float.

payments obligations and small forex reserves, there could be little doubt that the central banks would be unable to defend the pegs. Again, the fact that sharp currency depreciations occurred in the face of highly restrictive monetary and fiscal policies[10] suggests that the behaviour of private agents following the attack and the currency float was decisive and this was what a rational speculator would have tried to anticipate. The analytical implication of such an experience is fairly simple: given the prevailing state of economic conditions and trends, if a speculative attack, by putting pressure on financial markets, is expected to seriously undermine confidence of the average investor, the result is likely to be a currency crisis driven by self-fulfilling expectations.

The nature of economic forces considered here is similar to those Keynes (1936) emphasizes in connection with share price movements, viz., short term expectations and their fragility arising from investors' attempt to guess what the average investors' expectations are. We have, following the second generation models, only gone a step further and suggested why a rational currency trader should take into account the attack contingent changes in market expectations or herd behaviour, and how as a result a currency crisis may be marked by self-fulfilling expectations.

However, as in the case of the first and second generation models, in this case also the speculative attack is not devoid of any objective basis. In the canonical theories, the basis is persistent overvaluation of the pegged exchange rate due to expansionary policies or some other fundamental imbalances. In the second generation models, it is the perception that the government's concern for growth and full employment will make the defence of the currency too costly that lies at the root of speculative attacks. The Asian experience brings out the importance of two sets of factors in making expectations volatile. The first relates to the thinness of the external market for a country's financial assets and the difficulty or high cost of gathering reliable information of its real and financial sectors. The second consists of factors, both real and financial, which tend to make the country's external payments and liquidity position vulnerable. A

10 In Chapters 4 and 6 we have explained why these policies were inappropriate for countering the crisis. We have also suggested how in a few instances anticipation of such policies could have put pressure on financial markets. Be that as it may, what mattered in setting the crisis in motion was the behaviour of private investors.

constellation of these two sets of factors, reinforced by the anticipation that policies to be followed by the government in order to contain pressure in the currency market will inflict heavy losses on corporates and banks, makes the situation ripe for a speculative attack and the onset of a currency crisis.

GUARDING AGAINST CURRENCY CRISES

In the context of the Latin American currency crisis, economists have discussed extensively the importance of export competitiveness, avoidance of overvalued exchange rates for prolonged periods, as also prudent macroeconomic management in general and containment of budget deficit in particular. In all these respects, as we have seen, the Asian scenario before the crisis was free from any blemish. The second generation theories bring out problems the government may face in securing exchange rate stability along with macroeconomic objectives. The solution to this problem is not radically different from what is suggested in the Latin American context, viz., avoidance of overvaluation and prudent macroeconomic management. Again, to the extent the attack contingent crises, *a la* the second generation theories, are damaging to the economy, modes of their prevention are basically the same as what we shall suggest on the basis of the Asian experience.[11]

In Chapter 3 we have indicated policy initiatives required for reducing vulnerability of the real sector, especially on the trading front, to adverse shocks on account of cyclical or other factors. Some of these measures are aimed at correcting for co-ordination failure[12] at the domestic or the global level, while others are designed to reduce risk arising from unforeseen changes in world demand for

11 Note that if the pound was not overvalued and the contractionary forces operating in 1992 were cyclical, Great Britain could have defended the currency and followed an expansionary policy, supported by borrowing from the international market. However, the fact that the policy changes in the second generation theories occur following speculative attacks suggests that the post-attack equilibrium is generally worse (since the government could have followed the policies without any attack). For avoiding such a situation, the country needs to take steps to discourage speculative attacks.

12 Resulting in sectoral overinvestment or underinvestment.

or supply of tradables, even though this may involve some loss of output in the long run. However, at the final stage of our inquiry our focus is on operation and management of the financial sector, since not only does the Asian crisis throw new light on the significance of avoiding financial fragility, but the structural imbalance in the real sector of the crisis countries may also be traced to the nature of their financial system.

MODE OF FINANCING

Strengthening the financial structure of an economy to make it resilient to adverse shocks requires 'improvement' in the balance sheets of producers, of financial institutions, and of the economy as whole. Even an otherwise efficient firm may be threatened with bankruptcy if (a) its debt–equity ratio is very high[13]; and (b) it does not have ready access to sufficient funds to tide over temporary difficulties. Remembering that a major source of vulnerability of East Asia arose from exceptionally high debt–equity ratios of firms, it is not difficult to appreciate why bringing down the ratio constitutes a major plank of the reforms programmes being implemented in crisis countries.[14]

Second and no less important, even with a relatively low leverage ratio, a firm may encounter a liquidity problem if investment projects yielding their return over a long period are financed by short or medium term loans. Since the debt market was underdeveloped in East Asian economies, producers in the region relied mostly on bank loans for investment, not only in working, but in fixed capital as well. The problem, however, was that, their major source of funds

13 The reason is fairly simple: a high debt–equity ratio implies a large ratio of fixed expenditure of a firm in relation to its revenue and hence enhances the probability that the firm will be forced to default on its debt obligations in case of adverse developments. This, is apart from the tendency (called the moral hazard problem) for producers to undertake high-risk ventures when the major source of finance is debt, rather than equity. See Chapter 5 for an account of how the moral hazard problem can distort investment decisions and lead to a crisis. Also relevant in this connection is Rakshit (1998a).

14 In Korea, for example, the conglomerates were required to bring down their leverage ratio from 400 to 500 per cent prevailing at the beginning of the crisis to 200 per cent or less by end 1999.

being short term deposits, banks could extend long term loans only at the cost of impairing the health of their balance sheets and making them vulnerable to shocks borrowing firms were exposed to. Hence arises the need for paying close attention, to not only the ratio of credit to equity finance, but also to the maturity structure of debts in relation to the expected time profile of cash flows from the assets held by firms.

Third, ready access to funds is essential for a producer to ensure that temporary troubles do not force him out of business. Since a firm will generally find it too costly to meet such liquidity requirement by holding bank deposits, it is necessary for it to undertake some portfolio investment or enter into agreement with banks for overdraft facilities. In most emerging market economies, including the East Asian ones, portfolio investment of firms was difficult in the absence of well functioning bond markets. Development of secondary markets for debt instruments is thus required both for maintaining balance in the structure of liabilities and assets of firms, and for meeting their precautionary demand for liquidity.

Of particular importance are rules relating to corporate borrowing from the international financial market. A major source of malady of the East Asian firms, especially those in Indonesia and Korea, was their external loans without any forward cover. Enterprises, engaged in production and distribution, are generally ill-equipped to bear the risk arising out of changes in exchange rates and interest rates in international capital markets. Such risks are better borne by specialized financial institutions and it is important for corporates to rely on these institutions for their foreign currency requirement or to take forward cover whenever they borrow from abroad.

STRENGTHENING THE BANKING SYSTEM

Since the currency crisis has exposed serious limitations in the working of the East Asian banks, the focus of long term policy initiatives in the region is on banking sector reforms. One part of the reforms programme aims at strengthening supervision of financial intermediaries by the central bank or some other regulatory authority. The other part relates to rules banks are required to follow in order to strengthen their capacity to cope with unforeseen contingencies and to guard against adverse developments degenerating into a crisis. The basic rules for promoting the shock-absorptive capacity of banks and strengthening their balance sheet position are similar to those for producers; but in view of their highly sensitive position[15] and special characteristics of their operations[16], banks need to be extra cautious and take adequate precautions against exchange rate and market risk; avoid connected lending; adhere to norms relating to capital adequacy, provisioning, etc.; and follow standard accounting practices. No less important is the strict enforcement of these rules on the part of the monetary authorities, since it is the regulatory incompetence-cum-forbearance that permits banks in many a country to persist with unsound practices until they are pushed to the brink of bankruptcy.

MANAGEMENT OF EXTERNAL ACCOUNT

The contrasting experiences of China[17] and the crisis countries during the East Asian financial turmoil suggest that it is not simply the banking sector problem but its mixture with capital account convertibility that makes an economy prone to currency crises and contagion from the rest of the world. This perception has produced two sets of policy conclusions, the first fairly unanimous, the second quite controversial. There is broad agreement among economists on the need for strengthening the banking sector, since apart from acting as a bulwark against the currency turmoil, a well functioning financial system is crucial for allocative efficiency and sustained growth. By now economists have also come to recognize the folly of going in for full capital account convertibility of a country's currency before ensuring the resilience of the financial sector and putting an efficient regulatory system in place. However, economists disagree sharply as to whether countries, even with well functioning financial systems, should permit unrestricted movement of capital.

15 Failure of a bank, especially of a big one, (unlike that of a firm) can trigger off a systemic crisis through run on other banks. See Rakshit (1998a).

16 Not only does the overwhelming part of a bank's fund comes from deposits and other kinds of debts, but its earnings, unlike that of a producer, depend crucially on the customers' ability, enterprise and integrity.

17 Also relevant in this connection is the experience of India, which, thanks to limited capital account convertibility of the rupee, could weather the Asian storm without serious difficulties.

CONTROLLING CAPITAL FLOWS

The basic source of disagreement among economists on the advisability of controlling international capital flows is not too difficult to discern. Unhindered movement of capital across national frontiers, *a la* mainstream economics, raises productivity of the world's investible resources[18]; acts as a powerful vehicle for transferring knowledge or technology from one country to another; and enables nations, through cross-holding of assets, to reduce the risk of large fluctuations in their income and shift towards high-risk, high-return ventures in their domestic production.[19] However, recent events have led many an influential economist to regard these gains from capital movement as relatively minor compared to their cost in terms of the extreme volatility countries become subject to.[20]

The debate concerning the salubrious or deleterious impact of capital mobility has, nevertheless, produced some consensus on a few important issues. Countries can derive considerable benefit from international capital movements, it is generally acknowledged, when they are driven by economic fundamentals or relatively longer term prospects. Second, not only does foreign direct investment constitute an important mechanism of technology transfer, but such investments also tend to remain stable even in the midst of currency turmoil.[21] Third, it is the scope for easy and frequent cross-border movement of funds that makes ephemeral factors the major determinant of capital flows, encourages herd behaviour among investors, and lies at the root of self-fulfilling expectations, lacking any firm, long term foundations.

The Asian crisis was, in fact, aggravated, if not triggered off, by disproportionately large share of short term borrowing and foreign

18 Through deployment of capital to places yielding the highest rate of return. We have discussed the issues in some detail in Rakshit (2001).

19 See Obstfeld and Rogoff (1996a) and Acemoglu and Zilibotti(1997).

20 See Bhagwati (1998), Rodrik(1997) and Stiglitz (1998). Long before the Asian crisis Tobin(1978) advocated a policy of putting 'sand in the global financial gears'.

21 Thus, while net private capital flows in the Asian–5 countries came down from a whopping US$62.9 billion in 1996 to –22.1 billion in 1997, –29.1 billion in 1998 and –18.1 billion in 1999, the figures for net FDI in the four years were US$8.4 billion, 10.3 billion, 9.7 billion and 9.4 billion respectively (IMF, October 1999).

institutional investment (FII) vis-à-vis FDI in the aggregate inflow of external funds. In the US$62.9 billion net private capital flows to the Asian–5 during 1996, net direct investment was no more than US$8.4 billion, while (net) FII and 'other net investment', consisting mostly of short term bank loans, amounted to US$20.3 and US$34.2 billion respectively. Over the three subsequent years, FDI remained fairly stable[22], but the other two types of investment, especially bank loans, recorded massive decline and turned negative. During 1997, 1998, and 1999, net FII amounted to US$12.9, US$–7.3, and US$4.5 billion respectively, and the corresponding figures for 'other net investment' were US$–45.3, US$–32.6, and US$–32.0 billion.[23]

In the light of the theoretical considerations and empirical evidence noted above, even the most ardent advocates of capital control do not recommend restrictions on foreign direct investment or long term external borrowing.[24] The controversy centres around the need for and feasibility of controlling short term capital movements. The ingenuity of economic agents in exploiting legal loopholes, the ease and impunity with which they can (thanks to the internet revolution) effect clandestine financial transactions and incompetence, if not venality, of government administration in emerging market economies—all these are deemed to make measures for restricting cross-border financial flows quite ineffective. Such measures, it is also suggested, entail considerable cost, since they distort the market mechanism and result in inefficient allocation of resources.[25]

22 See the preceding footnote.

23 The Latin American experience, including the recent financial turmoil in Brazil, also confirms these characteristics of the three categories of capital flows.

24 This is not to suggest that such flows do not create any problem. However, we propose to ignore the problems here, our focus being on prevention of currency crises, without undue sacrifice of a country's long term growth potential.

25 By raising the cost of credit for working capital, exports and imports, restrictions on inflow of short-term funds tend to produce a negative impact on a country's economy. Even 'speculative' capital movements, when based on informed judgements, may play a positive role: by hastening the adjustment in currency and credit markets, speculators can enhance productivity of factors under the changing economic environment.

Efficiency gains from short term capital movements are, however, crucially dependent on the absence of herd behaviour and moral hazard, and on constant endeavour on the part of (leading) investors in tracking changes in economic fundamentals rather than 'in beating the gun' by outguessing 'the psychology of the market' (Keynes, 1936). As the increasing incidence of currency crises since the late 1970s strongly suggests, short term capital flows do not, in fact, take place under such favourable scenarios. Not only has the cost of transferring funds from one centre to another come down dramatically in recent years, but distribution of financial assets across a large number of countries by banks and pension funds has also reduced their incentive to devote resources for assessing the economic health of enterprises (or countries), and hence, given rise to serious moral hazard problems. No wonder, then, that empirical studies have failed to detect any beneficial impact of non-FDI capital inflows on their recipients.[26] Again, the experience of a number of countries like China, India, and Chile, not renowned for their administrative competence, shows that curbs on capital inflows are not too difficult to implement, and enable emerging market economies to weather financial storms raging in their neighbourhood. However, since outright ban and quantitative restrictions on even short term flows may create difficulties for producers and traders and tend to promote corruption, most economists favour a Chile-type scheme[27] of imposing taxes on inflow of foreign funds, with higher rates for inflows having shorter lock-in periods.[28]

26 Note that the overwhelming part of non-FDI capital flows consists of FII and short term loans from banks. A World Bank study (World Bank, 1999) for a sample of 18 countries did not show any statistically significant positive association between non-FDI capital inflows and productivity growth. Indeed, for the subsample of low-saving countries, the result was statistically significant, but 'the association was strongly negative'!

27 From May 1992 to May 1998, 30 per cent of all foreign borrowings in Chile were required to be held in the form of one-year non-interest bearing deposits with the central bank. Since the holding period was the same for all non-equity inflows, the implicit cost, in terms of interest earnings foregone, was higher for loans of shorter maturity period. The scheme was also transparent and left no room for discretion of the officials.

28 The plan suggested here, unlike that in Chile, covers both loan and equity inflows in order to discourage FII of a purely speculative nature.

ADEQUACY OF FOREIGN EXCHANGE RESERVES

Maintenance of 'sufficient' foreign exchange reserves, it has long been recognized, constitutes an important cushion against external shocks. The potency of such reserves in defending a country's currency has been demonstrated by the contrasting experiences of China, Hong Kong and Taiwan on the one hand and that of the Asian–5 on the other. At the end of October 1997, foreign exchange reserves held by China, Hong Kong and Taiwan amounted to US$139.9, US$91.8 and US$82.9 billion respectively. The result was that even while the Asian–5 currencies were undergoing a meltdown, China and Hong Kong were able to keep their exchange rates fixed against the US dollar. Taiwan let her exchange rate float in October 1997; but during the worst period of currency market meltdown, lasting from October 1997 to August 1998, the Taiwanese exchange rate fell from 30.4 to only 34.7 per US dollar. The source of this resilience is not far to seek. Not only do adequate foreign exchange reserves empower the central bank to ward off speculative attacks through intervention in the forex market, but the very existence of large reserves acts as a most effective deterrent against attacks on the country's currency.

How much foreign exchange reserves should the central bank hold? The question is prompted by the fact that holding of these reserves is not costless to the economy. By their very nature, the central bank's foreign assets need to be liquid[29] and their average yield is significantly less than the interest rate or return on foreign investment in the country. Hence arises the need for some cost–benefit estimates of holding forex reserves or maintaining them at, what economists call, the optimum level.[30]

In the absence of capital account convertibility, the currency market is driven primarily by trade flows[31] so that the central

29 These assets are generally held in the form of foreign currency and government securities.

30 At which net benefits of holding foreign exchange reserves are maximized. While costs of holding these reserves are not too difficult to estimate, serious problems arise in measuring their benefits, remembering that the major source of gains consists in smoothing out occasional, but temporary mismatches of inflows and outflows of foreign funds and avoiding volatility in the currency market. No wonder, then, that most central banks use some rule of thumb on the basis of their own and others' experiences.

31 Since the supply side of the foreign currency market reflects export earnings and the demand side payments required for imports. With capital

bank's task becomes relatively easy: monetary authorities have found that forex reserves amounting to 4 to 5 months' import bill are generally sufficient to take care of non-synchronization of export earnings and payments on account of imports. It is international capital flows in general, and FII or short term loans in particular, that make estimates of the optimum extremely difficult and force central banks to hold large foreign reserves for preventing currency crises. Indeed, in view of the fact that a substantial part of non-FDI capital inflows has to go into additional reserves, there are strong grounds for limiting such flows on the basis of their benefit–cost considerations.[32] While such controls should go a long way in reducing a country's vulnerability to currency turmoil and effecting substantial economy in the central bank's holding of forex reserves, it is also necessary to keep track of the maturity structure of other external liabilities (especially medium and longer term loans) and avoid bunching of payments obligations.

Finally for the reputation of the central bank. An important factor behind the rush for withdrawing funds from the East Asian economies was, as we have seen in earlier chapters, lack of reliable information, especially the revelation that the balance sheets hitherto published by the central banks were highly misleading.[33] Apart from the fact that maintenance and publication of accurate accounts (and their transparency) enable the central bank as also economic agents to take timely action[34], they also constitute an important bulwark against unfounded panic and speculative attack on a country's currency.

---

account convertibility, the currency market is dominated by inflows and outflows of foreign funds, with factors governing trade coming to occupy a peripheral role.

32 From a sample of 18 countries enjoying substantial capital inflows in the 1980s and early 1990s, it has been estimated that each US$1 of non-FDI capital receipt leads to only US$0.60 of additional investment in the economy, so that the country generally suffers a net loss on account of these inflows (World Bank, 1999).

33 The resulting loss of credibility led investors to suspect that the financial health of the economy was far worse than what it actually was.

34 Transparency of the external balance sheet can constitute an important factor in putting a timely damper on undue exuberance of foreign investors and hence in avoiding a surge of inflows culminating in a crash.

CHOICE OF EXCHANGE RATE REGIME

The central bank's choice relating to the exchange rate system is universally viewed as a crucial factor in promoting or undermining resilience of an economy to external shocks; but there is considerable disagreement on the exchange rate regime most appropriate for emerging market economies. An important source of currency crises, it is generally perceived, lies in pegging the exchange rate, and the consequent tendency over time for its overvaluation, and hence, erosion of the country's export competitiveness. Such a perception has produced two diametrically opposite policy recommendations. Rejecting the system of adjustable exchange rate pegs, one group of economists, including Dornbusch (1999), suggests the adoption of a full-fledged currency board system, but the other group goes to the opposite extreme and advocates a fully flexible exchange rate regime.

CURRENCY BOARD AND DOLLARIZATION

Even before the East Asian crisis, quite a few countries, for example Argentina, Hong Kong, Estonia, and Bulgaria, had already switched over to the currency board system[35] (CBS). Under this system (as in a fixed exchange rate regime) there is complete convertibility of the domestic currency at a fixed rate against the US dollar or some other major currency (for example, the mark in the case of Estonia and Bulgaria). The distinguishing feature of the CBS is, however, that the entire amount of the country's reserve money is backed by holding of dollars. The extreme version of this system is dollarization, under which the local currency is abolished and the US dollar circulates as the medium of exchange.[36]

Though under both the currency board system (CBS) and dollarization, the central bank loses its power of controlling money supply, the loss is total in the latter case. The reason is that while

---

35 At one stage during the Asian financial turmoil, Indonesia seriously considered adoption of the CBS as a way out of its troubles, but finally abandoned the plan.

36 Panama's monetary system was dollarized as early as 1905. In the aftermath of the Brazilian currency crisis in 1998, Argentina considered the option of becoming dollarized, but finally did not adopt the system. However, as a way out of her persistent economic troubles, Ecuador has recently replaced her currency by the US dollar.

absence of local currency leaves no scope whatsoever for pursuit of any monetary policy, under the CBS the central bank can affect money supply to a certain extent through raising or lowering the bank rate or the cash reserve ratio. Even when the CBS is considered impregnable and international investors do not perceive any exchange rate risk, non-homogeneity of the domestic and US financial assets, arising from differences in the interest rate, market or default risk, may produce inter-country interest differentials. Hence arises some scope for loosening or tightening domestic money supply. But this scope, it is not difficult to see, is extremely limited.

In many instances, the economic rationale of going in for the CBS or dollarization lies primarily in curbing domestic inflation. In fact, this is the main reason why such exchange rate systems have been widely advocated for the Latin American countries, given their long history of lax monetary and fiscal policies, hyper-inflation and capital flights arising from overvaluation or exchange rate instability. The CBS acts as a disciplining device on the authorities, and apart from eliminating exchange rate instability, provides a built-in mechanism against high inflation. When the gap between the domestic and the US price increases becomes large, the consequent overvaluation leads to an automatic decline in base money and puts a brake on price increases. Apart from the direct benefits accruing from price stability, the economy also gains through restoration of investors' confidence, prevention of capital flights[37] and inflow of foreign capital.

However, for the vast majority of developing countries including India, the currency board system does not appear to be an attractive option. Note that the CBS is very similar in its impact to the gold standard in its pristine form.[38] No wonder, countries adopting the CBS find it difficult to maintain full employment or internal balance when they are subjected to some negative shock or there are major changes in the demand or supply conditions of their tradables.

The benefits due to elimination of the exchange rate risk may also be much less than are generally presumed. To the extent the country experiences frequent bouts of unemployment and underutilization

---

37 Which were regarded as one of the major obstacles to Latin American economic development.

38 See Box 2.1, Chapter 2 for an account of the problems countries face under the gold standard in preserving external and internal balance.

of capacity on account of adherence to the CBS, it will be deemed unattractive to invest in, despite the absence of exchange rate volatility. Again, remembering that the commitment to the CBS can never be perceived to be 100 per cent and that the central bank has to build up and establish its reputation over a fairly long stretch of time[39], there can be severe speculative attacks on the country's currency when financial turmoils rage in the neighbourhood and the real sector of the economy is on a steeply downward course. Indeed, in order to preserve the CBS, the central bank then has to raise interest rates, and aggravate thereby the problems of unemployment and output loss.

That the aforesaid difficulties are not purely hypothetical is underlined by recent experiences of Hong Kong and Argentina. Despite possessing huge dollar reserves, Hong Kong raised domestic interest rates to astronomical levels following the outbreak of the Asian crisis. Indeed, the currency board system, as we have seen in Chapter 6, turned out to be a veritable albatross round the country's neck and she had to suffer from substantial decline in output and employment over the period 1997–9. We have also observed, how recovery of Hong Kong's real sector lagged way behind her neighbours' as a result of (a) sharp appreciation of the HK dollar vis-à-vis other currencies of the region, and (b) persistence with high interest policies. Argentina also had to endure a similar fate during 1998–2000. The country's malady during this period was due to contagion from the Brazilian crisis. However, while floating of the real in January 1999 practically marked the end of the crisis for Brazil and the country's GDP started showing rapid and sustained recovery fairly soon[40], production and employment in Argentina recorded massive declines in 1999 and remained depressed throughout 2000.

No less serious for developing countries can be problems of a long term nature, associated with the currency board system. First, given the difficulties of raising tax revenue in these countries,

---

39 Even when the CBS has been in place for a sufficiently long time, investors, remembering the fate of the gold standard (and of the Bretton Woods system, with all its safeguards), may harbour doubts regarding the central bank's commitment when the country is suffering from severe unemployment and depression.

40 See Rakshit (1999a).

seignorage or monetized financing[41] can constitute a none-too-negligible source of meeting the government's development and other expenditure.[42] Under the currency board regime, however, the entire reserve money, being held against an equivalent amount of dollar, constitutes a transfer of resources to the USA[43] —a transfer which a poor nation can ill afford on a continuing basis.

Again, the country adopting the CBS automatically subjects itself to the vagaries of the US economy and policies pursued by the Federal Reserve Board and the government of the United States. The system may work so long as the US economy enjoys steady growth and remains the major trading partner of the country concerned. However, these conditions are unlikely to be satisfied in the medium and the long run. Thus, if over time the nature of comparative advantage of the country changes and trade with the USA becomes relatively minor, having the same nominal exchange rate with other currencies as the US dollar can prove a major source of inefficiency and involve significant cost of adjustment in the pattern of trade and domestic production.

Finally, a currency board system reduces the central bank's ability to act as the lender of last resort. This heightens the probability of 'runs' on financial institutions[44] and of banking crises which, with

41 The increase in demand for additional reserve money as the economy grows over time implies that the government can finance part of its expenditure by printing currency without creating any inflationary pressure. Additional monetized financing beyond some level is inflationary and tends to reduce the demand for real balances. But upto a point monetized financing still raises the government's command over real goods and services as the increase in reserve money outweighs the fall in the demand for real balances. Hence the concept of maximizing seignorage.

42 The tax constraint, along with large interest payments on public debt, forces governments in many developing countries including India to cut back on their expenditure on social services and infrastructural investment. Under these conditons, monetized deficit, the safe limit to which is estimated to be about 1.5 per cent of full employment GDP, can be an important instrument for promoting economic and social objectives.

43 In the absence of the currency board system, when the government does not take recourse to seignorage, the additional reserve money reflects the central bank's advances to domestic producers and investors.

44 Depositors become much more shaky when they know that their bank, even though healthy, will go bankrupt in the event of a run, with no succour available from the central bank.

capital account convertibility, generally trigger off a currency crisis as well.

CLEAN FLOAT VERSUS DIRTY FLOAT

In view of the high economic cost of the currency board arrangement and of the fact that even adjustable pegged rates have been targets of speculative attacks, very often of a self-fulfilling nature, many economists favour a system of clean float, under which the exchange rate is left severely alone by the central bank. Under such a system, speculation against the currency reduces its sales price[45], but the exchange rate appreciates when traders subsequently want to buy the currency back in order to repay loans or restore the composition of their portfolio. These considerations are deemed to make costs of speculation higher, and hence, currency crises less likely under a pure float than in a pegged exchange rate system.[46]

We have also noted in Chapter 2 how exchange rate flexibility permits the government to attain both internal and external balance. Thus, when the country experiences a negative demand shock in its external sector, not only does the resulting depreciation serve as an automatic macro-stabilizer to a certain extent, but the government is also not constrained to pursue expansionary policies, and can let the exchange rate find its new equilibrium level corresponding to full employment of resources. A market driven exchange rate also makes easier the adjustment of the country's structure of production and investment in line with the country's changing comparative advantage.

The major problem with a clean float, as economist have recognized for long, lies in sharp fluctuations or instability of the exchange rate and the consequent risk, to which exporters and importers become subject. This produces an adverse impact on domestic industries catering to the export market or firms dependent for their operations on imported inputs. Traders, it is true, can guard against the exchange rate risk by entering into contracts for forward sale or purchase of foreign currencies; but given the thinness

45 i.e., there is a depreciation of the currency.

46 Under which the trader can buy foreign against domestic currency at a fixed rate and does not stand to lose much even if the attack is unsuccessful (so long as transactions costs are not too high). See Chapter 2 in this connection.

of the market for foreign exchange in emerging economies, the contracts tend to be quite costly and are available in most cases upto a period of six months. The result is that under a fully flexible exchange rate regime, relatively long term production and investment in export oriented or import intensive industries are difficult to plan, and allocation of the country's resources becomes sub-optimal.

It is also far from clear how far a fully flexible exchange rate regime is effective in guarding against the adverse economic consequences associated with currency crises. The post-Bretton Woods era has seen cycles of undue exhuberance and pessimism regarding the prospects of quite a few emerging economies. In such cases, a surge of capital inflows, unless tempered by central bank interventions in the currency market, tends to cause an appreciation of the exchange rate, an increase domestic consumption, a decline in export industries and allocation of resources in favour of non-tradables and import-substituting sectors—features which economists sum up by the sobriquet the 'Dutch disease'.[47] When the market turns pessimistic, the fall in the value of the currency creates serious troubles for domestic corporates and banks which have piled up substantial external liabilities in their balance sheets. Indeed, such balance sheet difficulties, as we have discussed earlier, can further undermine investors' confidence and degenerate into a banking-cum-currency crisis.

It thus appears, on balance, that an emerging market economy cannot afford a free float with no central bank intervention whatsoever. However, the East Asian turmoil, as also the experience of other crisis countries, suggests that while managing the float, the authorities need to take a few supplementary measures of safeguards. First, as argued earlier, the government has to exercise some control over short term capital flows, preferably through the market rather than quantitative restrictions. Second, the objective of the central bank should be to iron out sharp fluctuations and prevent significant over- (or under-) valuation of the currency. Third, even though the basic goal of the central bank's intervention in the currency market

---

47 In the case of the Netherlands the problem arose due to discovery of and large export earnings from petroleum. In recent times many oil exporting developing countries, particularly Nigeria, suffered from a similar fate following sky-rocketing of oil prices in the 1970s and their subsequent collapse in the 80s.

is quite clear, it should not announce a specific exchange rate target, so that currency traders are denied a one-way option and discouraged from mounting a speculative attack, based on mere rumour or self-fulfilling expectations.

INTERNATIONAL FINANCIAL ARRANGEMENTS: A GLOBAL LENDER OF LAST RESORT?

The East Asian currency crisis has underscored how in a globalized financial market even economies with strong fundamentals can be seriously buffeted by currency turmoil resulting from self-fulfilling expectations, and how easily the crisis spreads from one economy to another. These problems are similar to those present in the domestic banking sector, where a temporary liquidity crisis may well cause a 'run' on an otherwise healthy bank, or bank-specific difficulties set off a systemic crisis. At the domestic level, the twin problems are tackled by the central bank acting as the lender of last resort. Such considerations have led many an economist to advocate an arrangement under which the IMF or some newly constituted body can function as an international banker of last resort.

The plan for what amounts to a global central bank is not new[48], but there appears to be little likelihood of establishment of such an institution in the foreseeable future. The plan is bound to founder on the rock of strong opposition by the G-7 countries[49] in general and the USA in particular.[50] These countries would be quite unwilling to forego their dominance in international financial policy making and surrender their monetary policy autonomy to a supranational organization, presumed to look after the interest of the global economy as a whole. Again, in order to effectively play the role of the lender of last resort, not only has the control of world money supply to be vested with the organisation, but it must also have the requisite regulatory-cum-supervisory power over all national,

48 Keynes's plan for the International Monetary Fund was similar, but it did not find favour with the United States and other countries.

49 Consisting of the USA, Japan, Germany, France, the UK, Italy, and Canada.

50 Note that, thanks to the overwhelming importance of the dollar as a vehicle currency, and hence its large share in reserve accumulation of central banks, the USA has been able to invest at a decent rate despite a near-zero domestic rate of saving.

central, and commercial banks—something which is unlikely to be acceptable to most countries in the world.

There are also serious economic difficulties attendant upon a global economy operating with (virtually) a single currency. The major difficulty arises from the fact that phasing of cyclical fluctuations is generally quite different in various parts of the world: booming business conditions in some countries may go hand in hand with severe downturn in others. Hence, the monetary policy followed by the global central bank cannot simultaneously be appropriate for both sets of economies, and the burden of anti-cyclical policies is likely to prove too difficult for fiscal authorities alone.

While the scheme for a global central bank appears utopian at this stage, some progress may be made in reducing the vulnerability of emerging market economies without too radical a change in the existing international financial arrangements. As has been demonstrated time and again, the IMF's own resources are woefully inadequate, with the result that in times of crises it had to rely heavily on G-7 countries for providing financial support to the beleaguered economies.[51] Apart from the fact that decisions on bailout packages and their scale have often been influenced by political and not simply economic considerations, serious moral hazard problems have also been created by rescuing irresponsible lenders[52] and profligate borrowers. Hence, even if the IMF is not empowered to print global currency, resources available to the institution need to be raised substantially, taking into account the volume of international transactions on current and capital accounts.

Second, the IMF support to countries in trouble must be rule based and extended to those that follow international practices relating to transparency and regular publication of macroeconomic and financial accounts, and enforce prudential norms for banks and corporates. This condition should not be too difficult to impose, considering the fact that since the onset of the Asian crisis more and more countries have been trying to adopt international best practice norms in their financial sector, and have become aware of the need

---

51 In times of both the Mexican and the East Asian crisis, the IMF's own contribution to the rescue packages was quite small in relation to that provided by the major industrialized countries.

52 All of whom were from the US and other advanced countries.

for gathering accurate information and its regular and wide dissemination.

Third, the IMF support, if and when required, should be designed to restore macroeconomic stability and protect the vulnerable sections of the society, and not for providing succour to international lenders or to corporates and banks unable to meet their obligations. The task of designing a rescue package promoting these objectives is by no means simple, but the general principle is clear enough: bailout of an organization should be conditional on replacement of top management and scaling down cum rescheduling of repayments to foreign lenders.[53]

CRISIS MANAGEMENT

The measures suggested above are expected to be preventive, but do not rule out the emergence of currency turmoils. So far as crisis management is concerned, disagreement among economists is much sharper than in respect of measures for promoting longer-term resilience to shocks in the foreign exchange market. Particularly controversial has been the role of IMF sponsored policies in aggravating or resolving the East Asian crisis. The major and contentious issues arising in this context revolve around the following questions:

• Should there be temporary capital controls in the event of a serious crisis?
• What should be the package of monetary and fiscal measures for countering the crisis?
• Should the government embark on vigorous economic and structural reforms, especially in the financial and corporate sectors, in the midst of a currency turmoil?

53 A number of economists have drawn attention to the fact that IMF bailout encourages moral hazard problems in respect of government policies. Governments, to be sure, can, and have often been, quite profligate, piling up external debt without raising countries' capacity for its servicing. However, over the last two decades accumulation of external liability by emerging market economies has mostly been on private account, not due to government borrowing. Moreover, it is much easier to verify and monitor the government's balance sheet and trends of the items entering therein, than those for private corporates and banks.

CAPITAL CONTROL

When an economy is seriously rocked a by currency turmoil, temporary restrictions on capital outflows may prove quite effective in preventing a precipitous fall in the country's exchange rate and permitting inflow of essential imports. That is what Malaysia did in September 1998 in order to defend the ringgit against speculative onslaught. There is a good deal of disagreement among economists regarding the role of these controls in the Malaysian recovery (see Lane *et al*, 1999). There can however, be little doubt that on the heels of measures for curbing capital outflow, Malaysia could (or was emboldened to) pursue expansionary fiscal and monetary policies for countering the recessionary forces raging in the real sector.

The major argument against suspension of capital outflow is that, even when temporary, such measures lead to a loss of the country's reputation or credibility and consequently produce a negative impact on its future ability to access the international capital market. The argument does not seem very convincing. The hard nosed lender can distinguish between (a) a situation where the economy is beyond redemption or where rolling forward of all external debts will be of little avail in its recovery; and (b) the case where the troubles can be overcome if the country is provided some breathing space. In the second situation, while it is perfectly sensible for an individual investor to try to beat others in exiting from the troubled economy, though knowing fully well that such a scramble cannot but force the economy to default, every investor may well heave a sigh of relief at a temporary moratorium on withdrawal of funds, inasmuch as it enables the country to recover, and eventually honour, its external obligations.[54]

Recall that controls on non-FDI capital inflows in general and those on FII and short term borrowings in particular, have figured prominently in our list of preventive measures. Were such controls already in place, countries facing troubles on the external front would not have to renege on their payments obligations or to worry about their reputation. But for a country already burdened

---

54 This is yet another example of isolation paradox or fallacy of composition where results of individuals acting in isolation are worse than the outcome when everybody is forced to conform to some collective decision or rules imposed from above.

with substantial non-FDI liabilities, restrictions on capital outflows may prove a potent weapon in fighting speculative attacks on its currency.

Monetary and Fiscal Policies: The most controversial policy issue surfacing in the aftermath of the Asian debacle has been the type of fiscal and monetary measures required for crisis management. In general, pressure in the foreign exchange markets is sought to be reduced through an increase in interest rates. This raises the returns on domestic financial assets vis-à-vis their foreign counterparts and helps thereby in checking the outflow of capital or attracting fresh flows. After the outbreak of the currency crisis, all Asian countries, including the ones which did not seek IMF assistance, followed a highly restrictive monetary policy. Under the IMF bailout programmes, countries like Thailand had also to strive for fiscal correction in order to emit the right signal to international investors and meet the cost of restructuring their tottering financial sectors. Other countries also did not dare, for quite some time, to deviate from this well-trodden path.

Pursuit of these policies not only failed to prevent meltdown of Asian currencies, but the countries, as we have seen, also suffered from severe contractions in output and employment. It is for this reason that the Asian experience has raised serious doubts regarding the efficacy of the orthodox mix of monetary–fiscal measures for weathering an incipient or ongoing currency turmoil. We have discussed elsewhere in some detail[55] why the fiscal-cum-monetary squeeze in a country produces a negative impact on its neighbours[56] and can be seriously detrimental for the country's financial sector (apart from its real sector). The major deficiency of the IMF-sponsored policies, we have emphasized, lay in the neglect of two fundamental economic considerations.

The first involves the fallacy of composition: given the close trading and financial links among the East Asian economies, attempts on the part of each country to stabilize its currency market by raising interest rates to astronomical levels and following a contractionary fiscal policy could not but prove ruinous for the region as a whole.

55 See Chapters 4 and 6.
56 By reducing their exports and raising the inter-country interest differential.

Second, any policy that darkens the short-and medium-run prospects of the real sector of an economy, can hardly instil investors' confidence in the country's ability to discharge its future dues. To use a not-too-inappropriate analogy, a firm is unlikely to secure loans even if it offers to pay a very high rate of interest, if the rate is seen to be too burdensome, and the firm is facing, or expected to encounter, a serious demand deficiency problem.

The IMF itself has now recognized that its insistence on budgetary squeeze by the crisis countries was somewhat unwarranted[57] (Lane, 1999). A better approach would have been adoption of a two-pronged policy, with high interest rates for stabilizing the currency market, and fiscal expansion to neutralize the contractionary impact of monetary measures. However, such a policy, though attractive on paper, was unlikely to work in the Asian context. The basic reason lay in the weaknesses of financial firms and high leverage ratios of the corporates. Given these features, a high interest policy would put banks and corporates in serious distress and cause large-scale bankruptcies or a systemic crisis.[58]

The most effective way of dealing with a currency turmoil thus appears to consists in a combination of (a) temporary restrictions on capital outflows; (b) maintenance and strengthening of domestic credit lines; and (c) fiscal measures designed to prevent a slide of the real sector.

INTERNATIONAL CO-OPERATION

Note that the policy package suggested above does not include erection of direct or indirect import barriers, since such measures deepen the crisis elsewhere and constitute a negative-sum game. Our analysis also underscores the need for concerted action—in respect of fiscal, monetary, and exchange rate policies—by countries that have strong trading and financial links. Since such a course of action is of immense mutual benefit in times of crises, it should not

---

57 Given the fact that fiscal rectitude had been a hallmark of the Asian tiger economies, the IMF recommendations betrayed routine reliance on conventional wisdom without any serious attempt at appreciating the specificities of the problem at hand.

58 Note that expansionary fiscal measures push up interest rates further, remembering that additional government borrowing from the financial sector is not met by monetary easing.

be too difficult to evolve a consultative mechanism for co-ordinated policy plans and their execution.

STRUCTURAL REFORMS IN THE MIDST OF CRISES

The 1997–9 crisis, as we have seen, exposed some serious structural chinks in the armour of the East Asian economies, the most important of which were financial fragility, and building up of large capacity by corporates in several, often unrelated areas, on the basis of huge borrowing. It is for this reason that under the IMF assistance programmes the countries have been trying to carry through rapid and extensive reforms in both financial and corporate sectors. The major initiatives in this regard have been in the form of closure of non-viable banks; recapitalization of the surviving ones; adoption and strict enforcement of the Basle prudential norms; scaling down of debt–equity ratios of corporates; and restructuring of the business sector by arm-twisting companies to hive off units not closely related to their core operations and encouraging takeover or mergers of firms engaged in similar lines of business. Most of these measures should undoubtedly form part of a long term programme for promoting efficiency and reducing vulnerability of the economy; but their adoption in the midst of crises can be quite counterproductive. An increase in the capital adequacy ratio and enforcement of other Basle norms tend to reduce availability of credit to the commercial sector and can set off a string of bankruptcies among firms crucially dependent on bank loans for their operation.[59] Closure of a bank without simultaneously putting in place alternative arrangements for supplying credit to its borrowers will have a similar effect.[60] Requiring corporates to drastically bring down their debt equity ratio without developing an equity market puts even otherwise healthy firms in serious jeopardy. In fact, not only is the development of such a market quite time consuming, but even in economies with a long established equity cult, asking companies to substitute their debts for equities in the midst of a crisis betrays

59 Given the fact that banks are the most important, often the only, source of credit in emerging market economies.

60 By the very nature of credit disbursal process in banks, it is extremely difficult for firms to access a new bank at short notice for their credit requirement.

utter confusion between long term solutions to problems and requirements in times of emergency.[61]

It is for these reasons that (a) the timing and pace of reforms programmes have to be adapted to the phases of business cycles; and (b) steps for promoting long term goals, when taken in times of a crisis, should be accompanied by an effective programme for neutralizing their short term depressionary impact. The most important point to note in this connection is that, such an impact cannot be countered, as is often argued, by adopting an easy money or expansionary fiscal policy. The reason is that the effects of reforms measures are structural and take the form of ruptures in the credit delivery system, closure of firms or severe unemployment in particular sectors—effects which overall macroeconomic policies are ill suited to roll back in the short run.

---

61 In Korea the conglomerates were given more than two years to bring down their leverage ratio to below 200 per cent. What is more interesting, the requirement was met primarily by forcing banks to convert loans into equities—a step that was palpably contrary to the long term restructuring programme of the banking sector.

References

Acemoglu, D. and F. Zilibotti (1997), 'Was Prometheus Unbound by Chance? Risk, Diversification and Growth', *Journal of Political Economy*, 105, 5 August.

Agenor, P., J. Bhandari and R. Flood (1992), 'Speculative Attacks and Models of Balance of Payments Crises', *IMF Staff Papers*, June.

Amsden, Alice H. and Yoon-Dae Euh (1990), 'Republic of Korea's Financial Reform: What are the Lessons?', UNCTAD Discussion Paper no. 30, April 1990.

Asian Development Bank (1997), *Asian Development Outlook 1997 and 1998* (Oxford University Press: New York).

Banerjee, A. (1992), 'A Simple Model of Herd Behavior,' *Quarterly Journal of Economics*, 107, pp. 797–817.

Bank for International Settlements (1996), *Central Bank Survey of Foreign Exchange and Derivatives Market Activity*, Basle, May.

Bhagwati, J. (1998), 'The Capital Myth: The Difference Between Trade in Widgets and Trade in Dollars', *Foreign Affairs*, 77, 3.

Blinder, A.S. (1987), 'Credit Rationing and Effective Supply Failures', *Economic Journal*, 97, June.

Calvo, G.A. and E.C.G. Mendonza (1996), 'Petty Crime and Cruel Punishment: Lessons from the Mexican Debacle', *American Economic Review*, Proceedings of the American Economic Association, 86, 2, May.

Ding, W., I. Domac and G. Ferri (1998), 'Is there a Credit Crunch in East Asia?', Policy Research Working Paper Series, World Bank, June.

Dornbusch, R. (1999), 'Emerging Market Crisis: Origins and Remedies', *website: web. mit. edu/dornbusch.*

Eichengreen, B., A. Rose and C. Wyplosz (1995), 'Exchange Market Mayhem: The Antecedents and Aftermath of Speculative Attacks', *Economic Policy*, 21, October.

Flood, R.P. and P. Garber (1984), 'Collapsing Exchange-Rate Regimes: Some Linear Examples', *Journal of International Economics*, 17, August.

Flood, R.P. and Nancy P. Marion (1996), 'Speculative Attacks: Fundamentals and Self-Fulfilling Prophesies', NBER Working Paper 5789.

282   *References*

Flood, R.P. and Nancy P. Marion (1998), 'Perspectives on the Recent Currency Crisis Literature', IMF Working Paper No. WP/98/130.

Girton, L. and D. Roper (1977), 'A Monetary Model of Exchange Market Pressure Applied to Postwar Canadian Experience', *American Economic Review*, 76.

Government of India (1997), *Economic Survey*, 1996–7.

International Monetary Fund (1996), *World Economic Outlook*, May.

International Monetary Fund (1997), *International Financial Statistics Yearbook*, 1996.

International Monetary Fund (1997), *World Development Outlook*, December.

International Monetary Fund (1998), *World Economic Outlook and International Capital Markets*, December.

International Monetary Fund (1999), *World Economic Outlook*, October.

International Monetary Fund (2000), *International Financial Statistics Yearbook*, 1999.

Keynes, J.M. (1936), *The General Theory of Employment, Interest and Money*, Macmillan, London.

Krugman, P. (1979), 'A Model of Balance-of-Payments Crises', *Journal of Money, Credit and Banking*, August.

Krugman, P. (1994), 'The Myth of Asia's Miracle', *Foreign Affairs*, November.

Krugman, P. (1997), 'Currency Crises: National Bureau of Economic Research Conference'.

Krugman, P. (1998), 'What happened to Asia'? *website: web.mit.edu.krugman*

Kuznets, S. (1946), *National Product Since 1869*, National Bureau of Economic Research.

Kuznets, S. (1946a), *National Income: A Summary of Findings*, National Bureau of Economic Research.

Lane, Timothy *et al.* (1999), 'IMF-Supported Programmes in Indonesia, Korea, and Thailand: A Preliminary Assessment', Occasional Paper No. 178, IMF, Washington D.C.

McKinnon, R. (1973), *Money and Capital in Economic Development*, The Brookings Institution: Washington DC.

Modigliani, F. and M.H. Miller (1958), 'The Cost of Capital, Corporate Finance and Theory of Investment', *American Economic Review*, 48, June.

Obstfeld, M. (1986), 'Rational and Self-fulfilling Balance of Payments Crises', *American Economic Review*, March.

Obstfeld, M. (1994), 'The Logic of Currency Crises', *Cahiers Economiques et Monetaires*, 43, Bank of France.

Obstfeld, M. (1996), 'Models of Currency Crises with Self-Fulfilling Features', *European Economic Review*, 40(3–5), pp. 1037–47.

Obstfeld, M. and K. Rogoff, (1996a), *Foundations of International Macroeconomics*, MIT Press: Cambridge, Mass.

Rakshit, M. (1986), 'Monetary Policy in a Developing Country', WIDER, Helsinki, mimeo.

Rakshit, M. (1997), 'Money, Credit and Government Finance in a Developing Economy', in A. Bose, M. Rakshit, S. Sinha (eds.) *Issues in Economic Theory and Public Policy*, Oxford University Press, Delhi.

Rakshit, M. (1997a), 'Recent Monetary Trends: Understanding the Linkages,' *Money & Finance*, 2, pp. 42–71.

Rakshit, M. (1997b), 'Learning and Unlearning from the Thai Currency Crisis', *Money and Finance*, 3, September. Chapter 3 of the present volume.

Rakshit, M. (1997c), 'Crisis, Contagion and Crash: Asian Currency Turmoil', *Money and Finance*, 4, December. Chapter 4 of the present volume.

Rakshit, M. (1998), 'Retracing the Roots of Asian Troubles 1996–7', *Money and Finance*, 5, April. Chapter 5 of the present volume.

Rakshit, M. (1998a), 'Financial Fragility: Sources and Remedies I', *Money and Finance*, July–September.

Rakshit, M. (1998b), 'Financial Fragility: Sources and Remedies II', *Money and Finance*, 7, October–December.

Rakshit, M. (1999), 'Japan's Conundrum: Features and Alternative Hypotheses', *Money and Finance*, 8, January–March.

Rakshit, M. (1999a), 'The Decline, Fall and Recovery of Brazil 1997–9', *Money and Finance*, July–September.

Rakshit, M. (2001), 'Globalisation of Capital Market: Some Analytical and Policy Issues', in S. Storm and C.W.M. Naastepad (eds.), *Globalisation and Economic Development*, Edward Elgar: Cheltenham.

Reserve Bank of India (1997), *Report of the Committee on Capital Account Convertibility*, Mumbai.

Rodrik, D. (1997), *Has Globalisation Gone Too Far?*, Institute for International Economics: Washington, D.C.

Salant, S. and D. Henderson (1978), 'Market Anticipation of Government Policy and the Price of Gold', *Journal of Political Economy*, 86, pp. 627–48.

Shaw, E. (1973), *Financial Deepening in Economic Development*, Oxford University Press: New York.

Shiller, R. (1989), *Market Volatility*, MIT Press, Cambridge, Mass.

Stiglitz, J. E. and A.Weiss (1981), 'Credit Rationing in Markets with Imperfect Information', *American Economic Review*, 71(3), pp. 393–410,

Stiglitz, J. E. (1998), 'The East Asian Crisis and Its Implications for India', 19 May, Commemorative Lecture for the Golden Jubilee Year Celebration of the Industrial Finance Corporation of India, New Delhi, *website: www.worldbank.org/html/extdr/extmc/js-051998*.

Tobin, J. (1978), 'A Proposal for International Monetary Reform', Presidential Address to the Eastern Economic Association, *Eastern Economic Journal*, no. 4.

Triffin, R. (1960), *Gold and the Dollar Crisis*, Yale University Press: New Haven.

World Bank (1993), *The East Asian Miracle: Economic Growth and Public Policy*, Oxford University Press: Oxford.

World Bank (1997), *Private Capital Flows to Developing Countries: The Road to Financial Integration*, Oxford University Press: New York.

World Bank (1997a), *World Development Report 1997, The State in a Changing World*, Oxford University Press: Oxford.

World Bank (1998), *East Asia: The Road to Recovery*, Washington DC.

World Bank (1999), *Global Economic Prospects and the Developing Countries: Beyond Financial Crisis*, Washington DC.

World Bank, *World Debt Tables*, Various Issues.

Young, Alwyn (1994), 'Lessons from the East Asian NICs: A Contrarian View', *European Economic Review*, 38, 3–4, pp. 964–73.

Young, Alwyn (1995), 'The Tyranny of Numbers: Confronting the Statistical Realities of The East Asian Growth Experience', *Quarterly Journal of Economics*, 110, August, pp. 641–80.

Index